LEARNING, SPACE AND IDENTITY

01209 616182

Companion Volume

The companion volume in this series is:
Knowledge, Power and Learning
Edited by: Carrie Paechter, Margaret Preedy, David Scott and Janet Soler

Both of these readers are part of the second level Open University course E211 *Learning Matters: challenges of the information age*. This is an innovative course, which looks at the impact of new technologies on learning throughout life and in a wide range of learning situations. The course forms part of the Open University undergraduate programme.

How to apply

If you would like to register for this course, or simply find out more information about available courses, details can be obtained from the Course Reservations Centre, PO Box 724, The Open University, Walton Hall, Milton Keynes, MK7 6ZW, UK (Telephone 0 (0 44) 1908 653231). Details can also be viewed on our web page http://www.open.ac.uk.

LEARNING, SPACE AND IDENTITY

edited by
Carrie Paechter, Richard Edwards,
Roger Harrison and Peter Twining

P·C·P
Paul Chapman
Publishing Ltd

in association with

The Open
University

First published in 2001

 Paul Chapman Publishing Ltd
A SAGE Publications Company
6 Bonhill Street
London EC2A 4PU

SAGE Publications Inc
2455 Teller Road
Thousand Oaks, California 91320

SAGE Publications India Pvt Ltd
32, M-Block Market
Greater Kailash - I
New Delhi 110 048

British Library Cataloguing in Publication Data
A catalogue record for this book is available from the British
Library

ISBN 0 7619 6938 1
ISBN 0 7619 6939 X (pbk)

Library of Congress catalog record available

Typeset by Dorwyn Ltd, Hampshire
Printed in Great Britain by Athenaeum Press, Gateshead

Contents

Acknowledgements

The editors and publishers wish to thank the following for permission to use copyright material:

American Anthropological Association for Mark Warschauer (1998) 'Online learning in sociocultural context', *Anthropology and Education Quarterly*, 29:1, pp. 68–86;

Basic Books, a member of Perseus Books, LLC, for material from Seymour Papert, *The Children's Machine*, pp. 22–34. Copyright © 1993 by Seymour Papert.

Educational Technology Publications for B. Trilling and P. Hood (1999) 'Learning, technology, and education reform in the knowledge age or We're wired, webbed, and windowed, now what?', *Educational Technology*, 39:3, pp. 5–17;

International Society for Music Education for Akosua Obuo Addo (1997) 'Children's idiomatic expressions of cultural knowledge', *International Journal of Music Education*, 30, pp. 15–25;

Jessica Kingsley Publishers for Soraya Shah (1994) 'Kaleidoscopic people: locating the 'subject' of pedagogic discourse', *Journal of Access Studies*, 9:2, pp. 257–70;

The National Autism Society for T. Joliffe, R. Lansdown and C. Robinson (1992) 'Autism: a personal account', *Communication*, 26:3, pp. 1–14;

Open University Press for material from Stephen Brookfield (1993) 'Through the lens of learning: how the visceral experience of learning reframes teaching' from *Using Experience for Learning*, eds David Boud *et al.*, pp. 21–32;

Taylor & Francis for material from C. Comber and D. Wall (1999) 'The classroom environment: a framework for learning' from *Inside the Primary Classroom – 20 years on*, eds M. Galton *et al.*, Routledge, pp. 39–53;

Triangle Journals Ltd for material from J. M. Gore (1995) 'On the continuity of power relations in pedagogy', *International Studies in Sociology of Education*, 5:2;

Every effort has been made to trace the copyright holders but if any have been inadvertently overlooked the publishers will be pleased to make the necessary arrangement at the first opportunity.

Introduction

At the turn of the third millennium, enormous changes are taking place regarding how people learn. As we move into the 'information age' many individuals and groups have access to more information than ever before. In the West, vastly increased access to new technologies, coupled with a general move towards 'lifelong learning', also mean that we are learning for a much greater period of our lives than was traditionally the case. Learning is no longer regarded as something that happens in specifically educational institutions. We not only learn throughout our lives, but in a wide variety of places and spaces. These changes highlight the previously veiled relationship between learning, space and identity. The moves towards seeing learning as taking place outside as well as within the taken for granted spaces of the classroom, workshop and lecture theatre bring to our attention not just the question of how our learning is affected by the specific features of particular spaces, but also how we as embodied individuals are changed by our experiences in these spaces.

As we consider these issues, we also need to examine what is meant by the 'information age'. There is certainly an explosion in the information available to individuals in the West, particularly with the expansion of Internet access. What impact will this have on how people learn in the twenty-first century? How much will it unite people learning together across the globe, and how much will it exacerbate the divisions between rich and poor? How much will it enable increasing participation by informed citizens, and how much will it permit greater central control? To what extent will we be able to assess and assimilate this information, or will we find ourselves drowning in undifferentiated input? What we can say is that new technologies are having a profound impact on what we learn, and what we understand as 'learning'. This book explores some of these innovative practices but places them within a wider analysis which acknowledges the localised, contextual nature of learning and the social and cultural positioning of learners. In doing so it aims to provoke debate about the role of information and communications technologies (ICT) as tools for learning, disturbing some of the more universalised claims which have been made.

Increasingly, learning is being positioned both as a strategy for individual economic survival and career progression – we need to be adaptable to survive in the twenty-first century workplace – and as a means of personal, even spiritual, fulfilment and social inclusion. Alongside the growing importance attributed to learning is the opening up of spaces available for that learning. These are no longer bounded by educational institutions, as learning occurs, for example, in workplaces, through shared interests and

1

via the Internet. The advent of the 'information age' is affecting this in complex ways. The increased availability of ICT opens up new sources of information and sites, including virtual sites, for learning, as well as giving us the opportunity to adopt alternative, 'virtual' identities online. The space/time compression that results from the immediacy of e-mail communication has enabled us to learn with and from people living and working in different places and time zones. At the same time there is space/time compression of a different sort, as many people need to fit their learning into the small 'gaps' in increasingly complex, 'busy' lives. Learning is no longer confined to the time prior to our taking up roles as workers, parents and citizens, but is a lifelong activity, as we constantly adjust to social, economic and technological changes. Learning is also no longer just about what we know – the facts and concepts we think of as being in our heads. Increasing attention is being given to how we act, what values and beliefs we espouse, even how we look and feel. In other words, it is increasingly recognised that learning shapes the way we are, and that this in turn influences what and how we learn.

The introduction of new technologies, and in particular the resulting possibilities for our virtual presence in virtual spaces, highlights some key aspects of this learning. Because learning has been seen traditionally as something that takes place only in the mind, the fact that learning is something that happens to embodied learners occupying particular spaces has been generally ignored or played down. There has also been comparatively little emphasis on the relationship between learning and identity, both in terms of the relationship between how we see ourselves and what we learn, and in terms of the ways in which learning can change self-image and self-identity. As embodied learners, we are moulded and altered by learning experiences that involve both the mind and the body; they affect our view of who we are and who we might become. In virtual space, where we are in many ways disembodied, alternative identities can be developed, which are powerful and empowering, and which in turn will affect what and how we can learn about ourselves and others.

In this book we present a range of chapters which explore some of the issues around learning spaces, embodied identity and the processes of learning. They look at the relationship between these three areas through a number of lenses, seeing how it changes as we move into what some characterise as the information age. Some of the chapters concentrate on 'traditional' learning spaces and situations, some on those involving new technologies. All are concerned with learning in its many different forms throughout life. We have deliberately chosen to present a range of perspectives. We believe that the juxtaposition of these different views allows the examination of what is a complex area, and that complexity – not even that of the information age – cannot be 'grasped' simply or through universal characterisations.

The first five chapters focus on learning and how it is affected by the specific situations in which learners find themselves. Learning is not a general process, but takes place in space and time. We start with a chapter by Bernie Trilling and Paul Hood in which they identify and describe a move from the 'industrial' to the 'knowledge' age. The authors ask six basic questions about what this change means for education and how education needs to change in response. They then consider and critique a number of models of reform and suggest a new way forward, arguing that this arises directly out of the demands of the 'knowledge age'. They argue that this way forward is already transforming learning across the lifespan, and go on to look in detail at how educational technology can be used to support an alternative education model.

In Chapter 2, David Scott considers two theories of learning, symbol-processing and situated cognition, and looks at how they relate both to theories of knowledge and to learning situations. He argues that if we see learning as embedded in social situations this allows us to treat the practices of teaching and learning as subject to change as a result of what takes place in the learning situations themselves. In learning to take part in particular social practices, Scott suggests, we are also contributing to the development of the practices themselves.

In order for individuals to be able to learn about social practices, they need to have some understanding of what it is to be social, that is, they need to comprehend that other people, like themselves, have thoughts, feelings, intentions and so on. Without this understanding it is very difficult to function in the world. People with autism do not develop such an understanding in the same way as other individuals, and, indeed, many never do so at all. The next chapter, by Therese Joliffe, Richard Lansdown and Clive Robinson, focuses on what it is like to learn, at a later age than is developmentally usual, that other people have minds which influence what they do. In it, Joliffe, who has Asperger's Syndrome (an autistic spectrum disorder which combines normal or high intelligence with other characteristics typical of autism, particularly, for the purposes of this chapter, the lack of a 'theory of mind') describes how she learned about a variety of things that most of us take for granted, such as 'that people are supposed to be more important than objects' and that human speech is of more significance than other sounds. Joliffe still finds it difficult to understand what is going on in social situations, and she describes how this hampers her learning. We have included this chapter because it points up the enormous importance of social interaction for learning and the phenomenal amount of learning about this interaction that is taken for granted in discussions of social aspects of cognition.

Learning not only takes place within a cultural setting, it also involves developing understandings about that culture. In Chapter 4, Akosua Obuo Addo argues that, in many cultural groups, the process of teaching and learning music is important for imparting cultural knowledge. She contends that analysing folklore can provide us with information on cultural knowledge structures for educational practice in general and for curriculum content in particular. Children, she suggests, develop patterns of culturally

accepted human actions and relations, based on cultural knowledge structures as they are developed in society. The central question of the chapter
concerns how it is possible to introduce elementary school children in
Ghana to the cultural knowledge of that country through singing games.
Following a discussion of her theoretical position on culturally relevant
teaching and learning styles, Addo describes children's idiomatic expressions of cultural knowledge in their ways of knowing as demonstrated in
three teaching scenarios.

The next chapter, by Stephen Brookfield, looks specifically at the embodied nature of learning. The author outlines an approach to helping
teachers to reframe their practice by encouraging them to analyse their
visceral experiences as learners. He argues that our experiences as learners
provide us with a powerful lens through which we can view our own practices as educators in a more formalised and purposeful way. In particular,
he argues that experiencing what it feels like to learn something unfamiliar
and difficult will make it easier for teachers to support students' learning.

Next we have a series of articles that consider, from a variety of perspectives, the impact of ICT, and the resultant changes in space/time relations,
on learning and identity. In Chapter 6, Seymour Papert traces his personal
development and how it brought him to believe in the importance of particular ICT tools for children's learning. The chapter illustrates the ways in
which using computers in schools can change the ways that students can
learn, particularly through giving them a sense of doing 'serious work'; this
affects the ways in which they are able to perceive themselves as learners in
control of their own learning. The author reflects on his own learning in
many situations and applies this reflection to the processes of student learning in schools. He argues that the introduction of computers raises issues
not just about what to teach but about how to teach it, and suggests that the
importance of the written word to schooling is challenged by the use of new
technologies.

Complementing and in contrast to this chapter is one by Chris Comber
and Debbie Wall, which looks specifically at changes in space use in primary classrooms in the UK during the last 20 years of the twentieth century.
In it the authors demonstrate that, despite massive curriculum reform,
including the introduction of ICT, the ways in which space is used in
primary schools have changed hardly at all. They suggest that this is due to
a number of factors, including the constraints of building design, the need
for teachers to survive in conditions of rapid change, and the realities of
ICT use in classrooms where typically the one or two computers available
are sufficiently old to be considered obsolete.

In Chapter 8, Peter Twining considers the impact on learning of altera-
tions in the varieties of media through which that learning is mediated and
transacted. The author traces the development and design of a particular
ICT-based distance-learning course, showing how a variety of factors have
to be taken into account when selecting the appropriate learning media for
particular tasks. He argues that changing the balance of media used in a

course away from paper and towards new interactive media positively affects the quality of students' learning. In contrast to this is the next chapter, by Mark Warschauer, who specifically addresses the claims that online learning can transform education by promoting student-centred communication, collaboration and enquiry. He argues that the implementation of online learning is influenced by a range of sociocultural factors, and focuses on the ways in which a particular social context, in which students' identities are explicitly being moulded by the classroom situation, affects the way that ICT is used there. Through the detailed examination of a situation in which the sociocultural relationships and contexts inhibited the potential for change through the use of new technologies, Warschauer demonstrates that the use of new technologies in itself is not necessarily transformative of the learning situation.

We now move on to a group of chapters which focus on the relationship between learning and identity. In Chapter 9, Soraya Shah looks at how learning affects both one's sense of identity and one's ideas about personal achievement. Shah analyses her own experience within a poststructuralist framework and uses it to explore the politics of personal location, the concept of pedagogic space and the changing nature of identity. Focusing on her own return to education as an adult learner, she examines her perceptions of identity and self-development in relation to this process. Through this the author argues that identity is constantly being reshaped and is neither fixed nor singular; we have multiple identities which are in constant tension with one another.

Complementing this chapter, in Chapter 10 Roger Harrison argues that a distinctive feature of the curriculum innovations of profiling and recording achievement is the emphasis they place on developing personal qualities of autonomy and self-reliance. The rationale for these developments rests on the claim that personal autonomy is empowering for learners, and that self-reliance is a condition for survival in the contemporary work environment. Eliding economic necessity with liberal humanism has produced a powerful discourse which now occupies a central position in a 'progressive' agenda for educational reform. Harrison examines some of the assumptions buried in this discourse, questioning the relevance of the rational decision-making model which it supports. He then turns to alternative interpretations of the role of profiling and recording achievement, suggesting that they can be understood both as a form of social control and as a means of shaping learner identities. For teachers and learners this analysis opens up questions about how they might engage with or resist such learning technologies.

Finally, Jennifer Gore develops some of the issues of power in relation to learning, focusing specifically on how power relations impact on the embodied learner. In Chapter 11 she considers the ways in which power operates in regard to bodies across a range of pedagogic sites. Writing from a Foucaultian perspective, Gore identifies eight major techniques of power that can be found in educational sites, and shows how they operate in

school classrooms, in higher education institutions and in the more informal arenas of the feminist reading group and women's discussion group.
She argues that these techniques are common to all the locations.

This chapter brings us back to the central relationship of this book, that
between learning, space and identity, and to our focus on the physical as
well as the mental and emotional experiences of being a learner in particular learning spaces and situations. We must have a sense of the emotional,
embodied and social nature of learning as we move further into what some
describe as the information age. As more and more information is available
to us as individuals, we need to retain a sense of ourselves as part of a
group; as we are able to take up alternative, disembodied identities online
we need to remind ourselves that we remain fundamentally embodied and
that this embodiment is reflected in how we can learn. Above all, we have
to approach the use of new technologies both with a sense of excitement
and with critique. We need to go into the future with our bodies aware of
our physical and social environments and with all our physical senses, as
well as our minds, open.

1

Learning, Technology, and Education Reform in the Knowledge Age or 'We're Wired, Webbed, and Windowed, Now What?'

Bernie Trilling and Paul Hood

The year 2000 will mark the tenth anniversary of the arrival of the Knowledge Age in the United States. It will also mark nearly 20 years of efforts in the current round of education reform in the US. It's time to take a step back to a wide-angle view of the central roles learning and education will increasingly play in our new knowledge-based society. First, we will ask some basic questions about our newly arrived Knowledge Age, then we will survey the needed skills, theoretical supports, and main features of this new learning landscape. We will then focus briefly on three current models of reform – 'top-down', 'bottom-up', and 'systemic-mixed mode' – and their limited prospects for social traction and sustained change. Next, we will examine a fourth reform alternative, one that arises directly out of the new demands of the Knowledge Age. This 'turn-around' strategy is already transforming learning and training in the worlds of business, medicine, science, and technology, and is starting to do the same for public and private K–16 education. Finally, we will zoom in close on the critical work to be done in bringing the powerful toolkits of educational technology to the service of an emerging alternative education model.

At the Turning Point of the Knowledge Age

Where was the party?

It happened quietly, without fanfare or fireworks. In 1991, US spending for Industrial Age capital goods – things like engines, electrical distribution, metal-working and materials handling machinery, industrial equipment for mining, oil fields, agriculture, construction, etc., a total of $107 billion – was

7

Industrial Age:
Extraction => Manufacturing => Assembly =>
Marketing => Distribution => Products (& Services)

Knowledge Age:
Data => Information => Knowledge =>
Expertise => Marketing => Services (& Products)

Figure 1.1   *Industrial Age vs. Knowledge Age value chain*

exceeded for the first time in US history by the spending for information technology – computers and telecommunications hardware and software, which grew to a record $112 billion. This historic shift marked Year One of the Knowledge Age (Stewart, 1997, pp. 20–21). Since then, companies have spent ever more on equipment that makes, manipulates, manages, and moves the bits and bytes of information than on machines that perform similar operations on the atoms and molecules of the physical world (Negroponte, 1995).

The shift from an industrial-based to a knowledge-based society changes the fundamental processes and values added to each step in producing a product or service, the so called 'value chain' of work (see Figure 1.1).

Note that this does not mean that Industrial Age work in the world will (or can) ever go away. It does mean that with increasing automation and the export of manufacturing (and its environmental problems) to industrial-strength countries like China, industrial work in Knowledge Age countries like the US will continue to fade to low levels, whereas the need for knowledge work in these countries will continue growing well into the twenty-first century.

This turning point, decades in the making, forever tilts the balance of what is valued in our work and our society. This, in turn, changes what is needed to prepare for life and work in our society – the main concern of education.

At this transition, where the very purpose of education – cultivating knowledge and skills – becomes the centrepiece of our age, it is only appropriate to pause and take a fresh look at education and learning in our society and the new roles they will play as our Knowledge Age unfolds.

Six basic questions

Given the historic nature of this change, we must ask some basic questions:

1. Does this shift change the traditional aims of education in our society?
2. What skills will be necessary for success in the Knowledge Age?

Traditional Goals	Knowledge Age Response
Contribute to society	*Knowledge work, participation in the global economy*
Fulfil personal talents	*Actualize potentials with knowledge tools support*
Fulfil civic responsibilities	*Involved and informed democratic decision-making*
Carry tradition forward	*Build identity from and compassion for multiple cultures*

Figure 1.2   *Aims of education reconsidered*

3. What have we learned about learning that might help us gain these skills?
4. What does Knowledge Age learning really look like in practice?
5. How do we get there from here – which reform strategy will be effective?
6. How can we best apply learning technologies to support this alternative?

We will take up these questions, one by one, in the remainder of this chapter.

(1) Does this Shift Change the Traditional Aims of Education in our Society?

There are four traditional reasons why education is considered so essential to society. Education empowers individuals to contribute to society, fulfil their personal talents, fulfil their civic responsibilities, and carry tradition forward.

Though these broad, societal goals have not, in principle, changed, our cultural context most certainly has. Having entered the Knowledge Age, our response to each of these goals shifts dramatically and brand new sets of demands appear, challenging our entire education enterprise (see Figure 1.2).

Contribute to society

To contribute well to our Knowledge Age society, we need a new set of skills – knowledge work skills (more on this below). And now, when we apply these skills to our daily work, we participate in a vast, intricate web of global economic, informational, technological, political, social, and ecological interrelationships. We will all need to learn new ways to live and work in our highly complex, technological, information-rich world.

Fulfil personal talents

More and more of us are enjoying the benefits of powerful knowledge tools – computers and telecommunications hardware and software. They are enhancing our learning, our work, and our play. These 'amplifiers', 'storerooms', and 'sensory extensions' for our thinking and communicating are becoming 'power tools' for our personal development. But without strong societal initiatives to make these tools available to everyone, the existing disparities between 'knowledge rich' and 'knowledge poor' will only increase. And if the darker uses of these tools remain unchecked – addictive graphic violence and titillation, feelings of social isolation and even depression from over-immersion in electronic mediaspace, etc. – these negative effects may contribute to preventing many of our children from fully developing their talents (Healy, 1998; Papert, 1996; Postman, 1985).

Fulfil civic responsibilities

With freer access to a much wider spectrum of issues, facts, opinions, and conversations that electronic media and the Internet bring to us, our potential for involved and informed participation in the democratic process has never been greater. At the same time, the need to become a 'smart consumer' of information, to learn how to exercise discrimination and to filter the rushing media flood, has also never been greater (Tyner, 1998). And as fewer and fewer commercial media conglomerates control more and more of our sources of information, we must work ever harder to make careful choices from our abundant, daily media menu and to use critical judgement over our media diet.

Carry tradition forward

Increased worldwide mobility, immigration, and inter-marriage, growing economic opportunity, and other factors have led to a truly multicultural society in the US. With a diminishing majority soon joining a rainbow of ethnic and cultural minorities, the challenge now is for each of us to learn how to build and maintain our own identity from our given traditions, and from the pool of shared traditions, and at the same time, to learn compassion and tolerance for the identities and traditions of others. Though this is not entirely new to our 'melting pot' heritage, the scale and range of

Seven Cs	Component Skills
Critical thinking-and-doing	*Problem-solving, research, analysis, project management, etc.*
Creativity	*New knowledge creation, 'best fit' design solutions, artful storytelling, etc.*
Collaboration	*Co-operation, compromise, consensus, community-building, etc.*
Cross-cultural understanding	*Across diverse ethnic, knowledge and organizational cultures*
Communication	*Crafting messages and using media effectively*
Computing	*Effective use of electronic information and knowledge tools*
Career and learning self-reliance	*Managing change, lifelong learning and career redefinition*

Figure 1.3   *The seven Cs: Knowledge Age survival skills*

cultural and socioeconomic diversity is unprecedented. This will pose tough challenges to the preservation of social harmony in our society for a long time to come.

In short, though the traditional goals of education in our society remain the same in the Knowledge Age, the potential for reaching those goals, and for experiencing some stressful difficulties along the way, are both very high. The source of this stress has much to do with the inevitable lag between our powerful technical abilities and our very human inability to quickly shift habits of thought and social structures to meet new, large-scale challenges.

As we navigate this bumpy road into the Knowledge Age, we need to look closer at what the future will expect of us – what new sets of skills all learners will need to learn and all workers will need to apply to their work.

(2) What Skills will be Necessary for Success in the Knowledge Age?

Figure 1.3 outlines what we believe will be the key Knowledge Age survival skills, beyond the traditional, yet even more essential, three Rs. These seven skill sets represent a distillation of a wide variety of needs identified in a number of studies that examine future workplace skills (e.g., US Dept of Labor, 1992). Though there have been many ongoing efforts to cultivate these skills, they are still not yet recognized as priority education goals for all learners.

Critical thinking-and-doing

Knowledge workers need to be able to: define problems in complex, overlapping, ill-defined domains; use available tools and expertise, both human and electronic, for research and analysis; design promising solutions and courses of action; manage the implementations of these solutions; assess the results; and then continuously improve the solutions as conditions change. Fluency with the design process, project management, quality management, and research methods will all be important, as well as understanding the specific content knowledge of the field involved, which will be changing dramatically and will have to be continuously refreshed 'just-in-time'. Online information databases, quick e-mail access to experts, and web-based courses are a few of the tools that will help support this 'just-in-time' learning.

Creativity

Coming up with new solutions to old problems, discovering new principles and inventing new products, creating new ways to communicate new ideas, and finding creative ways to manage complex processes and diverse teams of people will all be highly prized Knowledge Age skills.

Collaboration

Teamwork will often be the only choice for solving complex problems or for creating complex tools, services, and products – multiple talents will be essential. From co-ordination and collaboration to compromise and consensus, the skills for effective, collaborative teamwork will be a necessary feature of work in the Knowledge Age.

Cross-cultural understanding

As an extension of teamwork, knowledge workers will have to bridge differing ethnic, social, organizational, political, and content knowledge cultures in order to do their work. In an increasingly multicultural society, a growing global economy, a world of increasing technical specializations, and a flattened 'network' organizational model, cross-cultural skills will become more and more valuable.

Communication

Knowledge workers will need to be able to craft effective communications in a variety of media for diverse audiences. Given the bewildering number of communication choices available – printed report, electronic document, magazine article, e-zine article, book, e-book, print ad, TV ad, web ad, phone call, cell phone call, Internet phone call, voice mail, telemarketing, fax, pager, web page, e-mail, snail mail, spreadsheet, simulation, database, multimedia presentation, slides, overheads, floppy disk, tape, video, CD, DVD, radio, TV, web-TV, teleconferencing, virtual reality – workers will be perpetually faced with choosing the right medium for the right message for the right audience, and with the challenge of doing it all as effectively and efficiently as possible.

Computing

Everyone in the Knowledge Age will have to be able to go beyond basic computer literacy to a higher level of digital fluency (Gilster, 1998; Papert, 1996, pp. 26-30) and comfort in using a variety of computer-based tools to accomplish the tasks of everyday life. Needless to say, those who master the knowledge tools of the Knowledge Age will be much more successful at school and at work than those who do not.

Career and learning self-reliance

In an age of 'at will' employment and increasing temporary and contract work, knowledge workers will have to manage their own career paths and their own continuous learning of new skills (Bridges, 1994). Since most work will be high-skilled, project-based work (as opposed to low-skill service work or factory line-work), the ability to manage a progressive series of shifts from one project to the next and to quickly learn what is needed to be successful in each project will all be essential to career survival and lifelong learning in the Knowledge Age.

As we look over this list of skills, an unsettling set of questions arises: How will we ever get to these new skills when we're still struggling with doing a good job on the three Rs? Where are these additional skills being learned in our existing education system? Where are the standards that set the learning of these skills as goals? Where are the tests and assessemnts that are measuring the learning of these skills? Where are the curricula and learning programmes that are building these skills from the earliest ages right through to adult education?

We must remind ourselves that, in many ways, we are still early explorers, having just arrived in this brave new Knowledge Age world. We have not confronted a set of large-scale changes as challenging as these

⇨ **Context:**   *Environmental learning*
⇨ **Construction:**   *Mental model building*
⇨ **Caring:**   *Intrinsic motivation*
⇨ **Competence:**   *Multiple intelligences*
⇨ **Community:**   *Learning communities of practice*

Figure 1.4   *The five Cs of modern learning theory*

since the Industrial Age steamed and cranked itself out of a centuries-old Agricultural Age back in the middle of the nineteenth century.

One can also argue, though, that we have seen these changes coming for quite a while (well before the *Nation at Risk* report in 1983) and that compared to the pace of change in the competitive business environment, education might be the last place to look for speedy action. We must also remember that education is firmly lodged in a political process in which it is far easier to secure support for quick fixes that attack symptoms than it is to find the political will to confront the root ailment of an elaborate education structure designed for an age that has just passed.

Despite the challenges, there are a growing number of school programmes and even whole schools where these new skills are being learned and where learners are being prepared for the knowledge work ahead (ASCD, 1997; Education Week/The Milken Exchange on Education Technology, 1998; Schauble and Glaser, 1996).

And, fortunately, what we've recently learned about learning provides substantial support for the acquisition of these Knowledge Age skills.

(3) What Have We Learned About Learning that Might Help Us Gain These Skills?

While there is still much discussion and debate over aspects of modern learning theory and how best to turn it into practice (Duffy and Jonassen, 1992; Perkins, 1992a; Resnick, 1996; Willis, 1998), a broad consensus has formed around a few key principles. We offer a very short summary list that highlights the major findings of over two decades of progress that educators, developmental and cognitive psychologists, neuropsychologists, learning and instructional theorists, sociologists, academic researchers, and others have achieved in adding to what we know about how we learn (see Figure 1.4).

Context

We have learned that context plays a very significant part in learning, that the environmental conditions for learning (objects, people, symbols, and their relationships) are much more influential than we've previously thought, and that the transfer of knowledge from one context to another is not often successful. The demand for more 'authentic' learning tasks that match real-world conditions comes directly from these findings, as well as the desire to have rich learning environments that offer a wide variety of contextualized opportunities for discovery, inquiry, design, practice, instruction, and constructive exploration. This approach coincides with the need to become proficient in solving real-world problems and to exercise critical thinking-and-doing in the Knowledge Age.

Construction

A great deal has been learned about how we build mental models, assimilate new experiences, accommodate changes to our models as we confront experiences that don't quite 'fit', and even hold important misconceptions about the world as necessary bridges to more 'accurate' models. These findings underscore the educational importance of constructing models, both physically (with wood blocks, *LEGOs*, etc.) and 'virtually' (drawings on paper and computer screens, simulation modelling with *SimCity*, etc.). These 'visceral and virtual' modelling activities provide strong external supports for the internal model-making going on inside our heads. We now can see just how important design, simulate, and build activities are in learning, for they match the constructive, modelling, and designing aspects of how we learn, and they also prepare us for the methods we will use to accomplish our future knowledge work (Papert, 1993).

Caring

We can rely on a rich literature of affective studies and reports from practice that clearly demonstrate the advantages of intrinsic over extrinsic motivation in learning and the development of deeper understandings (Covington, 1998). Recent project-based and problem-based learning programmes in which learners define their own projects (with careful guidance) and set the criteria for which they will be evaluated (student-generated rubrics that reflect current standards) have shown just how much learning can happen when students genuinely care about their work (e.g., The Project-based Learning Network; www.autodesk.com/foundation/pbl). This fully supports the Knowledge Age need to develop self-reliant and self-motivated learners and workers who have the persistence to creatively solve difficult problems and find answers to tough, complex questions.

Competence

Though there remains some lively debate over what exactly are the inherent 'modules of intelligence', there is now no question that competence comes in a variety of flavours and that intelligence is exhibited in a wide assortment of behaviours. Whether it's a triarchic mind (Sternberg, 1988), seven (or now '8½') intelligences (Gardner, 1983, 1993, 1999), or a society of interacting mini-modules in the mind (Minsky, 1986), we know enough now to encourage multiple learning approaches to match diverse learning styles and multiple ways of expressing understanding. This corresponds with the Knowledge Age need to benefit from multiple talents in the creative solving of problems in diverse teams, and in the sensitive design of services and products for diverse audiences.

Community

A strong case has been made for the social aspects of learning and the importance of learning from communities of practice (Lave and Wenger, 1991; Vygotsky, 1978; Wenger 1998). This extends the value of learning in context, discussed above, to the social and cultural realms of group interaction, peer and mentor relations, group culture, and the environmental influences of tools, settings, and techniques. Again, this firmly supports the Knowledge Age need to use collaborative community-based approaches to problem-solving and to learn from a variety of communities of practice in the pursuit of lifelong learning.

In summary, recent advances in theory indicate that the skill demands of the Knowledge Age are very consistent with the ways we naturally learn, solve problems, find answers to questions, and develop our abilities to think and act. Fortunately, there is a close match between theory and Knowledge Age needs; unfortunately, current educational practice does not often match modern theory.

(4) What Does Knowledge Age Learning Really Look Like in Practice?

From our analysis of educational programmes that appear successful in developing the Knowledge Age skills outlined above, and from programmes that are also successfully integrating information and knowledge tools into the fabric of everyday learning, we have derived a list of common characteristics of Knowledge Age learning practice. We have contrasted these methods with those of programmes that better fit the Industrial Age learning model, still the predominant mode of practice in our current educational system (see Figure 1.5).

From studying this chart, we can begin to draw a few conclusions. First, we are clearly looking at a paradigm shift in educational practice. So many of the behaviours beneficial for Industrial Age learning become their near opposites in the Knowledge Age. Where learning through facts, drill and practice, and rules and procedures was so adaptive in the Industrial Age, now learning through projects and problems, inquiry and design, discovery, and invention is more fitting for the times.

Industrial Age	Knowledge Age
Teacher-as-director	Teacher-as-facilitator, guide, consultant
Teacher-as-knowledge source	Teacher-as-co-learner
Curriculum-directed learning	Student-directed learning
Time-slotted, rigidly scheduled learning	Open, flexible, on-demand learning
Primarily fact-based	Primarily project- and problem-based
Theoretical, abstract principles and surveys	Real-world, concrete actions and reflections
Drill and practice	Inquiry and design
Rules and procedures	Discovery and invention
Competitive	Collaborative
Classroom-focused	Community-focused
Prescribed results	Open-ended results
Conform to norm	Creative diversity
Computers-as-subject of study	Computers-as-tool for all learning
Static media presentations	Dynamic multimedia interactions
Classroom-bounded communication	Worldwide-unbounded communication
Test-assessed by norms	Performance-assessed by experts, mentors, peers and self

Figure 1.5   *Industrial Age vs. Knowledge Age learning practice*

Second, we can see how difficult it really is to achieve systemic reform when the 'pull' of the older paradigm tends to reabsorb forays into the new order. Lacking a full-blown shift to Knowledge Age practice, the small advances we make in changing our methods eventually slip back into old and familiar Industrial Age habits.

Third, though we have emphasized the polarities, it is probably more accurate to view each pair of Industrial and Knowledge Age characteristics as a continuum. And though we are likely to see today many examples of fairly 'pure' Industrial Age practice, and far fewer examples of 'pure' Knowledge Age learning environments, we are even more likely to find a wealth of hybrid blends drawn from both columns. Even when the leap to mostly Knowledge Age methods has been made, the need for individual Industrial Age practices (like memorizing facts) will always remain. In the eclectic evolution of educational practice, previous methods don't entirely disappear, they are just used less frequently than the new ones.

A fourth observation is that Knowledge Age learning practices do correspond well with modern theory about how we learn. From project- and problem-based learning to collaborative and community-focused activities, from an emphasis on real-world learning in context to the increased focus on learner-motivated actions, Knowledge Age practices are well supported by modern learning theory (or is theory 'adapting' to the needs of the times?).

Fifth, at first glance, it looks as though Knowledge Age practice is quite dependent on modern knowledge tools – computers and telecommunications – to be really successful. But on closer inspection, most of the Knowledge Age characteristics (except the three specifically addressing the use of computers, multimedia, and communications) can be accomplished without the benefit of any of our modern tools. In fact, most of these practices were in place in Dewey's turn-of-the-century Chicago Laboratory School and later in the Dewey-inspired Progressive Education schools of the 1920s and 1930s in New York City, long before PCs and the Internet (Tanner, 1997). Though information and communications technologies are important catalysts for moving us into Knowledge Age learning methods, we must always remember that it's the practice and the results, not the tools, that make a difference. We can (and do) add lots of high-tech hardware and software to our classrooms without changing our practice, and end up with 'electronic horse saddles', no more effective (and most often less) than before in transporting our children into our high-speed Knowledge Age.

And last, but most importantly, this new paradigm for learning presents a tremendous challenge and opportunity to the professional development, both preservice and inservice, of our teachers. In many ways, it represents a redefinition of the teaching profession and the roles teachers play in the learning process (Fisher, Dwyer and Yocum, 1996; Sandholtz, Ringstaff and Dwyer, 1997). Though the need for nurturing, caring, compassion, and cultivating the best in our children will always remain at the core of teaching, the new demands of the Knowledge Age bring a whole new set of learning principles and behaviours into practice.

(5) How Do We Get There from Here? Which Reform Strategy will be Effective?

From teaching Titanic to learning 'Lifeboats'?

As we have seen, we are facing an unprecedented shift to a new kind of learning environment. It seems that moving deckchairs and polishing the brass on the Industrial Age teaching *Titanic* will most likely not get us to our desired destination. But inventing new high-tech learning 'lifeboats' looks like a difficult task, too, especially when the learning gear may need to be upgraded every six months or so. What is the proper reform vehicle that will carry education and learning on course to our Knowledge Age destination?

Moving deckchairs on the Titanic?

There have been three predominant approaches to improving our existing educational system: 'top-down', 'bottom-up', and 'systemic-mixed mode' (Murphy, 1990). Each has brought some degree of success to the reform of certain aspects of education, with most of the recent efforts focused on applying the more difficult 'systemic-mixed mode' approach.

- *Top-down*. Whether initiated at the national, state, or local level, the top-down approach has focused mainly on standards, assessment tests, accountability, and incentives to guide educational change efforts. Mandated structural changes, such as class-size reduction, have also been a part of this approach.

  A great deal of effort has been expended to create rigorous new standards and frameworks for all subject areas to expand the use of tests and assessments of both learners and teachers and to broaden the range of experimentation in creating incentive structures and structural changes to schooling. Despite these efforts, there remains a wide consensus that at the level of everyday practice in classrooms we are still not seeing the kinds of improvements, in test scores and other measures, that would indicate that these top-down reforms are working.

  The strongest criticism of this approach focuses on the core of its reform strategy – what we're testing and measuring. When we examine the knowledge and process skill needs of the age we have just entered (the 'seven Cs' beyond the three Rs), and then look at the predominantly fact-based testing of shorter-term memory that is still the main focus of our tests, we have a strong clue as to why many of these top-down reforms are not succeeding. A basic tenet of quality management states that 'you can only change what you measure'. Unless we begin to measure the kinds of skills needed in the Knowledge Age, we will never know whether our reform efforts are really helping or harming the development of these essential skills.

- *Bottom-up*. It is in using the bottom-up approach that we have seen a thousand flowers bloom. From creative teacher-led and even student-inspired innovations to whole school experiments in the re-invention of learning (e.g., Comer's School Development Program, Levin's Accelerated Schools Project, Sizer's Coalition of Essential Schools, etc.), and from research-based programme innovations (e.g., Success for All) to experiments in for-profit school management (e.g., the Edison Project, Advantage Schools, National Heritage Academies), we are witnessing a renaissance of bottom-up educational innovation.

The big question remains, though, can we really 'scale up' and sustain these innovations, which so often depend on the leadership of individual champions, on temporary excitement over participation in new change experiments (the Hawthorne effect), and more significantly, on temporary jolts of additional funding and support (grants and community donations) for programmes that are most often not sustainable after the money runs out?

- *Systemic-mixed mode*. Because of the limitations of both the top-down and bottom-up approaches, recent efforts have focused on combining the two, the so-called 'systemic' reform strategy (O'day and Smith, 1993). Top-down initiated leadership and support for the development and co-ordination of bottom-up initiatives, bottom-up initiatives that gain support and co-ordination from the top down, and many variations on these themes are all being tested in our recent wave of systemic reforms. Some of these mixed-mode initiatives (e.g., the Annenberg Challenge) are having important larger-scale successes, but the pace of change appears very slow and the challenges of sustaining hard-won reforms remain extremely daunting.

Leaping to the learning lifeboats?

With so many pupils in our classrooms, we must continue to improve our existing educational system. But shouldn't we also consider supporting the rise of an alternative system (Hill, Pierce and Guthrie, 1997; Schlechty, 1997), one that is more in tune with Knowledge Age needs and knowledge tools, and that is increasingly proving successful in business, science, medicine and technology research, and other knowledge-based institutions?

As we have shown, in education, there is an emerging profile of Knowledge Age learning in actual practice, thanks to the trailblazing work of pioneering teachers, trainers, educators, and students. We know that the skill demands of the Knowledge Age look quite different from those of the age we have just passed. The kinds of knowledge tools we now have at our disposal are much more powerful than those available even three or four years ago. What we now know about learning also supports the very styles of learning that will be necessary for success in the Knowledge Age.

These three Knowledge Age forces – the new demands for knowledge work skills, the new possibilities that our knowledge tools offer, and the support for new ways of learning from learning theory – are all converging on a new, alternative model of learning and education (see Figure 1.6).

What will this new Knowledge Age education model really look like?

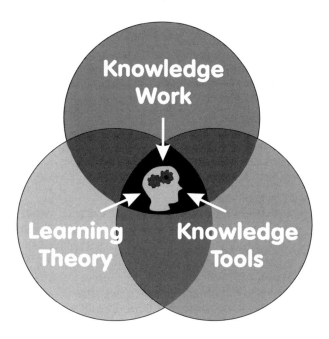

Figure 1.6   *The Knowledge Age learning convergence*

An alternative model: Knowledge Age community learning centres

From reviewing our earlier list of successful Knowledge Age practices (Figure 1.5), and the chart of Knowledge Age skills (Figure 1.3), and from observations of programmes that demonstrate these qualities (including business and industry examples which are much farther along than public education), we can begin to see some patterns and trends. Some of these new learning environments are starting to become 'extended learning centres' that look and feel more like rich cultural or community centres than schools (Dreyfoos, 1998).

With a little imagination and some creative speculation, we can begin to outline what some of these learning centres might become:

• A hybrid campus, open seven days a week, that houses a public school (or schools) as well as a variety of non-profit and for-profit (and partnerships of non- and for-profit) educational, social, health, community, and recreational organizations and small businesses, including a learning supplies store, copy centre, family-oriented restaurant, etc.; all locally orchestrated by a site co-ordinator and regionally managed by a regional executive management team in charge of negotiating contracts and maintaining educational balance and quality at all of the regional campuses.

- Small groups of similar-age learners starting and ending each day in their 'homeroom' where their primary learning adviser (still called 'teacher') presents the day's activity and class choices, leads reflective discussions on issues and topics of current interest, reviews progress toward mutually contracted goals, coaches and guides students through their learning hurdles, co-ordinates the resources and help needed, and provides caring support for the social and emotional needs of each of their homeroom learners.
- A rich schedule of 'live' instructional classes, presentations, demonstrations, field trips, and discussions led by local and distant (through teleconferencing) teachers, experts and other students in formal (classroom) and informal (meeting room) spaces.
- Small mixed age teams of learners working on a wide variety of projects under the guidance of 'project advisers' – teachers, parents and community members, with exhibits of past projects displayed throughout the campus – a dynamic 'museum' of project-based learning.
- A wide assortment of 'visceral' learning resources – well-stocked library-museum-lab-workshop-technology-art-construction spaces, multipurpose music-dance-theatre-recreation spaces, and outdoor garden-farm-biology-ecology spaces.
- Plenty of access to 'virtual' resources – portable computing with local network connections to learning and reference tools, productivity applications and personal databases, and global access to web-based information resources and conferencing tools.
- A wide variety of 'just-in-time' learning choices for students and teachers from web-based reference databases, libraries and resource centers, online courses, and online experts and mentors.
- Online, standards-based assessments and certifications of knowledge and skills mastery, including simulation exercises and electronic portfolio reviews by learning advisory teams that include students, teachers, and community experts; as well as in-person reviews of hands-on performance in authentic tasks by both teachers and students.

These Knowledge Age learning centres will extend into the community, with apprenticeships, local service projects, storefront, mini-businesses, neighbourhood projects, etc., as well as into the home through telecommunications. And the community will extend back into the learning centres with active community participation in a wide variety of projects and programmes.

Getting ready for the leap: the 'turn-around' reform strategy

Having taken a brief glimpse (albeit speculative) of where we think we are headed, we can now take a look at how we might get there – a reform strategy that will lead to this alternative education model.

The 'turn-around' reform strategy is based on promoting three important enabling trends – increased competition in education and training,
decreased educational costs from the use of educational technology, and
the effective use of performance-based educational practices and
measures.

Competition to traditional public schools is growing very rapidly. Char-
ter schools, private schools, for-profit schools, outsourcing of learning services to both non-profit and for-profit educational service providers, and
after-school tutorial programmes are all on the rise. There is a strong desire
on the part of entrepreneurs and the venture capital community to 'break
into' the multi-billion dollar school education market that is mostly 'locked
up' in governmental and non-profit programmes (Gay, Dobell and Dunlevy, 1998).

Though the risks of increased competition are high and must be carefully contained – threats to equal access and equal opportunity, the possible loss of democratic community control, the blurring of marketing and
learning under commercialization, etc. – the benefits of a well managed,
balanced level of competition may in the long run far outweigh the risks –
lowered costs and higher efficiencies; access to a much wider pool of cash
and management expertise from the for-profit community; the use of the
entire community as a classroom and learning laboratory; after school,
weekend, and summer learning programmes; on-campus health, social,
and recreational programmes and services; and wider learning choices for
students.

As information and communications technology costs continue to
plummet while technology performance soars, and as we increasingly
integrate these tools into our educational infrastructures and learning
practices, administration costs should drop as efficiencies rise, more
resources should be freed for classroom learning (currently in the USA
a little over 50 per cent of educational expenditures actually reach the
classroom), and more effective learning practices with integrated technology use should occur. This assumes, of course, that the increased
competition outlined above will force schools and other educational
service providers to continually transform their programmes and practices to benefit from the gains in performance and the lower costs of
technology.

Just as performance-based approaches are revolutionizing business and
industry – total quality management, portfolio-based assessments of em-
ployees, and electronic performance support systems with online knowledge databases and quick access to experts and mentors – applying these
practices to education will help focus change and reform toward the new
model. Much work will need to be done to adapt and develop these tools
and techniques for education and learning, especially in the tracking of
student performance toward meaningful standards and goals, and in the
devising and monitoring of common performance and quality measures for
all types of educational service providers.

The 'top-down, bottom-up, turn-around' reform dance

Public and private agencies, institutions, and programmes dedicated to improving education and training are facing a very perplexing situation. They must perform a very difficult and intricate reform 'dance'. They must combine top-down and bottom-up steps to more systemically improve the existing education system, while simultaneously executing 'turn-around' moves to prepare for leaps to an alternative education model still in its early stages (not an easy ballet!). And it is in this emerging alternative learning model that educational technologies will play an increasingly important supporting role.

(6) How Can We Best Apply Learning Technologies to Support this Alternative?

The gap between what our educational technologies can do and what they are actually doing in everyday classrooms and homes is still very wide. And some of the trends are truly disturbing:

- Educational software companies are merging into a few giant 'edutainment' mega-corporations which often abandon the more difficult high-investment, lower-profit 'edu-' development efforts in favour of lower-investment, higher-profit '-tainment' titles. (A recent case in point: The Learning Company, itself a product of multiple mergers, was purchased by Mattel, the toy-maker, best-known for the Barbie doll.)
- Large school-based education software developers like Computer Curriculum Corporation and Jostens Learning are struggling to develop new curriculum models as revenues from their large-scale, traditional drill-and-practice-style learning systems level off and start to fall.
- The web is starting to look much more like the world's largest shopping mall than a global library or communications medium, basing much of its revenue model on the same advertising strategy that has made so much of commercial radio and television of so little value to learning and to educational endeavours.
- Billions of dollars are being spent on connecting schools, libraries, and homes to the ever-expanding information infrastructure, while comparatively little is being invested in the learning content and support that will actually appear on our computer screens once they're connected.

On the positive side, there are promising tools for learning being developed by educational researchers and developers. (Center for Innovative Learning Technologies – www.cilt.org; Means, 1994); innovative uses of technology are appearing in many more learning settings each day (ASCD,

New Learning Environments

- **INFORMATION Content:** *Linked multiple media*
  - **Answers to:** Who? What? When? Where? How? Why?

- **LEARNING Challenges:** *Design and inquiry missions*
  - **Problems to solve:** Take apart, fix, improve, invent solutions
  - **Questions to answer:** Why do things work that way? Explanations

- **Learning SUPPORT:** *Virtual and visceral help*

Figure 1.7   *New learning environments*

1997; Education Week/The Milken Exchange on Education Technology, 1998 – www.milkenexchange.org); and the tools, environments, and methods for creating learning products are continuing to improve (Druin and Solomon, 1996).

'We're wired, webbed, and windowed, now what?'

What are the technology and content components of effective learning environments (Perkins, 1992b) that will help answer this question? We propose three integrated modules as the minimum for building effective Knowledge Age learning environments (see Figure 1.7): information content, learning challenges, and learning support.

Information content

Though there are many examples of multimedia CD-ROM encyclopedias covering vast areas of knowledge (like *Encarta* or the *World Book Enclyclopedia*), there are still very few multimedia reference works targeted at specific subject matter areas that are available to everyone on the web and that offer a structured gateway to other related web resources.

These subject-focused multimedia references must provide a simple interface that helps learners find answers to the basic questions asked about any subject – Who? What? When? Where? How? and Why?

Even more importantly, these reference resources must not be just static facts. Where possible, they need to use animations and interactive simulations to explain the processes and dynamics of the subject, with online links to community and expert resources for help in finding answers to the more difficult questions.

Learning challenges

The style of the learning activities in this environment must be consistent with Knowledge Age needs. Learning materials must provide more authentic design challenges where learners can collaborate on creating solutions to problems they care about.

Problem-solving leads to questions and the search for answers – learners then have a reason to use the informational resources available and a motivated context for learning. Multimedia stories and adventures can help keep the engagement level high, but these must be integral to the learning design and appropriate for the intended audience, not a thin marketing add-on. On-screen simulation activities and hands-on kits and construction materials must also be an integral part of the design so that there is a healthy balance between virtual interaction and visceral, real-world activities.

Though this 'inquiry through design' process (Baumgartner and Reiser, 1997) can provide a highly motivating context for learning, there needs to be strong support for getting past the necessary frustrations and creative blocks that are natural parts of the design and inquiry processes.

Learning support

Knowledge Age learners need support in developing their design and construction skills, their inquiry and answer-finding strategies, their creative and critical thinking skills, their project management skills, and their personal management abilities, such as setting goals, assessing their own performance, staying motivated and managing their own learning process.

Good trainers, teachers, mentors, counsellors and parents have been the traditional sources of this kind of support and will continue to be throughout the Knowledge Age. But more and more of this help can be delivered through web-based tools and databases, as well as through electronic contact with members of the relevant communities of practice.

We will need Knowledge Age tools for creating and sharing electronic portfolios of work on the web, for enabling multimedia discussions and collaborations, for getting quick help when needed, and for supporting all the stages of problem-solving, inquiry and design.

Top 10 Challenges for Educational Technology

In summary, we offer the following ten point 'challenge list' for educational technologists, curriculum developers, software designers and developers, learning materials publishers, engineers, technologists, scientists, educators, trainers, teachers, parents, students, and entrepreneurs who want to make a valuable contribution to Knowledge Age learners and workers:

1. We need more effective models of learning programmes that balance the 'virtual and the visceral' – effectively combining on-screen activities with hands-on construction kits, design challenges, probeware, discovery labs, and real-world explorations.
2. We need better web-based multimedia reference sites for learning, with simple interfaces and search engines, interactive simulations, comprehensive and updated guides to related web sites, and simple tools for learners and experts to use to contribute their ideas and comments to the knowledge base.
3. We need a wealth of high-quality, instructional, and constructional learning simulations and tools for the creation of simulations of all kinds, from games and scenario-based simulations to virtual construction kits and virtual simulators of complex environments and processes (Hood, 1997; Schank, 1997).
4. We need a quantum leap in ease of use and useful results in information searching, organizing, and reporting tools, especially for the web, and for databases of content knowledge and learning activities.
5. We need to make the entire database development, sharing, and maintenance process much simpler so that we can more easily create useful online knowledge bases; dynamic, database-driven web sites; personal learning history databases with multimedia portfolios of work; and large-scale education information systems that help us track Knowledge Age educational performance.
6. We need much better online collaboration and communication tools so that online discussions, live presentations with audience questions, groupwork, surveying and polling, and getting help online can actually be fun.
7. We need online learning assessment systems based on both the three Rs and the seven Cs that combine simulations, concept mapping, reflective essay questions, portfolio presentations, and the reporting of results from performance-based tasks. We also need a system to make it easy for content and learning experts to help review and comment on these portfolios and performance tasks.
8. We need more places for designing and constructing 'gizmos, gadgets, and useful things' – workshops, labs, 'garages', etc. – with real tools, construction materials, bins of parts, safe places to put things together and take things apart, and with access to online construction tips and exhibits of other students' inventions and experiments. This sort of constructive 'tinkering', so valuable to learning, is fast becoming an endangered species in our ecology of educational experiences.
9. We need to apply all of our educational technology talent to the challenge of preparing teachers, parents, and other helpers and learning guides to effectively integrate the use of all kinds of technologies, from hand lenses to supercomputers, into the everyday experiences of all learners.

10. We need to go outside, breathe deep, take a walk, smell the flowers, and forget about technology at least once a day.

Conclusion

We have seen some of the important work that must be done for technology to continue being an effective catalyst for learning and education reform. These are just a few of the needed pieces in a complex, 3-dimensional educational jigsaw puzzle of social, political, economic, infrastructural and, most important, human components.

The challenges that our Knowledge Age brings to learning and education are great, but the promise of a new Renaissance of learning and knowledge in our society is even greater. There is much good work to be done in helping to make this promise a reality for all lifelong learners and workers in our new Knowledge Age.

References

Association of Supervision and Curriculum Development (ASCD). (1997, November). Integrating technology into teaching (entire issue). *Educational Leadership, 55*(3).

Baumgartner, E. and Reiser, B. J. (1997). Inquiry through design: Situating and supporting inquiry through design projects in high school science classrooms. A paper presented at the 1997 Annual Meeting of the National Association for Research in Science Teaching (NARST).

Bridges, W. (1994). *Job shift: How to prosper in a workplace without jobs.* Reading, MA: Addison-Wesley Publishing Company.

Center for Innovative Learning Technologies; http://www.cilt.org

Covington, M. (1998). *The will to learn: A guide for motivating young people.* Cambridge, UK: Cambridge University Press.

Dreyfoos, J. G. (1998). *Full-service schools: A revolution in health and social services for children, youth, and families.* San Francisco, CA: Jossey-Bass Pubishers.

Druin, A. and Solomon, C. (1996). *Designing multimedia environments for children.* New York: John Wiley & Sons.

Duffy, T. M. and Jonassen, D. H. (eds.). (1992). *Constructivism and the technology of instruction: A conversation.* Mahwah, NJ: Lawrence Erlbaum Associates.

Education Week/The Milken Exchange on Education Technology (1998, October). Technology Counts '98: Putting school technology to the test (special supplement). *Education Week, 18*(5).

Fisher, C. Dwyer, D. C. and Yocam, K. (1996). *Education and technology: Reflections of computing in classrooms.* San Francisco, CA: Jossey-Bass.

Gardner, H. (1983). *Frames of mind: The theory of multiple intelligences.* New York: Basic Books.

Gardner, H. (1993). *Multiple intelligences: The theory in practice.* New York: HarperCollins Publishers.

Gardner, H. (1999). Are there additional intelligences? The case for naturalist, spiritualist, and existential intelligences. In J. Kane (ed.), *Education, information, and transformation* (pp. 111–131). Upper Saddle River, NJ: Prentice-Hall.

Gay, R., Dobell, B. and Dunlevy, A. (1998, November). *The age of knowledge: The growing investment opportunity in education, corporate training, and child care.* San Francisco, CA: NationsBanc Montgomery Securities.

Gilster, P. (1998). *Digital literacy.* New York: John Wiley & Sons.

Healy, J. M. (1998). *Failure to connect: How computers affect our children's minds – for better and worse.* New York: Simon & Schuster.

Hill, P. T., Pierce, L. C. and Guthrie, J. W. (1997). *Reinventing public education: How contracting can transform America's schools.* Chicago, IL: The University of Chicago Press.

Hood, P. (1997). *Simulation as a tool in education research and development: A technical paper.* Washington, DC: Council for Educational Development and Research.

Lave, J. and Wenger, E. (1991). *Situated learning: Legitimate peripheral participation.* Cambridge, UK: Cambridge University Press.

Means, B. (1994). *Technology and education reform.* San Francisco, CA: Jossey-Bass.

The Milken Exchange on Education Technology; http://www.milkenexchange.org

Minsky, M. (1986). *The society of mind.* New York: Simon & Schuster, Inc.

Murphy, J. (1990). *The educational reform movement of the 1980s: Perspectives and cases.* Berkeley, CA: McCutchan Publishing Company.

Negroponte, N. (1995). *Being digital.* New York: Alfred A. Knopf.

O'day, J. and Smith, M. (1993). Systemic reform and educational opportunity. In S. Fuhrman (ed.), *Designing coherent education policy.* San Francisco, CA: Jossey-Bass.

Papert, S. (1993). *The children's machine: Rethinking school in the age of the computer.* New York: Basic Books.

Papert, S. (1996). *The connected family: Bridging the digital generation gap.* Atlanta, GA: Longstreet Press, Inc.

Perkins, D. (1992a). *Smart schools: Better thinking and learning for every child.* New York: The Free Press.

Perkins, D. (1992b). Technology meets constructivism: Do they make a marriage? In T. Duffy and D. Jonassen (eds), *Constructivism and the technology of instruction: A conversation* (pp. 45–56). Mahwah, NJ: Lawrence Erlbaum Associates.

Postman, N. (1985). *Amusing ourselves to death: Public discourse in the age of show business.* New York: Viking Penguin.

Project-Based Learning Network; http://www.autodesk.com/foundation/pbl

Resnick, M. (1996). Toward a practice of 'constructional design'. In L. Schauble and R. Glaser, (eds.) *Innovations in learning: New environments for education* (pp. 161–174). Mahwah, NJ: Lawrence Erlbaum Associates.

Sandholtz, J. H., Ringstaff, C. and Dwyer, D. C. (1997). *Teaching with technology: Creating student-centered classrooms.* New York: Teachers College Press.

Schank, R. (1997). *Virtual learning.* New York: McGraw-Hill.

Schauble, L. and Glaser, R. (eds.). (1996). *Innovations in learning: New environments for education.* Mahwah, NJ: Lawrence Erlbaum Associates.

Schlechty, P. C. (1997). *Inventing better schools: An action plan for educational reform.* San Francisco, CA: Jossey-Bass.

Sternberg, R. (1988). *The triarchic mind: A new theory of human intelligence.* New York: Penguin Books.

Stewart, T. A. (1997). *Intellectual capital: The new wealth of organizations.* New York: Doubleday.

Tanner, L. N. (1997). *Dewey's laboratory school: Lessons for today.* New York: Teacher's College Press.

Tyner, K. (1998). *Literacy in a digital world: Teaching and learning in the age of information.* Mahwah, NJ: Lawrence Erlbaum Associates.

US Department of Labor, Secretary's Commission on Achieving Necessary Skills (SCANS). (1992). *Learning a living: A blueprint for high performance.* Washington, DC: US Department of Labor.

Vygotsky, L. L. (1978). *Mind and society: The development of higher psychological processes.* Cambridge, MA: Harvard University Press.

Wenger, E. (1998). *Communities of practice: Learning, meaning, and identity.* Cambridge, UK: Cambridge University Press.

Willis, J. (1998, May/June). Alternative instructional design paradigms: What's worth discussing and what isn't. *Educational Technology, 38*(1), 5–16.

Note: A special thanks to Bo DeLong of WestEd for her help in formulating some of the ideas in this chapter and for adding her considerable expertise in developmental, cognitive, and affective child psychology.

2

Situated Views of Learning

David Scott

Introduction

If we change our job, we are engaged in a new learning situation. However similar the two learning environments are, new skills are required and new knowledge has to be developed to allow us to function in this new environment. What are some of these new skills which have to be learnt? First, there are spatial skills, so that we have to learn where our place of work is, how the various parts of it are connected to each other, what the power relations between the different parts are, and indeed why these arrangements have been adopted and not others. If, for example, we have been used to working in an office with separate rooms and we now move to one which is open-plan, then we have to learn both a new way of working (we cannot do certain things which we did before such as playing music while we work) and we have to learn to communicate with other people in different ways (we cannot say certain things which we could have done before because other people may overhear us). This may be difficult for us because instead of acting instinctively, we have to think through what we do and this may cause us a certain amount of anxiety. We are also likely to make mistakes because we are moving between the old and new ways of communicating and working, and these mistakes may have repercussions for our future working practices. In addition, since we have to adopt a new way of working, this may make us less efficient in what we do.

Then there are the relations between people in the organisation which we have just joined. On the surface, we may very quickly come to understand the formal arrangements within the new setting; however, formal arrangements are not necessarily the same as informal and perhaps more significant arrangements. Our previous place of work may have adopted systems which accorded the greatest degree of influence to those highest up in the formal hierarchy; whereas our new place of work accords some influence to long-serving members of the organisation even if they have not risen very far up the formal hierarchy. We therefore have to identify how the formal and informal hierarchies work and in what ways.

In addition, our new organisation may operate through different systems of working, including how decisions are reached, to those in our old place of work. The time element may be important here and could involve matters to do with how quickly decisions are reached, how fast a piece of work has to be done; in short, how hard one has to work. There are, however, more significant problems for us to overcome and these have only been hinted at. These are to do with acquiring a mental representation of how those people we are working with understand the world. In order for us to do this we have to engage with them in various ways and if we decide that the best way to proceed is to adopt these new ways of working, then we have to assimilate these into our own way of thinking. As we do this we may experience conflict between the old and the new. However, there is a further process at work. We are not just passively replacing the old with the new; we are actively contributing to the development of the practice, as we are now a part of it. This process of enculturation is central to situated views of learning.

What this also suggests is that learning can be understood as participation in a social practice, in which both the learner and the practice are transformed. The last part of this chapter will argue that this social practice and others are differentiated and stratified, and these have powerful effects on what is learnt and how it is learnt. Before that, we need to discuss two opposing views of learning; the first of which has its origins in behaviourist and individualist perspectives – a symbol-processing approach. Having suggested that this approach is flawed, an alternative view – situated-cognition – will be proposed, and this understands learning as situated in knowledge-communities which provide the essential contexts for learning in them and about them.

Symbol-processing Views of Learning

Symbol-processing approaches understand the learner and the environment as separate; learning takes place within the human mind as the individual processes information they receive through their senses, assimilates that information and creates new ways of understanding. This approach has its origins in the philosophical theory of empiricism, which understands the world as given and then received by individual minds. It separates out language from reality, mind from body and the individual from society (Bredo, 1999). The first of these, the separation of language from reality, has a long philosophical lineage. After briefly describing this view of knowledge, an alternative view will be examined for the light it sheds on symbol-processing and situated-cognitive perspectives on learning.

Separating language from reality

Hacking (1981) suggests that the traditional image of science, i.e. one based on empiricism, can be understood in the following way. There is a real world out there. This real world exists regardless of whether the observer is observing it at the time or whether it is being described as such. Furthermore, there is a correct way of describing it. Scientific theories are superior to common sense understandings of the world. Science works by accumulating knowledge; it builds on previous understandings of the world and improves them. The ultimate purpose is to provide a complete understanding of both the natural and social worlds. Science makes a distinction between observation and theory. Observational statements are theory-less. This leads to the idea that there are facts in the world which can be collected regardless of the belief systems of the observer. Interpretation and theory-building are second-order operations and come out of and do not precede the accumulation of facts about the world. The correct way of conducting research is to test hypotheses developed prior to the data collection phase. Language is treated as a transparent medium; that is, words have fixed meanings and concepts can be defined unambiguously. A distinction is usually made between how truthful statements are produced (this involves concept formation, data collection and data analysis procedures) and how they are justified. Different criteria are thought to be appropriate for each. Finally, an assertion is made that the methods which are appropriate to the natural sciences are equally appropriate to the social sciences.

The most important of the points made above is the idea that facts can be collected about the world which are free of the value assumptions and belief systems of the collector. These facts constitute unequivocal and true statements about the world. Furthermore, learning comprises discovering what they are and developing adequate models to explain them. Winogrand and Flores (1986, p. 73) for example, suggest that the symbol-processing approach has the following characteristics:

> At its simplest, the rationalistic (i.e. symbol-processing) view accepts the existence of an objective reality made up of things bearing properties and entering into relations. A cognitive being 'gathers information' about these things and builds up a 'mental model' which will be in some respects correct (a faithful representation of reality) and in other respects incorrect. Knowledge is a storehouse of representations, which can be called upon for use in reasoning and which can be translated into language. Thinking is a process of manipulating representations.

However, this implies that we can understand the world as fixed by language and as language being a transparent medium for representing reality. As Usher (1997) suggests, language, thought and learning also act to construct the world or bring it into being. This of course does not mean that any individual can create the world in any way they like; but it does suggest that the source of understanding, learning and indeed, being, resides in communities of individuals who together construct particular worlds. Furthermore, it challenges assumptions that there is a world or reality out there which is separate from our knowing of it and that human beings have invented symbolic systems such as language and mathematical notation which mirror that reality – a view which has come to be known as representational realism – and reasserts the idea that research or learning acts to construct the world.

This notion of representational realism then misrepresents the process of how we act in relation to stimuli from our environment. Reality is not organised as such but requires the active efforts of the individual working in the world to make sense of it. The symbol-processing view of learning or mind is underpinned by this idea of representational realism. However, there is a more radical solution to the problem of the relationship between mind and reality and this is that representations of reality are not given in a prior sense because of the nature of reality, or because the human mind is constructed in a certain way, but as a result of individual human beings actively constructing that reality in conjunction with other human beings, some contemporary, some long since dead. This debate makes reference to the argument between constructivists and situated cognitivists, in that the former suggest that this active process of learning occurs in the mind, while the latter locate the process in society (Bruner, 1996). For situated cognitivists, categorising, classifying and framing the world has to be located in society and not in individual minds or in reality itself.

An example of this classifying process is the use of the notion of intelligence, and in particular the idea of a fixed innate quality in human beings which can be measured and remains relatively stable throughout an individual's life. This has come to be known as an intelligence quotient and is measured by various forms of testing, e.g. the 11+ test. The 11+ had a significant influence on the formation of the tripartite system of formal education in the United Kingdom as it was used to classify children as appropriate for grammar schools (those who passed the 11+), technical schools (those who passed the 11+ but were considered to be better suited to receive a particularly focused technical education), and secondary moderns (the vast majority who failed the 11+ and in the early days of the tripartite system left school without any formal qualifications).

Central to the concept of the intelligence quotient is the tension between the relative emphasis given to genetically inherited characteristics and the influence of the environment, or the 'nature versus nurture' debate. Many contemporary educationalists believe that children's early and continuing experiences at home and at school constitute the most significant influence on their intellectual achievement. However, early exponents of the argument that genetic inheritance determined intellectual potential saw intelligence, measured by tests, as the factor which could be isolated to produce a 'quotient' by which individuals could be classified. Regardless of environmental factors such as teaching and learning programmes or socio-economic variables, it was argued, some people were born with low levels of intelligence. Schooling could bring them to a certain level of achievement, but there would always be a genetically imposed ceiling on their capabilities. An extreme version of this belief was that intelligence, like certain physical characteristics, followed a normal curve of distribution, so that within any given population there were a set number of intelligent people and a set number of less intelligent people. It was further argued that those individuals who were most generously endowed were obviously more fitted to govern and take decisions on behalf of those who were less fortunate.

The use of IQ tests was widely accepted as a selective device among academics and the writers of government reports, including, for example, The Spens Report (1938) and The Norwood Report (1943), both of which influenced the writing of The United Kingdom Education Act of 1944. The 1944 Education Act incorporated the beliefs firstly that intelligence testing could reliably predict who would succeed academically at a later point in time, and secondly that children could and should be divided into categories based on the results and educated separately.

Soon after the 1944 Act was passed, the use of IQ tests to allocate places began to be discredited. One of the appeals of the policy was its supposed objectivity and reliability. If intelligence was innate and could be measured, then the tests would simply reflect this notionally 'pure' relationship, but this is not what happened. A number of other problems with this idealised concept became apparent. IQ tests should by definition be criterion referenced. If children had the intelligence, the theory went, then the tests would show it. All children who demonstrated their intelligence by achieving the designated mark ought to be awarded a place at a grammar school. In practice, Local Education Authorities set quotas for grammar school entrance. Furthermore, different Local Education Authorities set different quotas for passing (Vernon, 1957). The quotas also discriminated against girls and the argument was frequently made that since girls developed earlier than boys in their intellectual abilities, fewer girls should be given places in grammar schools because this would unfairly discriminate against boys who would catch up later.

A second problem with IQ tests was that if intelligence, as measured by the tests, was innate, then coaching and practice ought not to improve pupils' test scores. However, it was reported that pupils' performances were indeed enhanced by preparation for the tests, demonstrating that a supposedly free-standing assessment was being connected to the curriculum in contradiction to the intentions which lay behind it (Yates and Pidgeon, 1957). More importantly, Yates and Pidgeon's findings threw into question the notion of an innate and immutable intelligence quotient. Finally, the deterministic beliefs underlying the system implied low academic expectations for pupils who failed the 11+. A low IQ score at 11 ought to be a reliable guide to the rest of their school careers. However, it quickly became apparent that some of those who failed were capable of achieving high level academic success.

This complicated story illustrates one of the problems with a symbol-processing approach to the relationship between mind, society and reality. What was considered to reside in the nature of reality, i.e. innate qualities of intelligence in human beings, was shown to have undeniably social or constructed dimensions to it. Communities of individuals had constructed a powerful tool for organising educational provision, and given it credibility by suggesting that it was natural and thus legitimate.

Separating mind from body

Symbol-processing approaches to cognition also suggest a further dualism, between mind and body. This separation of mind and body locates learning and cognition in the mind, as the mind passively receives from the bodily senses information which it then proceeds to process. The mind is conceived of as separate from the physical body and from the environment in which the body is located. Learning is understood as a passive process of acquiring information from the environment and thus this view of cognition supports didactic approaches to teaching and learning. Situated-cognitionists argue that learning involves intimate and interactive contact with the environment which both contributes to further understanding for the individual, and changes or transforms the environment itself. In other words, knowledge is not understood as a passive body of items to be learnt about the environment but as an interactive process of construction.

Separating the individual from society

Finally, it is important to discuss the third dualism which critics of symbol-processing approaches have suggested is problematic. This is the separation of the individual from society. If a child or adult is given a task to do, the learner has to figure out for themselves what the problem is and how it can be solved. The task, moreover, is framed by a set of social assumptions made by the observer or teacher. The problem with the symbol-processing view is that an assumption is made that the task and the way it can be solved are understood in the same way by both learner and teacher. However, this is an assumption which cannot be made, and one of the consequences of making it is that the child who then fails to solve the problem is considered to be a poor learner, rather than one who has simply reconfigured or interpreted the problem in a way which is incongruent with that of the teacher or observer. The individual/societal distinction which is central to a symbol-processing view of cognition separates out individual mental operations from the construction of knowledge by communities of people and this leaves it incomplete as a theory of learning.

Bredo (1997, p. 32) summarises the symbol-processing approach in the following way, and at the same time indicates some of the problems with it:

> Each of these dualisms, such as the split between language and reality, mind and body, or individual and society is the product of a privileged description. Language is matched against a reality that is already described in terms of a certain vocabulary. An active agent or robot is similarly assumed to work with a certain

description of the environment that is fine tuned to the problems which are likely to arise. Individuals are judges and compared in terms of an interpretation based on a fixed framework for describing what is going on. Each dualism is based on the assumption that the proper space in which things are described is known. Everything revolves around this particular centre – the unquestioned framework of an external observer. The problem however, is that we generally don't know what the problem is in everyday life. We don't know how best to describe things or which vocabulary or orientation will be most helpful. Presupposing a particular description, vocabulary, or set of programming primitives amounts to adopting a fixed and unquestioning orientation before enquiry begins. Such a fixed orientation has blindnesses built in from the start. If the vocabulary or way of defining things can emerge from within the process of acting and inquiring, however, rather than being given from the outside, it may be changed and adapted as needed.

Situated Learning

Situated cognitive approaches were developed to solve some of the problems referred to above with symbol-processing approaches. Situated-cognition or environmentally embedded learning approaches understand the relationship between the individual and the environment in a different way. They view the person and the environment as mutually constructed and mutually constructing. As a result they stress active, transformative and relational dimensions to learning; indeed they understand learning as contextualised. These contexts are: knowledge, power, teaching and learning strategies, and structures of the learning environment.

Knowledge contexts

Usher (1997) suggests in relation to finding out about the world that knowledge has a con-text, pre-text, sub-text and inter-text. Research for him is a textual practice. Learning may be understood in a similar way. The context comprises the situatedness of the learner in the act of learning so that they are immersed in structures or significations of gender, sexuality, ethnicity, class, etc. Furthermore, the learner is situated within various pre-texts or discourses about the way the world is structured so that the learning strategy is always underpinned by pre-organised meanings. The pre-text always has attached to it a sub-text, in that the learning strategy and the knowledge which is subsumed within it are distinctive ways of knowing the world. Finally, each learning setting makes reference to other forms of learning, other knowledge constructs and other historical meaning formations – the inter-text.

An example from a formal learning situation will illustrate this. If a child is taught history in a formal setting such as a school, then that child is situated in particular discourses surrounding gender, ethnicity, sexuality and class, both in the subject matter of their learning and in the way that they are expected to learn what is being presented to them. Weiner (1990) for example, suggests that the United Kingdom National Curriculum History Syllabus is insular, chauvinistic and racially biased. She argues that it is both what is taught and what is not taught and the way what is taught is realised that constitutes discriminatory behaviour, albeit unplanned by the teachers concerned. Indeed, the teaching and learning strategy itself may be explicitly racist, again either through neglect, distortion or ideological bias. For example, curriculum materials have in the past included pictures and diagrams only of white children and have neglected children of other colours. Furthermore the child learning history is subsumed within particular learning strategies which act to organise the way they can see the world and its history. These pre-organised meanings are underpinned by particular conceptions of knowledge, ideas about what is appropriate to learn in formal settings, and views about which aspects of the culture should be passed on from generation to generation and in what way. For example, history may be taught as a series of 'facts' about the world, and this teaching strategy is then reinforced by assessment strategies which downplay the socially constructed nature of what happened in the past. Finally, the historical knowledge which is imparted and the way in which it is taught have a history, and refer to other ways of seeing the world.

An example from an informal learning setting is learning how to be a parent. What characterises this type of learning is that there is as yet no formal type of training which a putative parent has to undergo. It is an example of learning which is situated in the activity which is the subject of the learning. The knowledge of how to bring up a child is generated from the actual practice itself. However, this is misleading because the parent at the same time is immersed in various knowledge structures which provide the context within which they make parenting decisions. Firstly, they have memories, or at least remembered representations, of their own childhood. Secondly, they are surrounded by role-models, i.e friends and members of their family whom they may decide to emulate or perhaps work against. Thirdly, they are offered advice about how to bring up children from a number of different sources, for example, books and magazines, television programmes, relatives and friends. However, more fundamentally, they are immersed in particular discourses about parenting which act to close off other possibilities; these discourses reflect the way society is structured. Finally, the putative parent has a view about him or herself and how this relates to parenting. Parenting itself also takes place within particular environments, and these are arranged in different ways. Single parenting is a qualitatively different experience from parenting by two or more adults. We therefore need to understand learning how to be a parent as situated and as making reference to discursive structures or significations of gender, sexuality, ethnicity and class etc.; pre-organised meanings about parenting which reflect particular understandings about knowledge, i.e. views of childhood, adulthood, learning, identity and the like; and other viewpoints, discourses and knowledge structures which act as points of comparison. What this means is that learning is situated and that it has constructed or social features. As a result it can only be understood by making reference to those knowledge structures, discourses and practices which reflect particular time and space bound pre-occupations of particular communities.

Power contexts

Furthermore, these communities are stratified in various ways. First, some individuals in society have a greater influence than others in determining what counts as legitimate knowledge and what counts as illegitimate knowledge. Second, knowledge-gathering takes place in settings and environments in which individuals have different access to resources. The subject matter of learning is in part those differences and this means that power is a necessary construct in explanations of social life. Third, there are power dimensions of the learning situation itself. This is most obvious in formal learning situations where the teacher has a greater opportunity to impose his or her version of knowledge on the learner than the learner has to construct it for themselves. However, even in the most informal of learning situations there are power dimensions present, as the learner is situated within arrangements about knowledge, how it should be organised and how it should therefore be learnt which act to restrict the capacity of the learner to progress their own learning. Finally, learning acts to fix reality in a particular way which is never entirely justified and cannot be legitimated by reference to a notion of what the world is really like. This act of closure itself is a part of the reality within which the learner is embedded. By adopting a particular way of working, a particular understanding of knowledge, the learner is rejecting or turning aside from other frameworks and this itself is an act of power.

Teaching and learning contexts

However, within this general framework, learners have more control in some settings than in others. The teaching and learning strategy is constructed strongly or weakly (cf. Bernstein, 1985), where strong and weak are defined in terms of the capacity of the message system to restrict or allow different meanings, interpretations and actions. Each learning moment focuses on a particular aspect of knowledge, whether chosen by a teacher or not. This is made visible by the act of delivery. However, there are always invisible dimensions: what is not chosen and why it was not chosen are invisible.

The teaching device itself is weakly or strongly framed as well. If the teaching device is text-based, as in many forms of distance learning, it may allow the reader or learner the opportunity to interpret or read it in a number of different ways, or it limits these opportunities. On the other hand, oral commentary in the form of lectures, contributions to seminars, contributions to tutorials by the teacher operate in different ways. Again, this form of delivery is strongly or weakly framed. However, there are a number of differences when compared with text-based approaches. The spoken text is likely to be multi-faceted – that is, because of its greater informality and flexibility (it has not been subject to revision and redrafting) it is likely to incorporate a range of different modalities, i.e. at any one moment it may be more authoritative than at another moment. It is therefore likely to be more fragmented. Fragmentation allows the student a greater degree of choice because it surfaces for the attention of the student a range of possibilities which they can then make a choice about. The boundary between what is visible and invisible is also weakened.

The most common teaching device in formal settings involves student-teacher interchanges. Again, these may be strongly or weakly framed. If they are strongly framed, the teacher/student relationship may be such that the effect of the exchange is that the student is dispossessed of certain faulty, inadequate or insufficiently complex ideas, so that they now know or can do what was originally intended by the deliverer. However, there is another possibility, which is that the teacher does not have in mind a particular model of what the student should be able to do after the programme of study, and indeed is prepared to modify their teaching strategy in the light of what emerges. It is therefore weakly framed. The purpose of the exchanges is to dissolve, fragment or otherwise disrupt the models of knowledge held by the student, and, at best, the teacher. Here, there is no attempt made to provide a replacement, since the purpose is to provide disjuncture in the minds of students, and the responsibility for replacement is devolved to the student.

Structural contexts

Finally, there are the structural dimensions of the learning setting itself. These comprise in part particular spatial and temporal arrangements. Distance learning approaches are constructed in particular ways so that the learner is allowed some licence for when and where they choose to study. Face-to-face teaching settings are constructed in terms of timetables, sequences of learning, particular relations between teachers and learners and organised places where the teaching takes place. All these various forms of structuring influence what is learnt, how it is learnt and how that knowledge is used in other settings and other environments. Situated-learning approaches acknowledge that these arrangements for learning are constructed by communities of people. They also suggest that learning is itself a social practice which has the potential to transform the practice itself. What this means is that learning, knowledge and its outcomes have to be understood historically and as being socially embedded.

Conclusion

If we refer back to our original example of learning then it is possible to understand how in workplace learning, and more specifically induction into a new workplace, those features of a situated-learning approach which we have discussed above are present. We have suggested that these features or contexts are four-fold: knowledge, power, teaching and learning strategies, and structures of the learning environment. Induction comprises learning about the way members of the new organisation understand the various contexts, pre-texts, sub-texts and inter-texts which underpin the way it works, and then comparing them to their previous understandings of organisational life. Central to adopting a new way of working is to understand how the various power networks operate in the new place of work. Learning is likely to operate informally, though the new place of work may have arranged a formal induction programme. Regardless of whether this learning is informally or formally structured, how it takes place will allow the learner greater or lesser freedom to interpret the new rules which they are learning and contribute to their development. Finally, learning in this instance is located in time and place, takes on a particular form which determines what is learnt and may or may not contribute to successful induction. Situated-learning approaches reject the view that our representations of reality are given in a prior sense or that the human mind is constructed in a particular way which determines what and how we learn, but instead, argue that learning is embedded within arrangements made by particular societies. The source of learning is therefore particular social practices.

References

Bernstein, B. (1985) 'On Pedagogic Discourse', *Handbook of Theory and Research in the Sociology of Education*, New York: Greenwood Press.

Bredo, E. (1999) 'Reconstructing Educational Psychology', in P. Murphy (ed.) Learners, *Learning and Assessment*, London: Sage Publications.

Bruner, J. (1996) *The Culture of Education*, Harvard: Harvard University Press.

Hacking, I. (1981) 'Introduction', in I. Hacking (ed.) *Scientific Revolutions*, Oxford: Oxford University Press.

Usher, R. (1997) 'Telling a Story about Research and Research as Story-Telling: Post Modern Approaches to Social Research', in G. McKenzie, J. Powell and R. Usher (eds.) *Understanding Social Research: Perspectives on Methodology and Practice*, London: Falmer Press.

Weiner, G. (1990) 'The Framing of School Knowledge: History in the National Curriculum', Paper given at the British Educational Research Association Conference, Roehampton College, London, August.

Winogrand, T. and Flores, F. (1986) *Understanding Computers and Cognition*, Reading, MA: Addison-Wesley.

Vernon, P. (1957) *Secondary School Selection*, London: Methuen.

Yates, A. and Pidgeon, D. (1957) *Admission to Grammar School*, London: Newnes.

3

Autism: A Personal Account

Therese Jolliffe, Richard Lansdown and Clive Robinson

Preface

The person who wrote the account which forms the body of this chapter was diagnosed as autistic while a child and is still under the care of a consultant psychiatrist. The original was written to one person and the use of the second person pronoun has, therefore, been maintained. Editing has consisted mainly of cutting rather than altering the words written.

Introduction

From what I understood you wanted from our meeting, I have tried to give you all my ideas on things which I think you would be interested in. I have done this by mentioning not only what I feel to be my problems, but also what other people have pointed them out to be, as this I found to be an essential prerequisite to providing you with the advice you wanted.

I am very willing to help, but am a little worried about my particular problems and recommendations being taken to be the case for all people. My own feelings on the autistic syndrome and my experience with other people who have the same condition, is that despite all similarities in the behaviour, autism is a multiple problem and people so afflicted are afflicted to different extents in differing areas.

Not all my difficulties might be a result of my autism. I have other medical problems which include epilepsy and these could obscure the picture. I have been told that my autism is typical in many respects, but also my academic ability is very rare and this must make a difference to my condition.

In order to write this paper I have questioned people who know me well and knew me when I was very young. In the light of what others have to say about my problems and my own recognition of my particular difficulties, I have tried to give explanations for why I think and behave in certain ways. I know I am not qualified to provide my own explanations, but I thought it might be useful to try to obtain an insight into how I am thinking, as well as to the possible reasons behind my behaviour.

A Brief Review of My Life History

When I was young I was thought to have a hearing problem – it was noticed that I did not always respond to people when spoken to and I had difficulty in understanding what other people were saying and in learning to speak. In the space of one year I had four audiograms and it was decided that I did not have a hearing problem but it appeared that I had a slow response to sound: I was then referred to a hospital in London. Before the tests began I was thought to be suffering from aphasia, after the tests I was thought to be suffering from auditory agnosia and epilepsy. The latter diagnosis remained, but I was a little later seen at another hospital, where I was diagnosed as autistic. Since then the same diagnosis has always been arrived at by other psychologists and psychiatrists.

My mother said I was a very good baby – unlike my older sister I hardly ever cried. People rarely knew when I was awake, because I would be lying so quietly in my cot. I was the perfect baby because I made very few demands on her; a fact she once said she never really appreciated at the time, because she felt very unhappy after I was born. I can actually remember lying awake in my cot, along with what my cot looked like. I can remember being very interested in the colours in a picture which had been stuck on to the end of my cot. Although I can still remember what this picture looked like, I never actually understood what it was portraying at the time.

I spent a great deal of time alone in my bedroom and was happiest when the door was closed and I was by myself. I cannot remember ever thinking about where my mother, father, brother and sister were, they did not seem to concern me. I think this was because I did not for a time realise that they were people and that people are supposed to be more important than objects.

I used to, and still want to, put a big dark blanket over my head. This desire increases when I am with unfamiliar people and in unfamiliar surroundings. Doing this makes me feel much safer, but I used to get hot and run out of air and if I do it now I get told off.

Up to the age of seven or eight, I spent hours enjoying running my fingers over and scratching on the edge of my pillow case which had embroidery around it. I still do this now with different surfaces, especially if it feels good and makes a small sound, although I am frightened of some things, like polystyrene. I am frightened of its feel and the sound of it being touched.

I can remember, when I was bored, digging a hole in the wall which my bed was against. Over the few years I did this I had made the hole quite big. Also for a number of years I put my leg up against the bedroom wall and ran my heel down the wall. After a few years of doing this an arc gradually appeared on the wall paper. It must have been around ten centimetres thick.

When I was on my own I read books – hundreds of them. At first I just read them from cover to cover. Something made me feel I had to read them from beginning to end, without missing a single word. It was a long time before I actually understood and began to get any enjoyment from what I was doing.

I borrowed my older sister's Meccano set when I was six or seven and I made all the models in the construction booklet: a windmill, cement mixer, crane, merry-go-round and lorry. I found the wheels, cogs and chain most interesting of all the pieces. But as soon as I had made the models, which did not take long, the fun had ended and although I had made each one a number of times, I wished the book had a few more pictures of things to make.

I liked opening and closing the doors of some of my toy cars, and in particular watching the wheels as I turned them round. I used to put them one behind the other in a long line so that it looked like there was a long traffic jam, although this was not the intention; I used to put lego bricks into long lines as well.

I had hundreds of plastic toy soldiers. I put them in a big glass jar and I used to like quickly turning the jar and looking at the different colours and patterns.

I had a dolly and a dolly's cot, but pushed the dolly's head into the fire and burnt all its hair. My mother threw it out as it was ruined. I did not know what to do with the doll's cot so I got my father's hack saw and cut the poles off – my mother was very cross with me.

I had a round cardboard cylinder with metal on top. If I turned it over it made a noise of a cow. I remember enjoying playing with this, but other people got fed up with the same noise, and one day it seemed to vanish which made me very angry.

I had a cap gun and the bang at first frightened me. When I got used to the noise I liked watching the used tape come out and get longer and longer as it went bang. I also then started liking the bang sound and the small amount of smoke and its smell was interesting, but the noise got on other peoples' nerves, so nobody would buy me any more tape when I used it up. I had another gun which fired small gold plastic balls, about the size of a ball-bearing. This was not so interesting. It only went bang and fired the ball, so I pointed it out through the open kitchen door, so I could hear a small sound if it hit something hard. This was alright until my mother walked though and I hit her on her legs. After this my gun stayed in the shed on a high shelf.

One thing people did not seem to mind was my cutting up pieces of paper. The pieces had to be white and completely blank on both sides and I cut them into tiny pieces and kept them in a transparent box. I got very angry when my older sister emptied out my box and blew the pieces across the table. I also liked collecting the lids of tubes of Smarties. These were orange, green, blue, red and yellow and had a letter of the alphabet on. I had more orange ones and only a few blue ones and I never got all the letters of the alphabet. The only problem was that I wanted to take the lids off all the tubes of Smarties when I went to a sweet shop so that I could see what letter was underneath and this seemed to make other people angry.

I hated school. Parents of autistic children should never think about sending their children to ordinary schools, because the suffering will far outweigh any of the benefits achieved. The children just cannot tell anybody they are suffering and if you do end up with A-levels it does not really make people want you, so it seems that you cannot use the qualification to obtain let alone keep, a job. Although ordinary schooling enabled me to leave with a dozen or so O-levels and a few A-levels and then to obtain a degree, it is not worth all the misery I suffered.

The teachers pretended to be understanding but they were not. I was frightened of the girls and boys, the teachers and everything there. I was frightened of the toilets and you had to ask to use them which I was not able to do, also I was never sure when I wanted to go to the toilet anyway and the teachers got fed up with having to take me to the nurse to change me. It was mainly the women that were horrible, the men were a bit nicer. When I was at school I was kicked, hit, pushed over and made fun of by the other children. When I attended a place for autistic people, life was a little more bearable and there was certainly less despair.

However, once at university I was rarely teased, let alone kicked. I was allowed always to sit in my favourite places and when it came to my exams I was separated from the others in my favourite room, with the conditions as I liked them, because any change from my usual timetable was found to have an adverse affect on my work. I ended up with a high upper second degree.

There are certain things I enjoy, music is one, cantering on horseback is another: my consultant says the latter is because I enjoy the very rhythmical and rocking movement. I think he is right. But I do not ride any more because the lady whose horse I rode has now moved away and taken it with her. I used to really enjoy, and still sometimes do, looking at lights (but not very bright ones, like those used by photographers), shining metal and anything which sparkles, I also like spinning objects and watching them spin and enjoy the feel of certain surfaces.

I have spent most of my life attending hospitals for some reason or another. I have suffered from a great deal of stomach pain, which started from a very young age when I was unable to tell anybody. It occurs at anytime, but always when I know I have to go somewhere or do something which I know I will find very stressful. Sometimes the pain is so bad that my whole body becomes stiff and then I am unable to move. But I never suffer from stomach pain when I see doctors or visit hospitals, maybe because I have become so used to them.

What is it Like to be Autistic

When I was very young I can remember that speech seemed to be of no more significance than any other sound. For a time speech sounds seemed just to merge into one another without making any sense, a jumble of letters, hard to reproduce, let alone understand.

I began to understand a few single words by their appearance on paper. When I did begin to recognise odd words this was more comforting because I tended to recognise those words associated with things I liked. Then the reverse thing occurred, I began to associate the sound of particular words with things which I found unpleasant. I used to be very frightened of dogs because of their sudden movements and their barking. Every time I heard the word 'dog' I was not sure whether one was going to suddenly appear or not and because I could only understand single words at first and not the context, language acquisition began to take on a horrible side as well. Sentences still seemed to lack any clear definition.

It was ages before I realised that people speaking might be demanding my attention. But I sometimes got annoyed once I realised that I was expected to attend to what other people were saying because my quietness was being disturbed. I began to start to understand more than just a single word at a time when I realised that speech was sometimes directed at me. At the same time I started reading in my head and writing sentences at school. It was then I found that spoken language started to frustrate me. I was able to understand words better when they were on paper than when they were said out aloud, I did not realise at the time that I was different in this respect. I just tended to feel frustrated because the sounds of the words were so confusing and people expected me to understand speech.

Speaking for me is still often difficult and occasionally impossible, although this has become easier over the years. I sometimes know in my head what the words are but they do not always come out. Sometimes when they do come out they are incorrect, a fact that I am only sometimes aware of and which is often pointed out by other people.

One of the most frustrating things about autism is that it is very difficult to explain how you are feeling: whether something hurts or frightens you or when you are feeling unwell and you cannot stick up for yourself. I take Beta Blockers sometimes to reduce the physical symptoms of fear and although I can now tell people if something frightens me, I can never actually tell them when the event is occurring. Similarly, on several occasions when I have been asked what my name is by a stranger I cannot always remember it and yet when I am more relaxed I can remember phone numbers and formulae after just hearing them once. When I am very frightened by somebody or something, or I am in pain, I can often make motor movements and a noise, but the words just do not come out.

Sometimes when I really need to speak and I just cannot, the frustration is terrible. I want to kick out at people and objects, throw things, rip things up and break them and very occasionally scream. But I do not like to ruin any of my possessions, so in the end this sort of behaviour does not actually achieve very much. I usually end up just giving up in despair, and terrible it feels too. When I get like this no amount of trying to do anything about it makes any difference.

People's names are difficult to remember and say and I still get the names of similar objects confused, like sandals and shoes, dresses and skirts, knives and forks. Although I get the name wrong I do actually know what I mean. Also if I am in a situation where I have to talk to somebody about another person, when I refer to the person we are talking about and try to mention them by name, I seem always to give the name of the person I am talking to rather than the actual person I am talking about. Most of the time I am not aware of doing this, though others seem to notice it.

It is hard to reproduce and understand words that are similar in sound, like ball and bull, fend and vend, beam and bean, mum and numb, chase and case, bad and bag. Although people pick me up on any mispronunciations, they do not seem to notice that when they speak there is in every sentence words that are hard to distinguish, although after a bit of effort I can often work out what these words are from the context of the sentence. But when somebody talks to me I have to really try and listen carefully, if I am going to stand any chance of working out what the words are. At school and during my first degree I was helped by the fact that I could read up topics in advance, things were also written down on the blackboard, the work tended to follow a logical progression and because new material was being put across to students, teachers could not talk too fast, rather they seemed to leave gaps of a second or two between each sentence which enabled me to guess more accurately what I had heard. When I read books the problem of deciphering what the words actually are does not exist because I can see immediately what they are meant to be. Sometimes, though, it is very difficult to concentrate even just on reading, because things that frighten and worry me disturb my concentration.

I was once asked by somebody why I repeat the same phrase exactly as I had heard it and in a similar voice to the person who said it. I had no answer at the time. Being asked to write this paper I have had to think more deeply about myself than I have ever had to before. I now know that there are several answers. First, you have to work so hard in order to understand speech, that when the words eventually do go into your brain they seem to become imprinted in the way you hear them. Second, because trying to speak is quite an effort, particularly when you are just starting to learn to speak, it is all you can do to just try and reproduce what your good memory knows. Third, for a long time you have so little idea about speech and it is all such an effort that you seem to believe that the voice of the person used to say the words is the way you, too, have to say them. You do not seem to be aware that the words can be put across using all different kinds of voices and that there are alternative ways of expressing things. It was only from my academic work that I picked up the fact that there is more than one correct way of saying things. Fourth, sometimes I used to repeat the same words over again as this made me feel safer. Fifth, when I first started repeating back phrases exactly as I had heard them I think I did this as I was only able to come out with one or two words for myself so it seemed to be a good way of experimenting with longer sentences, even if they weren't thought out by me.

Throughout my life, I have had as much difficulty in trying to understand sounds, as I have had in trying to understand words. I have come to this conclusion quite recently, as I am still frightened of so many sounds that I cannot obviously be interpreting them correctly. The following are just some of the noises that still upset me enough to cover up my ears to avoid them: shouting, noisy crowded places, polystyrene being touched, balloons being touched, noisy cars, trains, motorbikes, lorries and aeroplanes, noisy vehicles on building sites, hammering and banging, electric tools being used, the sound of the sea, the sound of felt-tip or marker pens being used to colour in, and fireworks. Despite this I can read music and play it and there are certain types of music I love. In fact when I am feeling angry and despairing of everything, music is the only way of making me feel calmer inside.

I find it as difficult to understand the things I see as I do in trying to understand the things I hear. Looking at people's faces, particularly into their eyes, is one of the hardest things for me to do. When I do look at people I have nearly always had to make a conscious effort to do so and then I can usually only do it for a second. If I do look at people for longer periods of time, they usually claim that I seem to be just looking through them rather than actually at them, as if I am unaware that they are actually there. People do not appreciate how unbearably difficult it is for me to look at a person. It disturbs my quietness and is terribly frightening – though the fear decreases with increasing distance from the person. I have been trying to work on making eye contact whilst at hospital and whilst being treated by my consultant psychiatrist, but it has taken two-and-a-half years and has not been successful. My psychiatrist does not force me to look at him, although he insists on looking at me. He has explained that people might wrongly interpret my not looking at them as my being uninterested in them, that I am being untruthful about something or just rude. I am trying hard, because I do not want people thinking wrong things like this, but at the very best I can only look at someone for a couple of seconds. It is almost as bad having other people looking at me as it is me looking at them. I have only just recently realised that when I look at people and pictures, I am not looking at the whole but rather just the outline or a part. I *can* look at a picture completely, but only a small section at a time. It is the same with people's faces, I cannot take in the whole face in one go.

Once when I had psychological testing I was shown a number of faces all the same size and all black and white. Immediately afterwards I was shown two pictures at the same time, one of which I was meant to have just seen and I was to point this out. By the law of probability I had to get half right and I had to guess every one of them. Even though the lady said that I had just seen one of the two faces, I did not feel that I could recognise having seen this or really any of them for that matter. To me no one face seemed to have made any impression at all, they seemed like a mass of undifferentiated faces. Yet I could quickly and perfectly recognise as just having seen abstract words like 'and', 'at' and 'the', from a whole pile of such words, these seemed to have made a very good impression on me. But people, even the whole and not only just the face, do not seem to always make any proper sort of impression. I find it hard to recognise familiar people sometimes and I often do not notice a person in a room until they move and then it seems to disturb my inner quietness.

It may be because things that I see do not always make the right impression that I am frightened of so many things that can be seen: people, particularly their faces, very bright lights, crowds, things moving suddenly, large machines and buildings that are unfamiliar, unfamiliar places, my own shadow, the dark, bridges, rivers, canals, streams and the sea.

I always feel that I can understand things better through my fingers. Two of my relatives, one of whom is a clinical psychologist and the other a psychiatrist, both say that it appears that I am trying to compensate for my lack of auditory, and particularly my lack of visual understanding by making use of my fingers, sometimes, they said, just as though I was blind. My consultant psychiatrist said something like this as well because I was always pulling him and touching him in a way that his other patients would not have dared to. He said that most people would not realise that I was in fact actually communicating with him, even if it was in an unorthodox way.

On the other hand I tend not to like kisses, hugs and cuddles very much. If I do give anybody a hug and cuddle it has to be when I feel like it, not when they want it. The only person who gets a hug at the moment is my consultant psychiatrist. My GP says he is a very lucky man, but I do not understand what luck has got to do with a hug.

I usually find what other people call jokes very difficult to understand, so I rarely laugh at them. I do laugh occasionally, but it is rarely because I have found anything particularly funny, rather it is a repetition of the sound of somebody else laughing. It is interesting to try it out and makes you feel safer if you had heard this sound at a time when you actually felt a bit safer than you do at this moment. Similarly what other people call odd hand movements and what people refer to as grimaces are not meant to be annoying, they, too, give a sense of control, safety and perhaps pleasure.

Most people find that they can at least share their physical suffering with others, but nobody really understands what the emotional suffering of a person with autism is like, and there is no pain killer, injection or operation that can get rid of it or even at best relieve it even a little. Autism affects everything all the time. One person said to me once, 'It must be a blessing when you are asleep, at least you are not exposed to situations that you find frightening'. But this showed how little she and other people know about autism, because it will not even leave you while you are asleep. It affects your dreams and when they wake you up, you have to cope not only with what seemed a very real dream but a dark bedroom.

I once read that autism is a withdrawal from reality and somewhere else that autism is a problem in forming relationships and relating to other people. These were supposed to be the definitions, but they are both very misleading. Saying autism is a withdrawal from reality is incorrect because it implies that the person knew what reality meant in the first place before she withdrew from it for whatever reason. I feel it should have read, 'an inability to understand reality in the first place and that this itself leads to a person being withdrawn'. This is where the problem in forming relationships and relating to other people comes in. The latter is difficult to do because you have never been able to make any sense of reality, and thus cannot understand why you should, and how you should, form a relationship, not that you have just withdrawn from reality. Reality to an autistic person is a confusing, interacting mass of events, people, places, sounds and sights. There seem to be no clear boundaries, order or meaning to anything. A large part of my life is just trying to work out the pattern behind everything. Set routines, times, particular routes and rituals all help to get order into an unbearably chaotic life. Even when I want sometimes to take part in something, my brain just will not tell me how I should go about it, and contrary to what people may think, it is possible for an autistic person to feel lonely and to love somebody.

Normal people, finding themselves on a planet with alien creatures on it, would probably feel frightened, would not know how to fit in and would certainly have difficulty in understanding what the aliens were thinking, feeling and wanting, and how to respond correctly to these things. That's what autism is like. If anything were suddenly to change on this planet a normal person would be worried about it if they did not properly understand what this change meant. That's what autistic people feel like when things change. Trying to keep everything the same reduces some of the terrible fear. Fear has dominated my life. Even when things are not directly frightening I tend to fear that something horrible might happen, because I cannot make sense of what I see. Life is bewildering, a confusing, interacting mass of people, events, places and things with no boundaries. Social life is hard because it does not seem to follow a set pattern. When I begin to think that I have just started to understand an idea, it suddenly does not seem to follow the same pattern when the circumstances alter slightly. There seems to be so much to learn. People with autism get very angry because the frustration of not being able to understand the world properly is so terrible – sometimes it gets too much, then people say they are surprised when I get angry.

As it was a long time before I realised that people might actually be speaking to me, so it was a long time before I realised that I too was a person – if somewhat different from most others. I never thought about how I might fit in with other people when I was very young because I was not able to pick people out as being different from objects. Then when I did realise that people were supposed to be more important than objects and became more generally aware, things began to take on a new and more difficult light.

Objects are frightening. Moving objects are harder to cope with because of the added complexity of movement. Moving objects which also make a noise are even harder to cope with because you have to try to take in the sight, movement and further added complexity of the noise. Human beings are the hardest of all to understand because not only do you have to cope with the problem of just seeing them, they move about when you are not expecting them to, they make varying noises and along with this, they place all different kinds of demands on you which are just impossible to understand. As soon as you begin to think you are grasping how one of them works, something happens to change all this.

Life is such a struggle; indecision over things that other people refer to as trivial results in an awful lot of inner distress. For instance, if somebody at home says, 'We may go shopping tomorrow', or if somebody says, 'We will see what happens', they do not seem to realise that the uncertainty causes a lot of inner distress, and that I constantly labour, in a cognitive sense, over what may or may not occur. The indecision over events extends to indecision over other things, such as where objects are to be put or found and over what people are expecting from me.

It is the confusion that results from not being able to understand the world around me which I think causes all the fear. This fear then brings a need to withdraw. Anything which helps reduce the confusion (and a few people can actually be useful here) has the effect of reducing the fear and ultimately reduces the isolation and despair, thus making life a bit more bearable to live in. If only other people could experience what autism is like just for a few minutes, they might then know how to help!

Recommendations for the Child's First Few Visits to a Specialist

Because a person with autism has to cope with so much all the time, any change, even a different building or room, is frightening. The fear can be reduced.

When I was a child, the worst thing to happen to me was for my parents to drag me into a strange building, then into a strange room and then to be faced with somebody I did not know suddenly talking to me. Trying to be friendly towards a child straight away is unlikely to work. It is better to ignore him for as long as possible. From what I can remember I do not think that autistic children can interpret friendliness as being nice or even just realise when people are being friendly – although they probably can recognise when people are being nasty.

Because to an autistic person things are so complicated and frightening, it is far better to take things in stages. First getting used to the room, then your voice and appearance while not actually being directed at him and then finally you talking to him and looking at him.

The child should be allowed to see the consulting room first, without the professional actually being there. This is particularly important for the first few times. The parents should be with the child; this will make the child feel safer, even if this does not seem apparent. But it would be better for the parents not to 'hang on' to the child; autistic people do not like to feel restrained in any way, they would rather feel free to escape more easily from any horrible situation.

While alone in the room, the child has only to cope with the new sights and it is good to have time to become familiar with these. The longer the time given to this the more beneficial this will be but I realise that available space could be a problem. If you were to have two interview rooms a child could get used to a room while you were seeing somebody else.

Although this idea would not use up any extra time on your part, it would require an additional room and you would have to remember to show the child to the same room each time, otherwise it would not work.

When you enter, it would be good to talk fairly quietly to the parents and to be sitting as far away as possible from the child. This will enable the child not to feel overpowered and will enable him to get used to the sound of your voice (which is more frightening the louder it sounds) and also your appearance. If you are busy talking to and looking at the parents, the child is more likely to look at you. My own experience is that I tend to look at people when they are unaware of it. This enables me to get used to a person's appearance, without causing so much distress inside. Even if a child was not to look at you directly he could still get used to your outline from the edge of his field of vision.

If at first you just spoke to the parents and not the child, he might notice the fact that his parents seem to think that this different person is OK. If you do talk to the child directly it is best at first to keep it as brief as possible (more on this aspect later).

Having taken the autistic child time to get used to the room, I think it is important to mention, that if you were to move anything or change anything around then this actual change would probably generate some degree of fear. It does not matter how small the change is and even whether you have forgotten that you have altered the place of anything, an autistic person will probably notice it, and if he does, it will cause some distress.

Using the approach I have suggested above may not make you or the parents feel particularly happy, but I am sure it would make a big difference to the person with autism,

Recommendations for Parents and Professionals and Some General Points to Note

I do not now believe that autism can be cured because there are so many different factors – it seems to be a multiple problem. But I do believe that people with autism can be helped and that some of the therapies are better than others.

One form of treatment which I have had is Holding Therapy. To me the suffering was terrible and it achieved nothing. Some people who dislike this treatment argue that children submit out of exhaustion. I think this is true in many cases. A claim by proponents of this therapy is that the children are much quieter and better behaved for a little while afterwards. My quietness was due to exhaustion and to my being disturbed so much as a result of the experience that I was shocked into a state of terrified quietness, where I could not think or do anything much for a while.

There is something very special about music. It can be calming when all else fails and it seems to make the mind open up and become more receptive. Music therapy has never been used on me, but if I am autistic as everybody seems to think, then what I can say is that certain kinds of music really can help autistic people. When I attended a National Autistic Society centre before starting my second degree, I can remember two people who hardly ever spoke, but who could sing words perfectly. One of my relatives claims that when I was very young I would only speak when a certain kind of music was playing. This was classical, baroque, string, piano and some singing. Not only would I occasionally speak when these types of music were playing but apparently my behaviour was better and people said it was obvious that I was listening very intently to the music. In fact it was supposed to be the only time when I would let people anywhere near me. Maybe some children could be taught through first hearing the words sung.

I stated in an earlier section how speech seemed to be a jumble of sounds, so that the separate words with their separate meanings were for a long time impossible to differentiate. Too many requests in one sentence result in terrible confusion, distress, angriness and ultimately to withdrawal. Sentences need to be kept short because it is hard for autistic people to cope with one idea, let alone the possibility of more. Although, because of my academic work I can understand longer words, I do not think this is the case for most people with autism. The odd thing I have noticed is that I can now distinguish the sound of longer words actually better than I can the very short ones. But I feel that most autistic people would appreciate the use of simple words with gaps being left between sentences, so that they too can stand a chance in working out what words and ideas were being said as well. Even for me now I have often to try hard to work out what ideas are being put across.

People, particularly parents, need to say in short sentences EXACTLY what they mean, otherwise autistic people do not stand a chance in normal conversation and it might make them just give up. You mentioned to me at one point that you would 'lean on' a charity for some more money, but that you could not promise anything. I knew what you meant on this occasion, but most autistic people would not have known what you meant. Using odd words and expressions such as 'lean on' would really confuse and frustrate them.

When somebody starts to speak to me, I have nearly always lost the first few words before I realise that I am actually being spoken to. This happens so much that I have called them the 'waking up words'. It might be a good idea to repeat the first few words to a person with autism, particularly if you are giving them instructions to do anything. At the end of a sentence the last few words seem to make a stronger impression and are on occasions the only ones that can be meaningful. I often repeat what people are saying in my head, as if to try and get it clearer, and the last part always seems to stick, although the first part occasionally disappears. Most people would not think of repeating the first part of a sentence over again, so in my case, if I am unable to work out what this should have been, by using the rest of the sentence, then I become completely lost. There is a chance that other people who are autistic could be having this problem as well.

People with autism often carry out requests wrongly because they failed to understand the instructions properly. In order to ensure that they have understood exactly what was said, and if the person can talk reasonably well, it might be useful to get them to repeat back what you have said. However, if it is repeated back exactly then there is a good chance that they have not understood what you have said at all. You can tell whether they have understood what you were saying if they can repeat the instructions that you have given, correctly, but in a slightly different way, i.e. by using different words or in a different order. But this I think is extremely difficult for an autistic person to do and to grasp why you are doing it.

I sometimes still find it confusing when there is more than one alternative name for something – although this has lessened considerably. This I think is important to remember not just for yourself but to make parents aware of this problem. When introducing or referring to any new object, parents should always stick to just one name for quite a time, otherwise an autistic person will not understand what is being said and will become very confused and frustrated. After a very long time it would be OK to use different names for the same object. Parents need to be told to be consistent in the use of names.

I cannot give any reasons why, but I seem to be more frightened of things on some days than I am on others. On my bad days it takes much less to frighten me and I have more difficulty in behaving correctly. Other people with autism are probably like this as well. Parents need to be made aware that what is often called difficult behaviour, is in fact a direct response to the difficulties (fear and frustration) of life and that these difficulties stem from a very imperfect ability to understand sounds, sights and demands, of which human beings are the most complex.

Even when an autistic person can speak well, parents need to realise that their children can temporarily lose their speech if something frightens and worries them.

Because I did not respond to my name for a while, it tended to be used more and with more emphasis. When my parents were cross with me, they showed this by suddenly shouting out my name and the shouting has made me feel frightened. Ever since then I have become frightened if somebody suddenly shouts out my name, although it is OK when I am expecting to be called and it is OK if it is said more quietly. I think parents should be made more conscious of the effect of their behaviour on their autistic child. They should avoid shouting at their child unless it is absolutely necessary, because it is actually quite painful to hear shouting, and it is wrong if your name is made into something to be frightened of.

If parents complain that their children are bad at sleeping, it could be because the autism is actually affecting the child's dreams. If these dreams wake him up, it is very hard for him to realise that they are not real. It takes ages even with having a light put on afterwards to realise that what was experienced during sleep was just a dream. This still happens to me now. Most autistic children would not understand that there is such a thing as a dream anyway. Also if the bedroom is dark when you first wake from a horrible dream this adds to all the fear.

When I was young I hated my hair being brushed and washed, my teeth being cleaned and my nails being cut. I did not like people anywhere near me and I was cross that my quietness was being disturbed. However, if parents are sure that their child is not actually frightened, they should be very insistent for these are essential things to be done.

If it is possible to teach autistic people by feel then I think this should be used. I could not learn properly how to put a knife and fork on the correct sides of the plate from just being told how to. But when somebody put the items into my hands and placed my hands down on the table in the correct positions, I learnt for good, once these steps were repeated a few times. Similarly, it was years before I could put my shoes on the correct feet until somebody took hold of my hands and ran my fingers along the sides of my feet and then the sides of my shoes. After doing this a few times, I began to put my footwear on my feet by running my hands along the sides of my feet and then my shoes to match up the correct ones. Eventually I then learnt to go just by the look of my feet and the sides of my shoes. I even learnt to read by first running my fingers over the letters. If one thinks deeply then a lot of things could be adapted so that they can be learnt by feel.

Because life is such a confusing mass of sounds and sights it really helps an autistic person if he can get order into his life. It is important that the need for consistency mentioned earlier is maintained throughout each day as well as every day. This might be boring for most people but it is one of the few things that can actually relieve suffering a little. For me it is essential to have set times and places for everything. Parents could help their children to feel safer but they would probably find their own life very dull. A problem exists: if I am going to get better I have got to let things change. There seems then to be a trade off between keeping the order the same to minimise fear and in changing things to progress. I would suggest that the ordinary day-to-day tasks like having a bath, eating meals, washing hair and cleaning teeth should be all done at the same times and that a child should have a period of listening to music every day at the same time. There will then be some order and new things can be introduced in between.

If a parent takes a child to visit or stay somewhere, or in particular moves to a new place to live, then they should remember that the effect on the child is very great. A child should be shown every room or relevant part of the building. The different rooms or places should be shown slowly and with breaks in between; otherwise it will just appear a confusing and un-differentiated mass of frightening places. All the details should be pointed out and the whole process repeated several times, but also after appropriate breaks. This should reduce some of the fear and enable the child to get some order into his life. Similarly, if you know that you are going to have to take a child to a new place, where he may experience something unpleasant, then it is a good idea if you can take him before the event, in order to get him at least used to the sight of the place. This will have the effect of reducing some of the initial fear. Even if parents are going to look at new places to live, it is a good idea to take the child along. When you do eventually select a place, he will at least have seen it before and this will make his life a bit more manageable if he suddenly finds himself having to live in a strange place.

I find it very difficult to grasp social things and will only succeed in most cases if every tiny step, rule and idea is written down and numbered one after another in a column, then I have to go over these ever so many times in order to learn all these rules. But even this is no guarantee that you will always know how, when and where to apply things, as circumstances which are in any way different to how you learnt the rules will confuse. Some people have tried to teach me social things by linking similar ideas together, but this does not always work because the ideas seem to merge so that it is very difficult to differentiate which is which and how, when and where to apply these things because no one situation is identical to every other situation. I am afraid I have no good suggestions on how social things can be learnt. All I can say is that I prefer them to be written down in a column and numbered, but this is not likely to be of much value unless the autistic person can read – though I presume pictures portraying every little step could be used, but even these can be difficult for an autistic person to understand.

4

Children's Idiomatic Expressions of Cultural Knowledge

Akosua Obuo Addo

Introduction

Play activities, such as singing games, are simulations of social processes and expressions of intellectual processes (for example, observation, listening, spatial relationships, sequencing, and memorization). Children deliberately teach one another games and learn from one another; they think and express ideas while playing singing games. I argue that (a) cultural knowledge structures are evident in the performance and practice of singing games and (b) identifying and understanding the teaching and learning styles that underpin these music cultures facilitates the introduction of diverse music cultures in the general music class.

The central question of this chapter is: how can we introduce children in the elementary class to the cultural knowledge of Ghana through singing games? The chapter begins with a discussion of my theoretical position by considering research on culturally relevant teaching and learning styles and the implications for selecting curriculum content and structure in our global culture. This is followed by a description of the cultural context of singing games, and the method used to collect information for the chapter. Children's ways of knowing demonstrated during the performance of singing games in relation to three teaching and learning scenarios will then be discussed. Drawing on Gardner's (1985) categorics, the knowledge and skills demonstrated by the children during the performance and practice of singing games include intra- and inter-personal, memorization, motor co-ordination, language, tonal perception and rhythmic perception, numerical, and spatial skills. The final part details implications for professional practice.

Theoretical Position

With the emergence of learning theories based on social values, researchers argue that knowledge evolves from within a culture. Gardner (1985), for example, believes that each culture places value on the different aspects of intelligence that inform expressions of intellectual processes. Cross-cultural research shows that alternative thinking styles are evident among children of different backgrounds (Fiati, 1992). Intellectual processes constitute consciously held knowledge, skills, and ways of thinking or, more simply put, cultural knowledge structures. Therefore, to understand learning and suggest implications for teaching, it is important to study cultural knowledge structures. Interestingly, thirty years before Gardner's treatise, Kodály had proposed that his musical mother tongue, which is interpreted in many different ways today, was congruent with current theories of learning based on cultural knowledge structures (Chosky, 1981). To understand a music culture further, it is also important to study music learning within the culture (Chosky, 1981 on Kodály; Tracey, 1994).

Gardner's (1985, p. 57) belief that culture influences individual intellectual capabilities is shared by musicologist and educator, Kodály. Kodály believed that music educators world-wide could improve their music programmes by analysing their own country's music and including it in the music curriculum (see Chosky, 1981; Zemke, 1973). Ownership of music cultures becomes important in a nation with multi-ethnic cultures. In some of her previous work Addo (1996) demonstrated the manner in which children in Ghana identify with different music cultures and recreate music cultures on the playground as they are enculturated. The children eventually take ownership of these different cultures. Kodály identified structural similarities in the analysis of thousands of Hungarian folk tunes he had collected with assistance from Bartók. From this analysis, Kodály developed a sequence for teaching melody in Hungarian schools (Zemke, 1973). Numerous educators from other countries adopted both Kodály's sequence for teaching melody and Hungarian folk music. This was not what Kodály had intended, given his explicit argument that educators should use their own country's music in their music programmes. Osborn (1986, p. 2) examined Kodály's argument in a review of the Hungarian approach used in Canadian school music curricula. She suggested that pitch patterns of different cultures' traditional songs embody the metric and rhythmic structures of the particular language structure. She posited, therefore, that pitch-pattern characteristics differ across cultures (p. 220). Osborn, in agreement with Kodály, argued that Canadian music curricula should be based on Canadian folk music. Many countries, like Canada, are home to people of different cultures and therefore home to the new expressions of the music of these people. The music cultures of these countries embrace the cultures of many nations, and teachers continue to introduce different aspects of these cultures in their teaching. Whether labelled intercultural/multicultural or intracultural music programmes, the process of teaching and learning is as important for imparting cultural knowledge as the content of teaching. The analysis of folklore such as the performance and practice of Ghanaian singing games provides information for educational practice in general, and the curriculum content of cultural studies programmes in particular, with regard to cultural knowledge structures in performance events.

Cultural Context

This is an ethnography of Ghanaian children's singing games as a cultural resource in the elementary music class. Ghanaian cultural knowledge is the shared meanings in the Ghanaian social context, which includes indigenous cultures, cultures absorbed during the colonial era and cultures of recent global interactions. Music, dance, and language used in Ghana are influenced by these cultures. Indigenous Ghanaian society places importance on informal methods of enculturation. These informal methods are functional, in that they exist within the lived situation. The publicly shared meanings, and shared knowledge Ghanaians use to create, interpret, and understand social behaviours, drive the cultural situation and vice versa. In contemporary Ghana, enculturation occurs as colonial European values and contemporary global cultures are integrated with indigenous values in cultural expressions.

Material for this chapter was gathered during a six-month period in 1993 in the form of field notes, interviews with children from three schools, adults, photographs, audio and video tapes. Multimedia technologies were used for observation, participant observations, interviewing, analysing, and presenting the data in this study. Three schools situated in and around Cape Coast were selected for my study by the Central Regional Ministry of Education in Ghana. The schools were chosen to guarantee a socio-economic variability. Thirty-five children between the ages of seven and fifteen participated in the study. Fantis and Efutus ethnic groups dominate the otherwise heterogeneous population of the Central Region, Ghana. Situated in West Africa, Ghana has ten regions divided according to political administrative policies and other factors such as economic planning and convergent ethnic groups.

Children's Idiomatic Expressions of Cultural Knowledge

The performance and practice of children's folklore within or outside the school curriculum is significant to children's enculturation. A pattern of culturally accepted human actions and relations develop as children are enculturated into, for example, African society. These actions and relations are based on cultural knowledge structures which are both declarative or propositional knowledge, and procedural knowledge or skill (Bereiter, 1990) (see Figure 4.1).

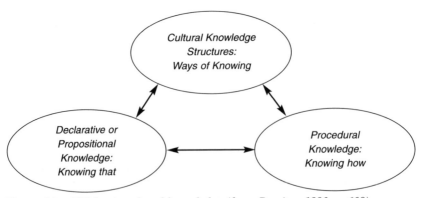

Figure 4.1   *Children's cultural knowledge (from Bereiter, 1990, p. 609)*

Cultural knowledge structures are of value to educational theory and practice in two key areas: (a) learning and teaching styles, and (b) the content and structure of the curriculum.

During my study, I observed three teaching and learning scenarios. In the first the children taught themselves singing games; in the second they taught me singing games (using a more overt teaching and learning style) and in the third the cultural studies teacher taught them conflict resolution skills in class. In all three scenarios, learning styles were marked by the following: (a) knowledge is uninhibited shared constructions, (b) knowledge grows when everyone is involved, and (c) knowledge is like 'midwifery'. I use midwifery as a metaphor for the urging which takes place during the performances of singing games. Usually at the birth of a child, the midwife and significant others coach the mother-to-be with words of encouragement. Occurrences of three learning styles are noted in the following discussion of three teaching and learning scenarios.

Scenario one: children teach and learn from one another

Invariably, whenever children at the three schools decided to play a new singing game, one child held the game's propositional knowledge, while the others had either no or only a vague idea of how it was played. For example, on one occasion, at the Ulesis School playground, I asked the children about particular games I had not seen them play, but which were played at the other two schools. (I wanted to know which games were popular across the three schools.) When I asked if anyone was familiar with the game, 'Pempena', played at Aardvark School, Adelaide (one of my key informants) put up her hand indicating that she knew the game. The other children then immediately gathered around her, ready to learn it. Knowledge is uninhibited shared constructions. The other children wanted to know what Adelaide knew, and she was prepared to share her knowledge. Since the practice and performance of singing games allowed children to share knowledge without reservation, the scenario was a healthy one for both teaching and learning.

If shared knowledge was important, so too, was the level of involvement in the game. As Adelaide used her own teaching style to share her knowledge with her peers, a distinct learning process emerged. Adelaide began by holding her playmates' hands and they in turn formed a circle to begin the game. Then, as was the case with children from the other two schools, they demonstrated a ritualized way of focusing during the performance of singing games – especially circle games (see Addo, 1996).

This activity called other children to the game and set its spatial organization. After the circle was in place, the children repeated the game's opening motif several times in order to gain everyone's attention. For these children it was important that everyone be fully involved in the game, that is, all participants observed one another. Knowledge grows when everyone is involved.

After the circle was formed, Adelaide extended her palms outward in a manner appropriate to the game and the other children followed suit. She then began to sing and clap the game. Observing and listening, the other children followed the sequence of hand claps and played along with Adelaide. The children were expected to learn as the game progressed, and Adelaide, acting as the leader, directed and facilitated the learning process through demonstration and verbal commands. Knowledge is like 'midwifery'. As they began to perceive the sequence in gestures and song, Adelaide's playmates joined her in correcting their peers. Adelaide's role as leader began to diminish as the other children acquired the knowledge necessary to play the game. They became both learners and teachers and through direct observation and experimentation demonstrated a number of skills. When all of the children demonstrated an understanding of the rules of the game, their performance was smooth. This style is Ghanaian cultural values in action – it expresses idiomatically a basic truth about what Africans consider important. An important basis for problem-solving is the weight given to consensus, agreement between people (Chernoff, 1979; Traccy, 1994; Nketia, 1974; Bebey, 1975). Tracey notes that Chopi music education is expected to teach 'how to move, how to correct, in "Chopi style", how to play and give power to others' (p. 275). This is also true in Ghanaian traditional music education processes and among these children.

Scenario two: children teach researcher singing games

When children at Ulesis Primary School first taught me a singing game, they used the method described in the previous section. The hand-clapping singing game they taught me was called 'Ziana Zina', and its performance demanded high levels of physical dexterity, numerical skills and precision. Beginning, as it does with gesture, counting and song, I found the game difficult to follow; I was expected to imitate the children, and as such, I could not master counting and other rules. A verbal description of the rules would have been helpful, as would have dividing the game up into sections. As it was, the only way I could understand what was going on was to ask questions. What became clear to me was the difference between adults' and children's ways of knowing.

The second time around, Adelaide decided that I should learn to play some skipping-rope games. She walked up to me and asked me to give the video camera to Vida, which I did. She then held my hand and brought me over to the rope.

It had become obvious to Adelaide and the other children that I did not learn in the same way they did. This was partly because I was no longer familiar with the gestures, songs, and sequencing of playground games. I had lost the spontaneity, physical dexterity, and co-ordination I had acquired while playing the games as a child in Ghana. Adelaide showed me how to play, section by section, and included verbal instructions such as 'This is the first part'; 'Let me show you the middle section'; 'Now let us do the last part'. However, she did not follow this sequence of events. She showed me the middle section first because the accompanying music provided me with substantial time to practise. She then taught me the tag at the end of the song followed by the beginning. Her friends urged my learning on with giggles and encouraging comments. Throughout the teaching the other children had opportunities to play, and this allowed me to step back and watch them do what I had just been taught. The skills demonstrated by Adelaide and the other children who taught me games were similar to those demonstrated when they taught one another. However, the teaching process was different. Because I was an adult, Adelaide broke the game down into sections and taught them in a sequence she believed would best enable me to learn. When I finally began to play the game correctly, all the children cheered.

The comments the children made as they taught me the singing game type, skipping-rope games are important, because this commentary reflects teaching and learning processes associated with adult traditional music performance. Through the running commentary, the children urged both performance and learning of the game. For these children learning is situated in the selection and collection of these urgings, which are much like a midwife's coaching of a mother about to have a baby. Grunts, verbal comments and other interjections from children participating in, or watching the game encouraged learning, and also communicated how accurately the participants were playing. They applied this same evaluative style when they taught me singing games. This is because learning is found in the accuracy of the relationship among the parts (Tracey, 1994). Also the role of the teacher is simply to motivate, guide and reward the students accordingly for their acquisition of musicianship and appropriate practices (Merriam, 1964; Turkson, 1989). In the next section I describe the extent to which urging comments were also part of a community member's teaching process. Knowledge is like 'midwifery'.

Scenario three: community member teaches

The local community member who taught cultural studies urged the children on during a classroom activity about conflict resolution. She began by presenting a scenario involving two friends having a disagreement. Selecting a student to play the part of one of the feuding friends, she demonstrated a method by which the argument could be resolved. The community member sang a song and used a handkerchief to wipe the student's face. She placed her hand around the shoulders of the student – her 'estranged friend', and walked with the student from one end of the room to the other, trying to win back the 'friendship'. By the completion of the walk, her 'friend' had embraced her, agreeing to make up. Combining hypothetical situations presented with music and dance performance is a popular educational strategy within traditional Ghanaian society. Knowledge is uninhibited shared constructions.

After the teacher demonstrated this conflict resolution method, two children volunteered to try the activity. The other children joined in by singing and making comments about the activity. An active and successful teaching and learning process was established. Knowledge grows when everyone is involved. After a few more children tried the exercise, the groups discussed the activity in detail. In this community member's class, learning was accomplished by doing, a practice similar to that exhibited by the children on the playground.

Co-operation, participation and co-ordination are undisputed qualities of Ghanaian cultural knowledge (Chernoff, 1979; Nketia, 1974). This is because in Ghana, like in other parts of Africa, one person defines another. This concept is transferred to music performance and practice situations as each player defines and complements the other. Whole-making is accomplished through participatory music-making. The community member's teaching style, which utilized question-raising and problem-solving, reflected traditional modes of learning.

Implications for Professional Practice

Whether knowledge is shared constructions, or involves every one, or is like midwifery, particular skills are needed to make knowing possible. In both covert and overt teaching and learning situations, the children in my study demonstrated intra- and inter-personal skills, memorization, motor co-ordination, language, tonal perception and rhythmic perception, numerical and spatial skills.

The three identified ways of knowing demonstrated by the children in Ghana resonate with children of similar backgrounds living in other cultures. Singing games do not represent a self-sufficient panacea for education, even though they combine different intellectual skills such as those outlined by Gardner (1985). Nonetheless, they are more than simply another educational device. Indeed, there are many ways in which singing performance can enhance teaching and learning, particularly, as is the focus of this chapter, the introduction of the cultural knowledge of Ghana in the elementary general music class. In what follows, I outline some implications for teaching and learning.

First, Kwami (1995) has suggested a model of cultural accessibility in teaching West African music in schools and colleges. He rightly proposes that in the initiation it would be better for music educators to begin with pieces that are close to what children listen to. Even though there is a general concern about the gradual disappearance of singing games on several playgrounds, children still know about singing games even if they do not know many. Singing games include movement as do many other forms of African music experience. Hence, I would add to Kwami's classification (see Figure 4.2).

Earlier, Kwami (1989) classified West African singing games as recreational syncretic forms. Then he categorized singing games on the bases of the socio-cultural constructs of age and gender. Using Kwami's (1995) revised classifications, singing games are a secular art form. In addition to the singing, movement and non-membraphonic instrumental component, singing games are created by children. Therefore, while it may not be possible to attribute a singing game to one composer, it is nonetheless the creative undertaking of children.

FORM	A	B	C	D	E
7. Religious indigenous					
6. Occasional					
5. Non-religious					
4. Traditional highlife					
3. Recreational syncretic					
2. Syncretic religious					
1. Secular art					

A = Singing
B = Movement or dance* (my addition)
C = Instrumental (non-membraphonic)
D = Instrumental (supporting drums)
E = Instrumental (master drum)

Figure 4.2 *Model of accessibility: form in West African music. Adapted from Kwami, R. (1995, p. 227)*

Second, a teaching style that encourages the expression of children's held knowledge is important for music educators. The children expressed and explicitly demonstrated some of their cultural knowledge in song and games. For example, when I asked the children about their games, they demonstrated consciously held as well as shared constructions of knowledge. This knowledge can be passed on in another cultural context, that is the general music class. Through play the teacher may discuss different aspects of Ghanaian cultural life, such as food, bedwetting, and religion. Knowledge is uninhibited shared constructions.

Third, there must be opportunities for co-operative learning through group work. Through group work and peer instruction, children can share their knowledge with one another, and teachers can begin to bridge the gap between classroom practice and playground activities. As previously mentioned, the performance and practice of singing games allows children to share knowledge without reservation, thus making the scenario a healthy one for teaching and learning. Interviewing and questioning by teacher or friends direct group activities. By implication, teachers are facilitators and this diminishes their role as the ultimate source of all knowledge. The children's desire to share may be transferred to classroom practice where the children, through group work and peer instruction, share their knowledge with others. Knowledge grows when everyone is involved.

Fourth, the teaching style should be one of continuous assessment. Judging from what occurs on playgrounds, continuous assessment involves verbal and gestured communications critical to children's education. Children in Ghana, because of the manner in which they process playground information, look and wait for verbal and gestured communications from their teachers and peers. Children in active learning situations are better able to learn when the teaching and learning style is active and marked by continuous assessment. An active teaching and learning style includes a dialogue of urging and acknowledging. Knowledge is like 'midwifery'.

Summary

Children in Ghana have particular learning abilities that they demonstrate during the performance of singing games. These learning abilities are driven by their consciously held knowledge, skills, and ways of thinking. Children's consciously held knowledge is related to the cultural context in which they live. This chapter is a presentation of three situated teaching and learning scenarios with suggested implications for professional practice. Singing games can be used in the elementary classroom as idiomatic expressions, reflecting the traditions of the culture and adult music culture within which they occur.

References

Addo, A. O. (1996). A multimedia analysis of selected Ghanaian children's play songs. *Council for Research in Music Education Bulletin*, 123, 1–27.

Bebey, F. (1975). *African music: a people's art*. Evanston, IL: Northwestern University Press.

Bereiter, C. (1990). Aspects of an educational learning theory. *Review of Educational Research.* 60(4), 603–624.

Chernoff, J. (1979). *African rhythm and African sensibility.* Chicago: University of Chicago Press.

Chosky, L. (1981). *The Kodály concept.* Englewood Cliffs, NJ: Prentice-Hall.

Fiati, T. A. (1992). Cross-cultural variation in the structure of children's thought. In R. Case. *The mind staircase.* Hillsdale, NJ: Lawrence Erlbaum.

Gardner, H. (1985). *Frames of mind: the theory of multiple intelligences.* New York: Basic Books.

Kwami, R. (1995). A framework for teaching West African music in schools and colleges. *British Journal of Music Education.* 12, 225–245.

Kwami, R. (1989). African music, education and the school curriculum. Unpublished doctoral dissertation. University of London, Institute of Education.

Merriam, A. (1964). *The anthropology of music.* Evanston, IL: Northwestern University Press.

Nketia, J. H. Kwabena. (1974). *The music of Africa.* Evanston: Northwestern University Press.

Osborn, F. E. A. (1986). A computer aided methodology for the analysis and classification of British Canadian children's traditional singing games. Unpublished doctoral dissertation. University of California, Los Angeles.

Tracey, A. (1994). African values in music. In A. Schmidhofer and D. Schuller (eds). *For Gerhard Kubik: Festscrift on the occasion of his 60th birthday.* (pp. 269–289). Main. Berlin: Peter Lang. Frankfurt am Maine.

Turkson, A. (1989). Music and games and early African childhood education. *African Music Education, 7,* 1–6.

Zemke, Sister Lorna. (1973). The Kodály method and a comparison of the effect of a Kodály adapted instruction sequence and a more typical sequence on auditory musical achievement of fourth grade students. Unpublished doctoral dissertation. University of Southern California.

5

Through the Lens of Learning: How the Visceral Experience of Learning Reframes Teaching

Stephen Brookfield

This chapter outlines an approach to helping teachers reframe their practice by encouraging them to analyse their visceral experiences as learners. Interpreting practice as a consequence of experiencing learning is probably done anecdotally by many educators when they draw upon memories of their own student experiences and determine that they will never perpetuate the outrages that were visited on them by teachers. In this chapter, I make the case that our experiences as learners provide us with a powerful lens through which we can view our own practices as educators in a more formalized and purposeful way. In particular, I argue that regularly experiencing what it feels like to learn something unfamiliar and difficult is the best way to help teachers empathize with the emotions and feelings of their own learners as they begin to traverse new intellectual terrains.

How I Learned to Stop Worrying and Trust My Experience: Notes for a Screenplay

Opening scene: Teachers College Swimming Pool, New York, November 1983

Spluttering, coughing out what seems like pure chlorine, I raise my head out of the water to see where I am. I know where I am in a larger sense – I'm in an Adult Swimming Class – but where am I in the pool? I also know that I've hit tiling (again) and that must mean that I've veered across the lanes and swum a width rather than a length of the pool. When I open my eyes, remove the chlorine solution and see that I'm at the other end of the pool from where I started a few minutes ago – that I've swum a length – I feel a startling jolt of pride, an unalloyed rush of pure happiness. I can't believe it – I've actually swum a length of a swimming pool! Me, who thought that practically all aspects of the physical, athletic world were closed to me. Me, who thinks of myself as a psychomotor dolt, someone whose limbs seem never to respond properly to signals from the brain. At some level, I believed I could never do this, never make it down from one end of a swimming pool to another.

Insight: The phenomenological meaning of a learning event can have little to do with supposedly objective measures of accomplishment. On almost any measurement scale available for assessing progress as a swimmer, my performance in swimming the length is pretty pitiful, not to say pathetic. People forty years my senior are zooming past me in the water as I splutter painfully down the designated slow lane in the pool. But that doesn't matter, or even register with me; my feeling of pride is so overwhelming as to make this first ever swimming of a length a critical high point in the phenomenological terrain of my experiences as a learner in the last ten years.

Cut to . . .

Scene two: A rainy, foggy night on an Italian auto-route, November 1989

As a sabbatical project I have decided, at the age of forty, to learn to drive a car. Initially, at the end of a five-month stay in Provence, my goal was to be able to negotiate the road from the farmhouse where we are living into the local town three miles away. However, six weeks after starting to learn under my wife's instruction (despite the marital risks this entails), I feel so confident of my newly developed skill that I take the wheel for large chunks of our journey to Bologna where we are going to spend a long weekend. Ignoring my wife's warnings that driving on a foggy, rainy night is stressful enough for experienced drivers on quiet back roads, let alone on an Italian auto-route, I insist that 'the only way to learn something is to do it'. Eventually, after several 'white knuckle' experiences (a nicely descriptive phrase referring to passengers gripping the dashboard in anticipation of their imminent demise), I accept that I'm placing the lives of our family in real danger by persisting any longer in driving. I let my wife take the wheel and I sink into a near catatonic state, a state I imagine resembles the falsely comforting enervation travellers trapped in snow drifts feel just before they slip into their last sleep.

Insight: Under the adrenalin rush induced by making much quicker progress than they had anticipated in a learning project, it is easy for learners to develop a vastly inflated and (sometimes literally) dangerously unrealistic notion of their capacities. This is the dark side of self-actualization, the often unacknowledged contradiction at the heart of much rhetoric about self-direction. After emerging from my catatonia, I am reminded of how important (and how difficult) it is for me as a teacher to balance a healthy and necessary emphasis on nurturing learners' tentatively emerging belief that they can accomplish something they had previously considered beyond their reach, with an attention to the dangers entailed by espousing the rhetoric of empowerment and letting them think they have the ability immediately to do anything to which they set their minds.

The point of these opening two scenes is also the point of this chapter; as a teacher, one of the most useful, and most ignored, sources of insight into your own practice is your own autobiography as a learner. Most important, perhaps, is the visceral nature of the experiences your autobiography represents. Any number of texts emphasize the importance of reflecting critically on the assumptions underlying practice and there is plenty of advice on methods that can be used to this end (Brookfield, 1987; Schön, 1987; Mezirow and Associates, 1990). But the stream of writing on reflective practice tends to appeal at a cerebral, rather than visceral level.

Letting Go: Using the Visceral Experience of Learning to Challenge Espoused Orthodoxy in Adult Education

In this section, I would like to draw explicitly on two experiential themes in my own autobiography as a learner that have influenced my practice as a teacher. The experiences described are visceral rather than cognitive and both of them contradict some aspect of the espoused orthodoxy of adult educational theory and practice into which I had been initiated (and which I had accepted uncritically) during my postgraduate study. I will describe general features of these experiences and then try to show how my reflections on them caused me to question and reframe some part of my practice as an adult educator.

Screaming for attention: participating in discussions

One of the most cherished tenets of adult educational practice is that discussion is an educational method that exemplifies the participatory, democratic spirit central to the field. In American adult education, I would argue that Lindeman's belief that discussion was the adult educational method *par excellence* (Lindeman, 1987) continues to this day. More recently, this belief that participating in discussion represents the quintessential adult educational experience has been strengthened by the critical and theoretical edge evident in writings by Freire (1970), Mezirow (1991) and Collins (1991), all of whom draw on the Frankfurt school of critical social theory in arguing (convincingly, in my view) that adult education's task is to create conditions in which authentic dialogue and communicative discourse can occur. At almost all stages of my own career, I have used discussion as my preferred method, viewing alternative approaches as supplements of essentially inferior status. As an educator, I am very comfortable leading discussions and this method is still one on which I rely greatly. As a learner, however, my visceral experience is very different.

The defining feature of my experience as a participant in discussion is that I feel a constant and overwhelming compulsion to perform; in other words, I feel impelled to make what I believe others would regard as a series of startlingly profound contributions. I see discussion groups as emotional battlegrounds with members vying for recognition and affirmation from each other and from the discussion leader. As a participant, my energy becomes focused on listening for someone else in the group to make a comment to which I can make some kind of reasonable response. In doing this, I tend not to listen for the merits of different arguments. I am concentrating so hard on finding a conversational opening, a place where I can make some relevant interjection, that any kind of reflective analysis of the accuracy of other members' contributions becomes almost impossible. So, in my case, one of the chief arguments that I would cite as an educator for using discussion – that it opens learners to considering carefully alternative perspectives and interpretations – is invalidated by my own behaviour as a learner. When I listen to a spread of opinion voiced within a group, I am not considering seriously the merits or accuracy of alternative viewpoints, so much as seeking an entry point where my voice might be heard.

The reason why I participate in discussions this way is because I have accepted the assumption that successful discussion participation should be equated with the number of verbal contributions one makes. Anyone who speaks a lot, so I reason, must be a good participant; and anyone who is silent must, by definition, be mentally inert. As an undergraduate and then graduate student, I learned early on that discussion groups quickly establish a pecking order of communication. The longer one stays silent, the harder it is to make that first contribution. With my own personal mixture of arrogance and introversion, I never contributed to discussions unless I was fairly sure that what I was going to say would be universally admired. So, once I found the conversational connection I was looking for, and I felt that I had thought enough about that point of connection to be able to make some contribution, I would spend minutes silently rehearsing my remarks. After deciding that my putative contribution was word perfect, I would summon up my courage and, with my palms sweating and my heart cannoning inside my chest, I would stammer out my rehearsed contribution, often only to find that during the time I was rehearsing my comments the discussion had moved on and what I was saying was now pretty irrelevant.

Over the years, the contradictions between my espoused theory of discussion and my experiences as a discussion participant have become more and more glaring. They have prompted me to change significantly aspects of my pedagogic practice. I now think much more carefully about why and when to use discussion, I make much more of an effort to evolve ground rules to guide discussion participation, and I am very careful to make explicit my ideas concerning what good discussion participation looks like. As a direct result of my own experiences as a learner in this format I am especially concerned, as a teacher, to make it clear to members that it is as important to listen carefully and critically to others' contributions as it is to make them oneself. I broaden the definition of participation to include not only the act of speaking, but also more silent contributions such as being a group recorder or summarizer, bringing a salient piece of research or polemic to the session for the group's attention, calling for periods of silent reflective analysis in the midst of heated debate, and zeroxing insights about the nature of previous discussion sessions that were contained in a participant's learning journal. Also, I'll try to remember to begin a discussion session with a new group by telling them that they don't need to speak frequently as a way of signalling their diligence, and that I don't equate active listening or silent reflective analysis with mental inertia.

Overall, my repeated experiences as a discussion participant have alerted me to the fact that participating in authentic dialogue, or meeting the minimum conditions of communicative discourse, is not something which comes easily to adults. As described by Collins (1991: 12), this kind of discourse is 'a kind of on-going, thoughtful conversation' in which 'all participants anticipate that their individual contributions will receive serious consideration from others. At the same time they remain open to changing or reconstructing their own stance on the problem under consideration in the light of what others have to say and on the weight of all relevantly identified information'. Since many group contexts of adult life are infused with considerations of power and status – we learn that success, conventionally defined, is often attained by flattering or mimicking those in power – it is naive for a discussion leader to imagine that adults can sign up for a course and engage immediately in democratic, critical, authentic, reciprocal, respectful discussion. Yet, as I reflect on my practice as an educator, I am embarrassed to realize just how much I have assumed that this capacity is innate, or easily awakened, and have missed entirely the dynamics and tensions of power differences, and the need learners feel to please the leader by mimicry, that have been such a feature of my experiences with this method as a learner.

Practising what you preach: the importance of credibility and authenticity

Allied to adult education's traditional reverence for the use of the discussion method is the emphasis placed in the field on small group exercises. Most variants of small group exercises ask participants to offer some part of their experiences for analysis by other group members. When people hear the term 'andragogy', they probably equate this with some form of small group exercise, and, in the USA at least, a regular reliance on the small group method is generally taken as evidence of adult education's admirable learner-centred, democratic, collegial character. In my own practice, I have often moved to some kind of small group task as early as possible in the belief that doing so sends a strong symbolic message that my ideas and experiences are not the most important resources in the learning group. Indeed, I have often opened the first meeting of a course by telling participants that as adults they probably have the skills and knowledge they've come to learn, it's just that they're not aware that they already possess these. My task, I continue, is to help them realize that they already know much more than they think they do, and I urge that they look to their own experiences, rather than to my supposed expertise, as they negotiate this course. As I make this speech, I have often taken a quiet pride in the fact that such acknowledgements of the value of learners' experiences show me off to good personal advantage; as a self-deprecating, collegial, down-to-earth sort who has no time for academic pomposity.

During my years of behaving this way as an educator, I was also witness-ing this kind of interaction from a participant's view, without ever connect-ing the two in my mind. I would often show up at professional gatherings, academic conferences and in-service workshops eager to learn something from the person or persons advertised as leading a particular session. What caused me to choose one session or workshop over another was the fact that leading the event would be a particular individual, whose word-of-mouth reputation, published work or conference biography promised that my time would be well spent. Yet, when this same person, citing 'principles of good adult educational practice', came into the session and announced that we, as participants, already knew what we thought we had come to learn, and that we were going to form small groups and spend the first portion of the event taking an inventory of all the valuable experiences we had accumulated, my first reactions were to feel annoyed and cheated. I had come primed to learn from this person, and I would say 'how dare he or she put the emphasis right back on me'.

This question would quickly be followed by a rueful admission to myself that I was falling into the same teacher-dependent, passive modes of learn-ing which I was trying to avoid perpetuating in my own students. So, for quite a few years I would say to myself, 'alright, so I'm temporarily feeling cheated by this person's throwing the emphasis for my own learning back on to my shoulders, but this only goes to show just how deeply those despicable other-directed, dependent ways of learning are internalized, even in supposedly progressive educators!' But the feeling of being cheated never really went away and, as a result, a new interpretation began to emerge; one which is, incidentally, confirmed in many adult learners' crit-ical incident reports, interviews and learning journals (Brookfield, 1990a). This interpretation runs as follows.

Before educators can ask groups of strangers to turn to each other, form small groups and reveal something about their own experiences, those educators must somehow model the process themselves. They must take the initiative, through their actions, of setting an emotional tone for small group work. Teachers must earn the right to ask people to reveal aspects of themselves to strangers, by first doing this publicly in front of their learners. Teachers' actions, whether they like this or not (and most adult educators I know detest this idea) are granted enormous symbolic significance by learners. So for an adult educator to walk into a room full of strangers and to ask them to 'share their insights and experiences' with each other in small groups, without first having done this himself or herself in front of the whole group, is to miss entirely a crucial moment in terms of creating the right emotional tone under which authentic discourse can occur. I realize now that I, and others, are sometimes right to feel cheated when the first thing that happens is that we are put into small groups. It is as if the leader has asked us to be open about some aspects of our lives, but has personally refused to do this. There is often a consequent sense that the leader sees herself or himself as somehow above the fray, as possessing a superiority of insight, a private analytical line on truth. There is also the suspicion that the leader has some kind of hidden agenda that will be revealed at a later point, by which time we will have spoken things that, in terms of this agenda, make us look stupid.

As I think about learning episodes in my life that have held, or do hold, enormous terror for me, I realize that one of the most important factors which pulls me through these activities intact is my trusting in the educator's credibility and authenticity. When I feel that someone has some valuable skill, knowledge, experience and insight, and when I know that he or she is being open and honest with me, I am much more willing to try to do something which holds great threat for me, and to risk failure in the attempt. I have, for example, resisted for many years trying white water rafting; but if I am ever cajoled into taking a white water rafting trip, the last thing I want is to be on the river bank one morning with the distant sound of churning rapids pounding in my ears listening to the instructor tell me that I already know how to do this, that the instructor will learn as much from me as I will from him or her, and that the other fear-stricken novices in the group are as valuable a resource as the leader's experiences. What I need to hear is that the leader has navigated this stretch of river, or others like it, a thousand times, and that if I just learn some basic rules of survival I'll stand a much better chance of making it through this experience physically and psychologically intact.

Insight: What I have drawn from this and other similar experiences as a learner is that small group work can be enormously beneficial when the leader of the activity models the qualities of openness and honesty he or she hopes will characterize the small group interactions. Small group work has to be timed carefully, and progressively minded adult educators like myself have to resist the temptation of hurtling precipitously and mindlessly into such exercises. I have also come to realize that when an educator gives participants (particularly those who are terrified at the prospect of doing something they would much rather avoid) the sense that they are in the hands of someone whose experience in this area is of considerable breadth, depth and intensity, the level of anxiety surrounding the new learning is considerably reduced (though never entirely eliminated). These insights have directly influenced how I approach teaching critical thinking (Brookfield, 1987, 1990b).

My approach to teaching critical thinking is one which emphasizes participants' exploring their own autobiographies, using their experiences as the raw material for critical analysis. I rely a great deal on small group exercises, conducted in triads, through which participants are asked to choose critical incidents which illustrate the kinds of assumptions that have framed their actions, and which they have accepted uncritically. One of my own framing assumptions regarding how critical thinking can be developed is that since it is enormously difficult to stand outside of one's own interpretive frameworks through an act of one's own mental volition, this activity is usually best conducted in small group formats. In earlier years, I would move as quickly as possible to small group exercises in which participants told stories about high and low points in their experiences, and then invited other triad members to tell them what assumptions they thought were embedded in those stories.

Reflecting on my own insights as a workshop participant in small group exercises, I began to realize that I was missing an important step. Now, before asking groups to engage in any analysis of critical events in their own lives, I am careful to understake this activity in front of them. I try to earn the right to ask them to think critically about their own experiences by first inviting their critical analysis of my own actions. I speak, as honestly and descriptively as I can, about a high or low point in my life as an educator and then invite participants to give me their best insights about the uncritically accepted assumptions they see informing my choice of that particular event as good or bad, and about the assumptions they see embedded in the specific actions I describe. Very frequently I discover a dark side to the 'high' events I choose as learners make interpretations and detect assumptions which cast my conduct in much murkier light than I would wish. Since making this key change in my practice, I have often had people come up to me and tell me that seeing me first take the risk of inviting critical analysis of my own hidden, taken-for-granted assumptions encouraged them to be more honest in their subsequent small group exercises than would normally have been the case.

In an interesting commentary on the reluctance of adult educators to see their practice as teacher-centred as well as learner-centred, Collins (1991) argues that 'it is more efficacious to think in terms of engaging thoughtfully with theory and, then, putting ourselves into practice rather than putting theory into practice' (p. 47). This is a nice turn of phrase which is full of rich implications for the development of educators. It means that we must take seriously the consequences that our own actions have within a group and that we should stop pretending that how we behave has no symbolic or political significance. As someone who is asked quite frequently to advise on faculty development and in-service education, I believe that the best use of often limited time is for teachers to find ways of studying how their actions are perceived by learners. Realizing how crucial it is for me as a learner to trust an educator's basic credibility and authenticity – in particular, for me to feel that the actions and words are consistent – has made me much more attuned to making sure that I don't espouse one way of working and then behave in a way which contradicts my avowed beliefs. Better to make no promises at all than to commit to some way of working and then fail to follow through. I am now painfully aware that the extent to which I model the application of critical analysis to my own beliefs and actions is sometimes directly connected to learners' willingness to behave in the same way.

Scrutinizing our biographies: critical checks on generalizing from experience

The kinds of subjective, idiosyncratic experiences outlined in this chapter cannot, of course, be considered as the only basis for developing a practical theory of teaching. Indeed, there are very real dangers in relying on one's autobiography as a guide to action. So much of our experience is irredeemably context-bound; what are thought to be well-grounded insights culled from reflective analysis of experiences in one context can be rendered wholly invalid in another context. As Usher and Bryant (1989) point out in their analysis of the processes of practical theory development, experience without critical analysis can be little more than anecdotal reminiscence; interesting, but unconnected, experiential travellers' tales from the front lines of practice. Simon (1988, p. 3) also recognizes the conservatism inherent in much rhetoric on experiential learning and asks 'how can one avoid simply celebrating personal experience and confirming that which people already know?' If experiences like the ones I have described are going to have a serious, continuing influence on practice, they need to be submitted to two different forms of critical review.

First, formal theory has an important contribution to make in helping to convert situationally specific, informal hunches into well-framed theories of practice. Collins (1991, p. 51), for example, writes that 'serious commitment to adult education as vocation implies that its practitioners as intellectuals should be prepared to read and enagage with theoretical texts as they begin to theorize their own practice' and argues that 'serious engagement with theoretical models improves our potential as reflective practitioners, which in turn manifests itself in actual performance' (p. 47). To Usher (1989), formal theory serves as 'a kind of resource and "sounding board" for the development and refinement of informal theory – a way of bringing critical analysis to bear on the latter' (p. 88). In the process of practical theory development, the inductively derived, situational insights regarding practice which are embedded in particular contexts and experiences can be reviewed through the more universalistic lens provided by formal theoretical perspectives. Hence, it is important that these formal perspectives be developed as carefully as possible.

Secondly, assumptions derived from experience that frame practice can be submitted to a form of collaborative scrutiny; that is to say, educators working in similar and allied contexts can compare their hunches, instincts and intuitions. In this way, educators can gradually become more sophisticated at recognizing contextual cues – events and features that signal those times when certain assumptions should be held in check and those times when they can confidently be used as provisional guidelines for action. In my own in-service and faculty development workshops with teachers, I have experimented with the critical incident technique as a means of helping them uncover the assumptions that undergird their habitual ways of acting and reasoning about their practice (Brookfield, 1992). After assumptions have been identified through a process of small group analysis, I ask group members to pick out those assumptions on which there exists the greatest amount of agreement. When these assumptions have been identified, group members are asked to take each assumption in turn and to draw on their experiences to find three invalidating circumstances (the number is arbitrary); that is, to find three factors, events or variables that, if they existed, would make following these commonly held assumptions a risky prospects. For example, one common assumption that surfaces with teachers can be stated as follows: 'praising learners for work well done strengthens learners' desire to engage in further learning'. When teachers have examined their own experiences of giving praise, they have identified various invalidating circumstances that, if they are in place, would call this assumption into question. The three most frequently mentioned invalidating circumstances are:

1. When the praise is given so fulsomely that learners infer that they are so expert at the task or subject matter involved that there is no more learning that needs to be done.
2. When the method of giving praise is so laconic and understated (perhaps the praiser equates giving praise with not publicly tearing another's efforts to shreds) that it is not explicitly recognized by the learner as praise and therefore has no encouraging effect.
3. When there is something in the cultural background of the learners that makes the public receiving of praise an uncomfortable experience for them.

Through exercises such as those described, practitioners can serve as reflective mirrors for each other's informal theories, helping to focus attention on those parts which have the greatest validity across contexts, and on those parts which are unique to a specific setting.

References

Brookfield, S. D. (1987) *Developing Critical Thinkers*. San Francisco, CA: Jossey-Bass.

Brookfield, S. D. (1990a) *The Skillful Teacher*. San Francisco, CA: Jossey-Bass.

Brookfield, S. D. (1990b) Using critical incidents to analyse learners' assumptions. In Mezirow, J. and Associates, *Fostering Critical Reflection in Adulthood*. San Francisco, CA: Jossey-Bass.

Brookfield, S. D. (1992) Uncovering assumptions: The key to reflective practice. *Adult Learning*, 3(4), 13–14, 18.

Collins, M. (1991) *Adult Education as Vocation*. London: Routledge.

Freire, P. (1970) *Pedagogy of the Oppressed*. New York: Continuum.

Lindeman, E. C. L. (1987) The place of discussion in the learning process. In Brookfield, S. D. (ed.) *Learning Democracy: Eduard Lindeman on Adult Education and Social Change*. London: Routledge.

Mezirow, J. (1991) *Transformative Dimensions of Adult Learning*. San Francisco, CA: Jossey-Bass.

Mezirow, J. and Associates (1990) *Fostering Critical Reflection in Adulthood*. San Francisco, CA: Jossey-Bass.

Schön, D. A. (1987) *Educating the Reflective Practitioner*. San Francisco, CA: Jossey-Bass.

Simon, R. (1988) For a pedagogy of possibility. *Critical Pedagogy Networker*, 1(1), 1–4.

Usher, R. S. (1989) Locating adult education in the practical. In Bright, B. (ed.) *Theory and Practice in the Study of Adult Education: The Epistemological Debate*, pp. 65–93. London: Routledge.

Usher, R. S. and Bryant, I. (1989) *Adult Education as Theory, Practice and Research: The Captive Triangle*. London: Routledge.

6

Personal Thinking

Seymour Papert

A course on psychology I took as an undergraduate left little residue in my mind, except for a homily on objectivity delivered in the first lecture. We were warned that many of us might have enrolled under the erroneous impression that the course, being about psychology, would provide an occasion to explore the psychological issues in our own lives. Those who had come for this reason were advised to consider whether they really wanted to be there. The starting point for the study of scientific psychology was, we were told, the skill of distancing oneself from the object of study. We would have to work hard to learn how to keep intuitions based on our own experiences out of our thinking about the psychological issues we would be studying.

Without a doubt there is a need in any discipline for skill in distancing oneself from the object of study. However, the more significant lack in the study of education is quite the opposite: there is too much distancing.

Yearners have tirelessly protested the way that School's curriculum distances knowledge from the individuality of the student. Beyond this, the quest for a science of education has led to ways of thinking about teaching that exclude the teacher as a person, and ways of thinking about education research that exclude the researcher as a person. My protest starts by situating my own work on educational innovation in my life experience.

My critique of School and yearning for something else began very early. In elementary school I already knew quite clearly that my best intellectual work was done outside the classroom. My resentment of School was mitigated only by the fact that I loved two teachers and had a handful of friends who participated with me in activities I considered to be more valuable. The most important of these was a newspaper produced by a 1930s version of desktop publishing. My printer was a homemade gelatinous block to which ink could be transferred from a glossy master sheet and thence to sheets of absorbent paper. The newspaper was important for me in many ways. Above all, it gave me a sense of identity. Adults asked one another, 'What do you do?' and I could think of what I 'did' as something more personal and distinctive than 'going to school'.

Besides this, the newspaper made connections with several areas of intellectual and social development that would shape my high school years and beyond. I developed a sense of myself and a little skill as a chemist. My printing system was initially based on an article in Arthur Mee's *Children's*

Encyclopedia but evolved over time and through many experimental variations. I developed a sense of myself as a writer, and I had to shoulder financial and managerial responsibilities that were no less real for being on a very small scale. And, perhaps most important in its subsequent impact on my life, the newspaper slowly drew me into the beginnings of political activism in the highly charged atmosphere of Johannesburg, where I lived from age seven through my mid-twenties.

The particular facts of my story are unique to me as an individual; the general principles it illustrates are not. Reading biographies and interrogating friends has convinced me that all successful learners find ways to take charge of their early lives sufficiently to develop a sense of intellectual identity. A fascinating example is Jean Piaget. The case has a mild irony in that this man, so often quoted as the authority on what children cannot do because they are not at the appropriate stages of development, published his first scientific article at age eleven! What does one make of this? Devotees of Piaget often view it reverently as an early sign of his genius. In fact the short paper, which reports a sighting of a rare bird in the Swiss mountains, does not contain any logical patterns that would be surprising in an average child of eleven. I am inclined to think of the publication as being as much a cause as a consequence of Piaget's exceptional intellectual qualities, though, of course (in what he would have called a dialectical sense), it is surely both.

Piaget's article did not just happen as a consequence of some quality of his mind. He explains it as a simple intentional act. He wanted to be allowed to use the college library in his small Swiss town, and wrote and published the article to make the librarian take him seriously enough to give him permission to do so. What I find most impressive in the story is not that a boy of eleven could write a report about a bird but that this same boy of eleven took himself seriously enough to conceive and carry out this strategy for dealing with the librarian. I see in it young Jean preparing himself to become Piaget. He was practising taking charge of his own development, something that is necessary not only for those who want to become leading thinkers but for all citizens of a society in which individuals have to define and redefine their roles throughout a long lifetime.

In stark contrast with the image of Piaget the child constructing Piaget the adult, School has an inherent tendency to infantilize children by placing them in a position of having to do as they are told, to occupy themselves with work dictated by someone else and that, moreover, has no intrinsic value – school-work is done only because the designer of a curriculum decided that doing the work would shape the doer into a desirable form. I find this offensive, in part because I remember how much I objected as a child to being placed in that situation, but mainly because I am convinced that the best learning takes place when the learner takes charge, as the young Piaget did. Thus my antennae are always out for initiatives that will allow the purpose of School as a place for learning to coexist with a culture of personal responsibility.

This must not be confused with the faddish idea that what children learn should be made 'relevant' – so, teacher, don't just make them add numbers, pretend you are shopping in the supermarket. Children are not easily duped. If they sense that they are being made to play a silly game, they will be discouraged from taking themselves seriously. I liked a little better what I saw at the Lamplighter School in Dallas, where the fourth-grade children actually had real responsibility for operating an egg business. They bought the feed, cleaned the coops, collected and sold the eggs, and kept the profit, if there was any, at the end of the year. If they ended up with a loss, they had to explain themselves to the next class. But even this allowed very little opportunity for real initiative and only a minor sense of doing something really important.

A deeper sense of doing something important in itself is visible in the project 'Kidnet', developed in a collaboration between the National Geographic Society and Robert Tinker, who is responsible for developing some of the best uses of computers for learning science. This project engages middle school students to collect data about acid rain. The individual schools send their data across electronic networks to a central computer where it is integrated and sent back to the local sites, where it can be analysed and discussed in the context of globally important problems. The project hints at a vision of millions of children all over the world engaged in work that makes a real contribution to the scientific study of a socially urgent problem. In principle, a million children could collect more data about the environment than any socially affordable number of professional scientists.

This is infinitely better than School's ritualistic worksheets and demonstration experiments, if only because the students feel they are engaged in a meaningful and socially important activity they really care about. However, what I like most is the opportunity it offers the students to break out of its own framework to engage in more self-directed activities. One way that students break out quite frequently is to use the expertise acquired in the project to engage in local environmental campaigns. Another example that pleased me particularly was expressed by a student who had worked out a plan to bypass the use of children to collect data by automating these operations. He explained that the children could then devote themselves to more important environmental work! This student could not actually implement this plan with the means provided by his school, but he was close: in a few years such projects will use hardware and software flexible enough for this student's plan to be widely implemented.

A different example of computers giving children the opportunity to develop a sense of doing serious work is that of two fifth-grade boys with very different interests, one in science and the other in dance and music, who came together to create a 'screen choreography' by programming a computer set up in the back of the classroom. What they were doing may not have been relevant, but it certainly felt vitally important to these boys and was seen as such by their teacher, who encouraged them to take time from regular class work for their project. Watching them, I was reminded of the newspaper I worked on as a child. I guessed that they were growing as independent intellectual agents, and anyone could see that they were learning what was for their age an unusual amount of mathematics and computer programming.

This discussion, which intermingles learning incidents from my life and Piaget's with incidents from the lives of children in contemporary schools, represents an alternative to the methodology favoured by the dominant 'scientific' school of thought. Researchers, following the so-called scientiic method of using controlled experiments, solemnly expose children to a 'treatment' of some sort and then look for measurable results. But this flies in the facc of all common knowledge of how human beings develop. Although it is obvious to me that my newspaper played a profound role in my intellectual development, I am pretty sure that no test would have detected its role by comparing my 'performance' the day before I started and three months later. The significant effects emerged over a much longer period, to be measured, probably, in years. Moreover, an experiment that gave a hundred children 'the experience of producing a newspaper', even if continued for several years, still would miss the point of what happened to me. The significant engagement was too personal to be expected to operate as a mass effect; I fell in love with my newspapering (as I did with mathematics and other areas of knowledge) for reasons that are as personal and in a sense as unreproducible as those that determine any kind of falling in love.

The method of controlled experimentation that evaluates an idea by implementing it, taking care to keep everything else the same, and measuring the result, may be an appropriate way to evaluate the effects of a small modification. However, it can tell us nothing about ideas that might lead to deep change. One cannot simply implement such ideas to see whether they lead to deep change: a megachanged system can come into being only through a slow, organic evolution, and through a close harmony with social evolution. It will be steered less by the outcome of tests and measurements than by its participants' intuitive understanding.

The most powerful resource for this process is exactly what is denied by objective psychology and the would-be science of education. Every one of us has built up a stock of intuitive, empathic, commonsense knowledge about learning. This knowledge comes into play when one recognizes something good about a learning experience without knowing the outcome. It seems obvious to me that every good teacher uses this kind of knowledge far more than test scores or other objective measurements in daily decisions about students. Perhaps the most important problem in education research is how to mobilize and strengthen such knowledge.

One step toward strengthening it is to recognize it. The denial of personal intuitive knowledge has led to a profound split in thinking about learning; the split recalls the theory that each of us has two brains which think in fundamentally different ways. By analogy, one might say that when it comes to thinking about learning, nearly all of us have a School side of the brain, which thinks that School is the only natural way to learn, and a personal side that knows perfectly well it is not.

A second strategy for strengthening the personal side and breaking the stranglehold of the School side is to develop a methodology for reflection about cases of successful learning and especially about one's own best learning experiences. Analogies with two events in the history of aviation – a case of true megachange – will clarify my thinking.

People who dreamed about making flying machines looked at birds in the same spirit as I want to look at examples of successful learning. But it was not enough simply to look and copy. Many were misled into thinking that the essence of bird flight was the flapping of wings. Even the great Leonardo was drawn into the vision of an ornithopter, a machine that would look like a bird and fly by flapping birdlike wings. This was not the way to make a flying machine. Nevertheless, it was the observation of birds that provided the secret. My analogy here concerns John Wilkins, a seventeenth-century bishop, scientist, and founder of the Royal Society. Wilkins could not have been the first to observe that birds could fly without flapping their wings. But he was one of the first to see the importance in this otherwise banal observation. He was right. The simplicity of a gull soaring without a visible movement of its body became the model that eventually led to formulating the principle of lift, the concept underlying both the understanding of natural flyers and the making of artificial flyers. We have to learn to see successful learning through the prism of such powerful ideas.

The second event happened as an indirect result of the first. The year 1903 – when a powered airplane first flew successfully – was a turning point in the history of transportation. But the famous flyer made by Wilbur and Orville Wright did not prove itself by its performance. The duration of the best of several flights that day was only fifty-nine seconds! As a practical alternative to the horse-drawn wagon, it was laughable. Yet imaginative minds could see in it the birth of the industry that would lead to the jumbo jet and the space shuttle. Thinking about the future of education demands a similar labour of the imagination. The prevalent literal-minded, 'what you see is what you get' approach measuring the effectiveness of computers in learning by the achievements in present-day classrooms makes it certain that tomorrow will always be the prisoner of yesterday. Indeed, the situation in education is often even worse than judging the effectiveness of airplanes by the fifty-nine-second flight. It is more like attaching a jet engine to an old-fashioned wagon to see whether it will help the horses. Most probably it would frighten the animals and shake the wagon to pieces, 'proving' that jet technology is actually harmful to the enhancement of transportation.

I have in my files a large collection of scientific papers reporting experiments that try to measure 'the effect of computers on learning'. It is like measuring the flight characteristics of the Wrights' flyer to determine 'the effect of flying on transporation'. The significance of the flyer could be appreciated by hard imaginative work based on understanding the principles, such as 'lift', which lay behind the design. In order to find the corresponding principles for learning, we have to look into ourselves as much as at computers: principles such as 'taking charge' and 'intellectual identity' and 'falling in love' (as I used in talking about my newspaper) have come to play that role in my own thinking as a direct result of observing myself when I seemed to be flying intellectually. The incidents in the rest of this chapter highlight some others.

As I grew up, learning became a hobby. Of course any hobby involves learning, but most people are more interested in what they learn than in how the learning happens. In fact, most learn without giving a thought to learning. I often go to the other extreme. I learned to juggle, to fly a plane, and to cook, not only because I wanted to do these things but also because I wondered what the learning would be like. Though I came to love all these hobbies for their own sake, part of my pleasure in them has always been that of observing myself learn and making up theories about how I do so. A good example of this process is how I learned to make croissants.

When I got croissant-making right after many, many failures, I allowed myself some elation but then began to worry about what had happened. One day I couldn't do it, the next day I could! What had changed? In order to reconstruct the moment of transition, I tried to recapture the state of 'inability' I had been in the day before. At first I thought in terms of external factors such as the proportions of ingredients, the times of rising and resting, and the temperatures of dough, working surface, and oven. But varying these did not seem to account for my prior uneven results.

When I eventually did relive the key moment, I had learned about much more than making criossants. The difference between before and after lay in feeling the degree of 'squishiness' of the butter through the squishiness of the pastry dough and through my heavy marble rolling pin. Trying to capture this deliberately seemed at first like the princess and the pea. I tried many times. It was only when I decided that I had enough and would give up for the day that a breakthrough happened. On my marble slab was a last parcel of butter wrapped in dough. Wondering what to do with it, I playfully flattened it with the rolling pin, relaxed, without trying to do anything in particular – and all of a sudden I felt distinctly the structure of the mass of matter. Once I felt it, I knew 'in my fingers' how to make a croissant, and now when I try after an interval of several years, the knack always comes back by the second batch – though if I had to do it on a school test I would fail, because I need the spoiled first try to get the feel for the successful second one.

When I retell such experiences to an audience of educators, I always hope that someone will be annoyed by my talk of criossants and say: 'What has this to do with grammar or maths or writing business letters? Naturally in cooking you have to learn to feel the relationship of your body to matter. But maths is not about feeling relationships of your body to numbers.' I like this reaction because it brings out into the open something that lurks in the culture and allows me to confront it.

A few years ago I would have begun with the rejoinder: 'You think that maths does not have anything to do with the body because you are not a mathematician; if you were you would know that mathematics is full of gut feelings and all sorts of kinesthetics.' Today I would say it the other way around: 'The reason you are not a mathematican might well be that you think that maths has nothing to do with the body; you have kept your body out of it because it is supposed to be abstract, or perhaps a teacher scolded you for using your fingers to add numbers!' This idea is not just metaphysics. It has inspired me to use the computer as a medium to allow children to put their bodies back into their mathematics.

My favourite example is an invention called 'the turtle'. You can think of this as a drawing instrument whose simplest use will become clear from the following scenario. Imagine that you are looking at a computer screen. On it you see a small turtle, which moves when you type commands in a language called 'turtle talk', leaving a line as it goes. The command 'Forward 50' causes the turtle to move straight ahead a certain distance. 'Forward 100' will make it move in the same direction twice as far. You soon get the idea that the numbers represent the distance it moves; they can be thought of as turtle steps. Now if you want to make it go in a different direction, you give it a command like 'Right 90'. It stays in the same place but turns on itself, facing east if it had previously been facing north. With this knowledge you should easily be able to make it draw a square. If that's easy for you, you can think about how to draw a circle, and if that's easy, you can try a spiral. Somewhere you will meet your level of difficulty, and when you do I'll give you this piece of advice: put yourself in the place of the turtle. Imagine yourself moving in a square or a circle or a spiral or whatever it may be. You may resist for a while because you are tense and trying too hard, as I was with my croissants. But when you let yourself go, you will find that there is a richer source of mathematical knowledge in your body than in classroom textbooks.

Learning to speak French was one of my most instructive learning experiences. Although this was not a case of learning for its own sake – I went to live in Paris to complete my doctoral research in mathematics – my professional purpose was interlaced with playful learning experiments. For example, I developed a relationship with an eight-year-old boy who was delighted to be my 'professor'. He was young enough to be 'studying French' at the same time as I was. Although he was a native speaker, he was learning spelling and grammar at school and was acquiring vocabulary at an appreciable rate. I was able to compare the speed and pattern of my progress with his, and in doing so established a curious fact: by any measure I could think of, I was learning faster. I could have attributed the discrepancy between this observation and the common linguistic sluggishness of adults to some kind of special 'gift for languages'. I didn't. I explain the discrepancy by the fact that I was learning French mostly like a child but could also take advantage of some sophisticated ideas that a child would not know. On the one hand, I was open to playful immersion; on the other,

I could make occasional use of formal linguistics. Somewhere between the two was the fact that my learning of French seemed to be facilitated by experimenting (or playing) not only with French but also with learning itself. Studying one's own learning process – as the example of croissant-making also shows – can be a powerful method of enhancing learning. In any case, looking back I see an important root of my present ideas in this recognition of the advantages of combining childlike and adultlike ways of learning.

Although my mathematical research in Paris earned me my PhD, the Parisian discovery that had the biggest impact on my life was Jean Piaget, who at the time was giving a course at the Sorbonne. I got to know him and was invited to work in his centre in Geneva, where I spent the next four years and became passionately interested in children's thinking. If the key ideas in this book first crossed my mind then, however, they were in the most nebulous guise. In particular, I made no connection that I can remember between my own learning and the process of intellectual development of children on which we worked at Piaget's center. The reason is significant: we were all too serious and too formal about children's thinking. Of course we thought about their play; it was Piaget who coined the oft-quoted line that play is child's work. But no one in that environment was looking at the other half of this pithy aphorism: the idea that work (at least serious intellectual work) might be adult's play. We thought of children as 'little scientists' but did not think much about the complementary idea of viewing scientists as 'big children'.

Following the four years in Geneva, I became a professor of mathematics at MIT. Many factors made the move attractive. There was the prospect of access to computers and of working with Marvin Minsky and Warren McCulloch, as well as a wonderful sense of playfulness that I had experienced there on brief visits. When I finally arrived, all this came together in all-night sessions around a PDP-1 computer that had been given to Minsky. It was pure play. We were finding out what could be done with a computer, and anything interesting was worthwhile. Nobody yet knew enough to decree that some things were more serious than others. We were like infants discovering the world.

It was in this situation that I thought about computers and children. I was playing like a child and experiencing a volcanic explosion of creativity. Why couldn't the computer give a child the same kind of experience? Why couldn't a child play like me? What would have to be done to make this possible?

These questions launched me on a new quest guided by the Robin Hood-like idea of stealing technology from the lords of the laboratories and giving it to the children of the world. A first step in the quest was to recognize that one of the sources of the technologists' power was the veil of esoteric mystery woven around the idea of programming. The situation is quite analogous to the way priests of other ages kept power from people by monopolizing the ability to read and write, and by keeping what they considered the most powerful knowledge in languages the common people could not understand. I saw the need to make computer languages that could be 'vulgarized' – made available to ordinary people and especially children.

This has turned out to be a long and difficult task. Computer languages, like natural languages, cannot be 'made'; they have to evolve. What could be made was a first shot at such a language, named Logo, which would serve as a starting point for a longer evolution that is in fact still continuing.

[. . .]

7

The Classroom Environment: A Framework for Learning

Chris Comber and Debbie Wall

Introduction

Primary classrooms are remarkably crowded places. This much has always been true, but in recent years the pressure on space has increased. Pupil numbers, having dipped in the 1980s, gradually rose again during the 1990s, so that earnest debates about 'class size' have once more entered the educational and political arenas.

It is not simply a matter of numbers which determines the level of congestion, however, it is also one of the physical space in which teacher and pupils are obliged to work. Both the dimensions of the room in which learning takes place and its overall design have implications for the way in which teachers organise its layout. Some have the luxury of spacious rooms, which allow for adaptation and movement, while others are obliged to work in confined or awkwardly shaped spaces which place particular constraints on the degree of flexibility available. While the dimensions and design of a classroom are fixed, and therefore largely beyond the control of the teacher, the challenge is, and has always been, to make the optimum use of what space and resources are available. In the following pages, we examine the ways in which teachers went about this task, and the impact of curricular reform and shifts in educational philosophy since the first ORACLE studies.

The 1976 Classroom

By the time of the first studies, the pre-war image of the primary classroom as a place where children sat behind serried rows of desks had virtually disappeared. Children mostly sat together in groups around desks or tables brought together to form larger working areas. The teacher, meanwhile, no longer stood in front of a blackboard, or instructed the pupils from behind a centrally positioned desk, but instead moved around the room interacting with pupils as individuals or as members of their group.

This form of organisation reflected the philosophy of the time which emphasised the child as being at the 'heart of education' (Plowden, 1967, para. 1) and which extolled the principle of individualisation, while recognising the educational and social virtues of collaborative learning. As the ORACLE research established, however, this proposition was never seriously tested, and the surface appearance in these classrooms of activity, discovery and interaction – the Plowden ideal – was somewhat illusory. Pupils spent most of the time at their working base rather than moving around the class, and communicated only infrequently either with their teacher or with others in their group. In this situation levels of distraction were relatively high, interaction between pupils was relatively low, and such communication as there was rarely had much to do with the task in hand. This discovery led to a refinement of the original ORACLE observation schedule to take account not only of where and how children were seated, the pupil's 'base', but also of who they worked with, their 'team'. Subsequent research which used these categories confirmed that, while children mainly *sat* together in groups, they *worked* on their own for most of the time (e.g. Hargreaves, 1990).

Classroom Organisation and Attention to Task

In the light of such findings, there followed a growing interest among researchers in the relationship between seating arrangements and time on-task (e.g. Wheldall and Lam, 1987; Yeomans, 1989; Hastings *et al.*, 1996). Given that, in most primary schools, a single classroom has to serve multiple functions, requiring flexibility on the part of both teacher and children, the goal of such research was to examine the impact of varying the physical classroom organisation on the level and nature of communication. The general but consistent finding from these kinds of studies was that, where children were required to be sitting down and engaged in individual work, the level of on-task work was substantially higher when seated in rows than when grouped around tables.

Furthermore, the research suggests that the greatest beneficiaries of such arrangements may be those who are most likely to be distracted in a group situation (Wheldall and Congreve, 1981). Nevertheless, as Hastings *et al.* (1995) point out, to use these findings to support a return to 'rows with everything' position would be to 'miss the point entirely', which is that, in order to encourage effective learning, teachers need to use a variety of organisational approaches to ensure that 'seating organisation reflects teaching intentions and task demands'.

There is, therefore, a considerable body of research, from ORACLE 1976 onwards, which indicates a clear relationship between classroom seating arrangements and the pupils' involvement in the task. The recent shifts in thinking about the nature and purpose of primary education, and the policy changes which have followed, have further emphasised the importance of this link. The National Curriculum, with its clearly delineated subject areas, programmes of study, attainment targets and assessment procedures, was designed to provide a common curricular structure which had hitherto been absent in the primary classroom (Bennett *et al.*, 1980). Later pronouncements concerning the most appropriate teaching methods and classroom organisation for its successful implementation (Alexander *et al.*, 1992), coupled with the introduction of more exacting inspection procedures and compulsory end-of-Key Stage testing, have brought considerable pressure to bear on primary teachers to alter their practice. How, then, have teachers in these various environments responded to demands placed upon them by this period of policy-led reform? In particular, what has been the impact of these changes upon the way that teachers make use of the classroom environment they find themselves in?

The 1996 Classroom

The schools in the present study ranged from the very old to the relatively new. The oldest was a cramped, high windowed early Victorian building, designed at a time when teachers lectured from the front, and pupils were seated shoulder to shoulder behind rows of fixed desks, which were often bolted to the floor. The most recently built schools were, on the other hand, spacious, light and modern open-plan units, the design of which is variously claimed to be influenced by the so-called progressive ideology of the 1970s, the result of financial necessity, or a practical response to the move towards de-streaming of the primary classroom.

Of the twenty-eight classrooms observed, twenty-two were of the type generally referred to as 'box like', the key characteristics of which were that they were discrete rooms defined by walls and a door which closed them off from the rest of the school. As we shall see, however, this term should not be taken to indicate a uniformity of shape or size. The remaining six classrooms, or more accurately 'home units' were part of open-plan teaching spaces.

Given this diversity, what was remarkable was that, regardless of the shape, size or original purpose of the classrooms observed, the organisation within them had hardly changed in twenty years. Children were still mainly to be found 'seated in groups around flat-topped tables or desks drawn together to form working surfaces', just as they were in 1976.

It would appear, therefore, that two decades of classroom research, curriculum reform on an unprecedented scale, and a shift in educational thinking which has produced calls for a return to whole class teaching and more subject specialisation has had almost no impact on the way in which teachers organise the pupils. Within this general picture of stability, however, there have been some variations beyond the arrangement of the pupils' working surfaces, and in the following section we briefly examine three features of the primary classroom and their effects on the organisation of the classroom: the teacher's desk, the 'carpet area' and the computer.

The Teacher's Desk

What of the teachers themselves? How do they organise their 'space' in the primary classroom, and how do they operate within it? In earlier times, it was the teacher's desk which dominated the class, symbolising both the authority of the teacher and a pedagogic style of teaching. Positioned at the front, and often in the centre of a raised platform, it afforded an uninterrupted view of the class, so that the pupils, like the inmates of Bentham's panopticon, were acutely aware that their activities could be observed at all times.

By the 1970s, however, the central positioning of the desk, and its powerful symbolism, had all but disappeared; it was often to be found instead placed in a corner of the room. Although the majority of teachers still preferred to situate it in such a way as to be able to monitor the class when necessary, the 1976 ORACLE study showed that teachers spent most of their time moving around the class, going from pupil to pupil, monitoring children's activities or 'housekeeping'. The desk therefore became something akin to a 'base' to which the teacher returned periodically to collect or replace materials, to mark or plan work, to register the class, or occasionally served as a place for children to come to read to the teacher, or to queue for information or clarification of instruction.

In some ways, little appears to have changed since that time. In only a quarter of all observed classrooms in the present study did the teacher's desk occupy a traditional centre-front position, and even here teachers were rarely observed 'teaching-from-the-front'. Occasionally, children were brought out to gather around the desk for a demonstration of some kind, reflecting to some extent the increasing importance of science and technology in the curriculum, but in general the teacher's desk appears to have much the same function in the modern primary classroom as it did twenty years ago, irrespective of its location.

However, although teachers were still mobile for much of the time, they were less likely than their ORACLE 1976 counterparts to interact with individual pupils, or to be silently monitoring the class or organising materials, and they were much more likely to be addressing the whole class. We have seen that in the main teachers have not been busy rearranging the children's desks into rows, neither have they returned to a front of class style of delivery. What, then, is the context in which this increase in whole class interaction is taking place?

The answer to this question is a complex one. In the context of the present discussion, however, one clue lies in the use of communal spaces in the primary classroom, the 'carpet area'.

The Carpet Area

The carpet area or reading corner represent spaces which have traditionally been marked off as a place for shared activities which often involve the whole class and the teacher (see Figure 7.1). In the 1970s these areas were often used by teachers when they wanted to talk to the whole class, particularly first thing in the morning to take the register, outline the morning's activities and so on. The children would often gather again at the end of the day to sit and listen to a story read by the teacher. Beyond these shared events with the teacher, a carpet area was also used spontaneously by children who required additional work space, or as a place for silent reading.

In 1996, these carpeted areas continued to be an important part of classroom life, and even in the case of some modern classrooms that were carpeted throughout, a space was often marked out in some way. What was particularly interesting, especially in the light of the shift towards the use of whole class teaching discussed above, was that in many classrooms this area was used more frequently than in ORACLE 1976 times, so that children were sometimes brought out from their desks to 'sit on the carpet' mid-way through lessons for whole class instruction or discussion.

One possible cost of increasing class-based activity is a rise in the kind of behaviour defined as 'partially co-operating and partially distracted'. Where a discussion or instruction is relatively lengthy, for example, it becomes difficult for the teacher (and indeed the observer) to determine whether or not the children are fully engaged or not, allowing some pupils to 'melt into the crowd'. However, teachers reported that bringing the children out to the carpet area so that the children were close to them allowed a greater degree of control over the pupils' behaviour and attention.

The strategy can also be seen as pragmatic. Since pupils are still mainly seated in groups around tables, addressing the whole class in this situation necessarily involves a measure of 'talking to the back of children's heads', making it difficult for the teacher to engage directly with all of the pupils, or to monitor behaviour. The alternative would be to ask some of the children to twist around so that they all faced the front. Bringing them out to the carpet obviates the need for either tactic. Having said this, seating children in groups is, of course, a strategy in itself, so that the argument for the practicality of one arrangement over the other becomes rather circular.

There is, however, another, perhaps more powerful purpose behind these communal gatherings. The relationship between teacher and pupil in the primary classroom develops over the period of a whole year, and in some instances longer, which allows for a more intimate, relational style than is possible in the secondary classroom, where a teacher might interact with the class for no more than an hour or two per week. In other words, teachers are able to retain what Moyles (1995) calls the 'cosy togetherness'

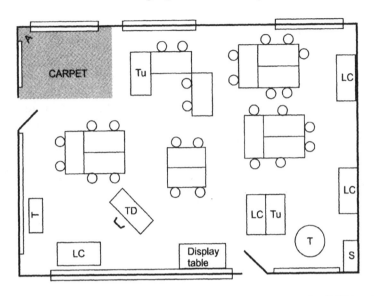

Figure 7.1   *Typical classroom layout. Source: adapted from Moyles (1995, p. 14)*

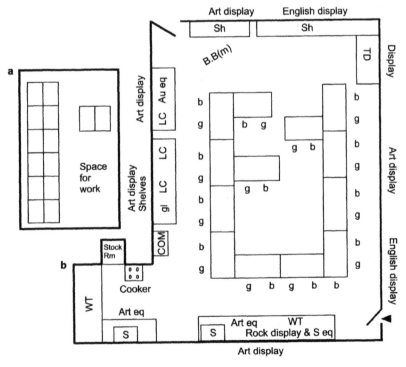

Figure 7.2   *'Horseshoe' layout*

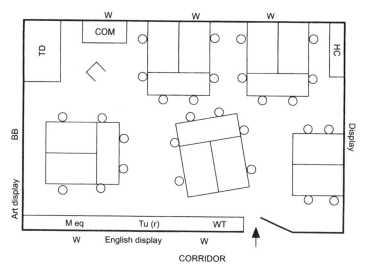

Figure 7.3   *'Shoebox' layout*

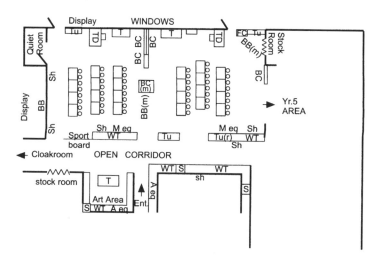

Figure 7.4   *Open-plan layout*

Key

A	Armchair	HC	High cupboard	Tu	Tray units
A eq	Art equipment	LC	Low cupboard	Tu(r)	Tray units (resources)
Au eq	Audio equipment	M eq	Maths equipment	W	Windows
BB	Black/White board	O	Pupils' seating	WT	Worktop
BB(m)	as above (mobile)	S eq	Science equipment	⋁⋁⋁	Folding door
BC	Bookcase	Sh	Shelves	Ⓢ	Sink
COM	Computer	TD	Teacher's desk	⬚	Teacher's chair
gl	Globe(s)	T	Table	——	Wall

Source of key: adapted from Alexander *et al.* (1989, p. 248) of sitting together, while still meeting the demand for more whole class interaction.

Information Technology

One major development since the 1976 study was conducted is the increasing importance of Information Technology (IT), and much has been written about its potential impact on the organisation of learning and the implications that the increasing use of computer-mediated activities have for the role of the teacher (e.g. Somekh and Davis, 1997). What effects has this had on organisation within the primary classroom?

In most of our sample schools the answer is very little. Most of the primary classrooms in our sample confirmed the general findings of the McKinsey survey of IT provision in the UK (McKinsey & Co., 1997) which showed a national average of one computer for every seventeen pupils, and that in 40 per cent of primary schools the ratio was 1:20 – that is about one per class. What is more, many of the computers that schools did have were obsolete. In the present study, although there was often a dedicated space for a computer, occasionally accompanied by a printer, much of the equipment was relatively old, of varying make, of low specification, and rarely used, so that out of almost 1,000 records of curriculum activity, just twelve recorded the use of IT. Indeed, in a number of classrooms, IT had seemingly taken the place of science, which, according to an account by Ridley and Trembath (1986, p. 110), 'was lost somewhere in the detritus of a nature table and fishtank'. It would seem, therefore, that primary schools may have a little time to wait yet before the 'Information Age' significantly affects the organisation of most primary classrooms.

Despite the tremendous changes in primary education in the previous decade, then, we see that, with a few general exceptions, the layout and use of the primary classroom of the 1990s is remarkably similar to that of the 1970s and 1980s. We are not suggesting, however, that teachers have somehow failed to deliver the National Curriculum, or that practice has not changed at all in two decades. There has clearly been a reluctance to make major changes in the geography or utilisation of the classroom environment, however, and such shifts as we have so far identified represent a rather subtle movement.

Some explanations for this position are offered later in this chapter, but in the meantime, we move beyond the general picture to examine in a little more detail three of the classrooms in the present study. These examples demonstrate the flexibility of teachers when presented with particular organisational challenges, and we examine the different ways in which each teacher went about meeting them.

As we have already said, all but six of the classrooms in the present study conformed to one of the four types of 'box' classrooms described by

Alexander *et al.* (1989), the chief variation between which was the number and location of workbays (a 'typical' box primary classroom, an amalgam of these four, is depicted in Figure 7.1). Nevertheless, classrooms come in all shapes and sizes, and some of those in the sample were much more conducive to flexible organisation than others.

The first example is of an L-shaped room (see Figure 7.2). The smaller part of the 'L' was unsuitable for teaching purposes, and was therefore used as a storage area. This left a rectangular teaching area of about 9 by 6 metres. The presence of fixed storage cupboards down the longer side of the room further reduced the space available, resulting in a fairly awkwardly shaped area to accommodate twenty-eight Year 6 pupils. Because of the teacher's approach to this situation, we call this classroom the 'horseshoe'.

Classroom 1: the 'horseshoe'

Largely in response to the restrictions imposed by the dimensions of the room, the teacher decided to experiment with a 'U' shaped, or horseshoe, arrangement of the children's tables. As an alternative to isolating pupils with behavioural difficulties by placing them next to the teacher's desk, children who required additional monitoring, in some cases for a temporary period, were seated at tables arranged at right angles to the 'U' formation and thus facing the front of the classroom. The same arrangement pertained for children with certain learning difficulties. As far as possible, boys and girls were seated next to each other, the pairings carefully selected, and regularly changed, as part of a deliberate policy to encourage interaction, a strategy which has been found to be particularly effective in raising the level of time on-task (Wheldall and Olds, 1987).

McNamara and Waugh (1993) suggest that this U-shaped arrangement, commonly found in further and higher education but unique among the primary classrooms observed in the present study, is the most effective for allowing the three main working styles, individual, group and whole class, with a minimum of modification. The horseshoe pattern was indeed maintained for many activities, for example class discussions and for most written work, and it also facilitated working in pairs. However, the teacher also used other arrangements according to the demands of the curriculum, exemplifying the 'fitness for purpose' ethic advocated by Hastings (1995), particularly when the task required or was designed around small-group work. The tables were rearranged in smaller blocks for these purposes, as well as a variety of other arrangements for particular curriculum activities. For example, one task required several pairs or small groups to collaborate with one another to design and make a large mural. The tables in the classroom were pushed together to form one long 'boardroom table' for the main sections of the artwork, with separate areas for the organisation and distribution of materials, and for designing the border for the mural (see Figure 7.2a). Working for about an hour a day over several days, the children had become adept at quickly breaking down the horseshoe to construct this and a variety of other arrangements and at reforming it just as efficiently.

This 'flexible horseshoe' strategy thus proved to be an extremely effective means of making the most of a fairly unpromising situation. Interestingly, having moved in the year following the observational study, to a larger classroom in which the seating layout initially conformed to the more typical group style, the teacher in question reported difficulties in getting the class to work together. Mid-way through the second term, having reverted to the horseshoe arrangement, she found an almost immediate improvement in the level of collaboration between the children, and in her ability to communicate effectively with the pupils. The somewhat anecdotal nature of this evidence makes it difficult to separate cause and effect – for example, the confidence developed with using the U-shape may have been temporarily lost when the teacher transferred to the new room. Nevertheless, the strategy was clearly successful in the observed classroom.

In the second example, the limitations of space were even more extreme, imposing severe restrictions on the scope for flexibility, and for this reason, we call the room the 'shoebox'.

Classroom 2: the 'shoebox'

The Key Stage 2 classrooms were located in an early Victorian building, constructed in an era when pupils were taught but not heard, and which retained most of the features of the original design. If coniditions were cramped at the time of its construction, then the variety of teaching approaches demanded by the modern curriculum rendered the situation in the school even more difficult. The building was divided by a narrow corridor which also served as a makeshift cloakroom and breaktimes were staggered in order to cope safely with the number of pupils who used the small playground. A recent OFSTED inspection report acknowledged that the cramped nature of the classrooms restricted opportunities for teaching and learning, drawing attention to the lack of adequate storage space and the fact that a lack of water supply to most classrooms adversely affected practical activities.

The observed classroom measured just over 7 by 6 metres. As in the previous example, there were twenty-eight pupils in the class, and as Figure 7.3 shows, the scope for reorganising furniture under these conditions was extremely limited with space at such a premium. There was no sink in the room and very little storage space in which to put materials and resources, much of which was stacked on top of a worktop which ran along one side of the class, the only surface in the room available, apart from the children's tables. Underneath the worktop was stored a variety of mathematics equipment, cubes, blocks, scales, measuring equipment and so on. The only other storage space was a high 'wardrobe' style cupboard positioned in a corner of the room, directly behind two pupils' seats. The high Victorian window ledges were used to shelve extra books and National Curriculum documentation. The only area dedicated to a specific activity was a small space against the wall where the computer was located. Much of the wall space was uneven white painted brick, which had proved to be less than suitable for displaying work.

The response of this teacher was to use the space efficiently and, in some cases ingeniously, so that, although the size of the room meant that it was impossible to create work bays for different activities, the teacher successfully taught all curriculum activities in the space available.

The strategy for achieving this involved a high level of organisation. In order to save space, personal equipment trays were integral to the pupils' tables, which meant that they did not have to move around the classroom to collect materials. The children were assigned to specific groups for each activity. A sign affixed to the board indicated the seating arrangements for each successive task. Some flexibility was built into this system depending upon the nature of the task. In science, geography, history and technology, for example, pupils were often given choices as to where they sat, whereas they had set places for the core areas of maths and English.

The teacher had contrived to find a small 'carpet space' for whole class activities. However, since there was not enough room for the whole class to sit on it together, for example when the teacher was reading a story, those children with seats nearest to the front of the class stayed where they were. For tasks such as spelling, groups of pupils interacted with the teacher on a rotating basis, each coming in turn to sit on the limited open carpet area. By using these various devices, the teacher had been able to introduce, in a severely restricted space, a level of flexibility which allowed for individual, group and classwork, and which could be tailored to different curriculum activities, without any rearrangement of the furniture.

This account and the preceding one demonstrate a high degree of flexibility on the part of the teachers in question. Both cases represent a considered and deliberate response to a difficult situation, overcoming the constraints of an inadequate or difficult classroom environment. In each class, a kind of partnership developed, an understanding between teacher and learners that co-operation and organisation were required, which was fundamental to the success of the strategy. This is not to say, of course, that such understandings cannot develop in classrooms where conditions are rather more suitable, but in the case of an inadequate or difficult classroom environment, it would seem to be a prerequisite if the teacher is successfully to deliver the full curriculum.

Our final example is of quite a different environment, an open-plan area. Three of the schools in the sample were built on open-plan principles, and most, like the Victorian school described above, had retained the major features of their original layout. Open-plan schools were mainly constructed during the 1970s, and although the origin of their design is contested the series of spaces of different shapes, sizes and purposes were clearly created to encourage the use of space and resources 'leading to co-operation between teachers and flexible grouping of children' (Bennett, 1976), that is, team teaching and the integrated day.

Detractors of open education saw these schools as the repositories of an extreme and damaging form of progressive practice. However, as Brogden (1986) argues, the reality rarely matched the rhetoric: a number of studies showed that there were wide variations in pedagogy that were little different from those found across primary education in general.

Nevertheless, the requirement to deliver a 'broad and balanced' curriculum in the 1990s, and the calls for more whole class teaching and for greater subject specialisation in the upper years of KS2, creates considerable logistical problems for teachers in schools that have retained an open-plan design. How did teachers in our example cope with these new demands in an environment designed for a quite different approach to teaching and learning?

Classroom 3: the open-plan

Figure 7.4 depicts the home-unit for two Year 6 classes in one of these open-plan schools. This unit was part of a larger L-shaped space which served four classes altogether (two Year 5 and two Year 6). Furniture served as space-dividers between the four units, with bookshelves and a mobile blackboard also arranged as a partition and demarcation line. Low cupboards and worktops further separated the Year 6 from the Year 5 areas, and helped to define a corridor which ran around one side of the whole area, allowing access to each of the home units. On one side of this corridor was a practical art area, which was shared by Year 6 pupils, with worktops, sinks and shelving for materials. There was also a well-equipped technology room at the end of the Year 5 unit which was suitable for small group activity.

In the basic seating plan, the children all faced the same way behind three long rows of tables with seven or eight children to each row, an apparently contradictory and somewhat inefficient use of a space designed for flexibility. However, this seating arrangement was used for specific activities requiring individual work, and the layout was frequently reorganised, for example for art and craft, or for activities which involved collaborative group work. On some occasions, the whole year group worked together on a single project, for example in technology sessions, where children organised themselves into working groups. The tables were also rearranged when the Year 6 children divided into ability groups for mathematics.

This interesting combination of open-plan flexibility and traditional structure was also to be found in the approach to teaching. The teachers in the school described their arrangement as 'team teaching', and while this may not have conformed to a purist definition of the term, there was considerable evidence of a genuine collegial approach within and between year groups. The teachers planned together and worked on a two-year rolling programme for Levels 2–5 of the National Curriculum so that, for example, a teacher would take a class in Year 5 and continue to work with that class throughout Year 6. Moreover, the pupils sometimes moved to the teacher rather than the other way round; this was deliberately introduced as part of a strategy for transition to secondary school, which also allowed a particular unit to concentrate resources for different curriculum areas. Thus, for example, a Year 6 class went to a Year 5 teacher's home-unit for all science lessons, while their own teacher taught a Year 5 class.

Similar exchanges were observed between geography and PSE, while in history each teacher taught their own class but shared resources across the whole year group. In Years 5 and 6, for example, four teachers taught subject-based work in history, geography, science and technology, allowing each teacher, in the words of the KS2 Co-ordinator, 'to teach one thing four times, instead of four things once'. This system of 'teaching swaps' crossed year groups and extended downwards as far as Year 3.

The 'quiet room', a common feature of most open-plan schools built in the 1970s, was a place where groups of children could work away from distractions when necessary. In the present example, this area tended to be mainly used for special educational needs support. On one observed occasion, however, the whole class squeezed into this small room to listen to the end of a story which had been disturbed by a Year 5 class returning from a different activity. This episode, although rare, demonstrates one of the problems associated with the use of open-plan areas for more structured teaching of the kind now demanded by the National Curriculum, namely the maintenance of an appropriate noise level in which children can work without distraction.

Nevertheless, it would appear that, in general, the open nature of the classroom units did facilitate 'team arrangements' which teachers found both flexible and effective. Although open-plan areas were designed for the sharing of resources and working spaces, and to enable classes to move easily to common areas, or for teachers to move to classes, an early criticism of this system was that it increased the amount of 'evaporated time', the time lost during in transitional activities (DES, 1972). Ironically, therefore, the school designed originally to facilitate an open educational approach enabled a flexible response to the changing demands of a much more prescriptive curriculum.

A Conservative Culture?

Earlier in this chapter we raised the issue of teachers' apparent resistance to changing their practice, despite public exhortation to do so, and in the wake of a completely restructured primary curriculum. We have presented three examples of classroom organisational strategy, each of which demonstrates considerable flexibility and, in the case of the open-plan classroom, a high level of collaboration. While these were the exceptions rather than the rule, we do not intend to imply that flexible approaches were not to be found elsewhere. Variants of many of the approaches described above could be found, to varying degrees, in a number of the classrooms in the sample. Nevertheless, it is an inescapable fact that for most of the time, in most of the classrooms, children sat together in groups, and that despite some rather general modifications, the typical layout of the primary classroom has hardly altered in twenty years.

Are we to conclude, therefore, that teachers are as conservative in matters of classroom organisation and layout as Cuban (1984) suggests they are in their teaching strategies? Some, like Alexander (1997), argue that the grouping principle has such a 'powerful doctrinal status' for primary teachers that they refuse, or are unable, to consider any other arrangement, and if we accept this proposition, it would appear to be a strong enough force to override a considerable rise in whole class teaching. An alternative, and more cautious view, is that unless teachers feel that they have some sense of ownership over the process of change they will operate according to what Doyle and Ponder (1977) call the 'practicality ethic', where the benefits of introducing an innovation are weighed against the personal cost. Only when teachers see a clear sense of the usefulness and purpose of the new curriculum will there be a shift towards its adoption at anything other than a utilitarian level. Beyond this, only when teachers have begun to feel that they have some control over the direction of the innovation, will they move towards fully integrating it into their professional practice.

This model presupposes some element of choice, however, whereas the National Curriculum was, in effect, a technical innovation that was imposed on teachers, with little or no guidance as to how to implement it. In this situation, it is hardly surprising that, teachers draw upon familiar, tried-and-tested practice. Although, as Simon argues, 'tinkering' with the primary curriculum has continued more or less unchecked since the 1940s (Galton *et al.*, 1980), the pace of educational reform in the past decade has been rapid and continuous. Teachers simply have not had the time or opportunity to get accustomed to one demand before a new requirement is upon them, let alone begin to feel that they have a real stake in the process. The first response in such situations is to 'bolt on' each new development to existing (and familiar) practice. The idea that teachers would, in the face of relentless change, dismantle the traditional and familiar framework in which they work is deeply unrealistic. This is not conservatism, therefore, but basic survival.

References

Alexander, R. (1997) *Policy and Practice in Primary Education*, 2nd edition, London: Routledge.

Alexander, R., Willcocks, J. and Kinder, K. (1989) *Changing Primary Practice*, Basingstoke: Falmer Press.

Alexander, R., Rose, J. and Woodhead, C. (1992) *Curriculum Organisation and Classroom Practice in Primary Schools*, London: Department of Education and Science.

Bennett, N. (1976) *Teaching Styles and Pupil Progress*, London: Open Books.

Bennett, N., Andreae, J., Hegarty, P. and Wade, B. (1980) *Open Plan Schools*, Slough: NFER.

Brogden, M. (1986) 'Open Plan Primary Schools: Rhetoric and Reality', in Cohen, A. and Cohen, L. (eds) *Primary Education: A Sourcebook for Teachers*, London: Harper & Row.

Cuban, L. (1984) *How Teachers Taught: Constancy and Change in American Classrooms, 1890–1980*, New York: Longman.

DES (1972) *Open-Plan Primary Schools*, London: HMSO.

Doyle, W. and Ponder, G. (1977) 'The Practicality Ethic and Teacher Decision Making', *Interchange* (8), 1–12.

Galton, M., Simon, B. and Croll, P. (1980) *Inside the Primary Classroom*, London: Routledge & Kegan Paul.

Hargreaves, L. (1990) 'Teachers and Pupils in Small Schools', in Galton, M. and Patrick, H. (eds) *Curriculum Provision in the Small Primary School*, 75–103.

Hastings, N. (1995) 'Seats of Learning?', *Support for Learning* 10(1), 8–11.

Hastings, N. and Schwieso, J. (1995) 'Tasks and Tables: The Effects of Seating Arrangements on Task Engagement in Primary Classrooms', *Educational Research* 37(3), 279–291.

Hastings, N., Schwieso, J. and Wheldall, K. (1996) 'A Place for Learning', in Croll, P. and Hastings, N. (eds), *Effective Primary Teaching: Research Based Classroom Strategies*, London: David Fulton.

McKinsey & Company (1997) *The Future of Information Technology in U.K. Schools*, London: McKinsey & Company.

McNamara, D. and Waugh, D. (1993) 'Classroom Organisation: A Discussion of Grouping Strategies in the Light of the "3 Wise Men's Report"', *School Organisation* 13(1), 41–50.

Moyles, J. (ed.) (1995) *Beginning Teaching: Beginning Learning*, Buckingham: Open University Press.

Plowden Report (1967) *Children and their Primary Schools*, report of the Central Advisory Council for Education in England, London: HMSO.

Ridley, K. and Trembath, D. (1986) 'Primary School Organisation: Some Rhetoric and Some Reason', in Cohen, A. and Cohen, L. (eds) *Primary Education; A Sourcebook for Teachers*, London: Harper Rowe Ltd.

Somekh, B. and Davis, N. (eds) (1997) *Using Information Technology Effectively in Teaching and Learning: Studies in Pre-service and In-service Teacher Education*, London: Routledge.

Wheldall, K. and Congreve, S. (1981) 'Teachers and Behaviour Modification: What Do They Think of it So Far?', in Wheldall, K. (ed). *The Behaviourist in the Classroom*, Birmingham: Educational Review Publications.

Wheldall, K. and Lam, Y. (1987) 'Rows versus Tables II: The Effects of Two Classroom Seating Arrangements on Disruption Rate, On-task Behaviour and Teacher Behaviour in Three Special School Classes', *Educational Psychology* 7(4), 303–12.

Yeomans, J. (1989) 'Changing Seating: The Use of Antecedent Control to Increase On-task Behaviour', *Behavioural Approaches with Children* 13(3), 151–60.

8

ICT and the Nature of Learning: Implications for the Design of a Distance Education Course

Peter Twining

Introduction

This chapter explores the impact of new technology on learning, using the specific context of an Open University (OU) course to illustrate some of the issues. It describes how evidence about the impact of information communication technology (ICT) on learning based on the existing literature and an analysis of this OU course compare with the realities as revealed by developmental testing of that course.

Over the first 25 years of its existence the OU developed a course model for distance education that proved to be very effective (Daniel, 1997; Lane, 1999). This model was based on high quality course materials combined with a strong support network. The course materials typically consisted of paper-based resources (e.g. Study Guides, Readers), television or video programmes, audio cassettes or radio programmes and, for some courses, home kits (e.g. a microscope and slides). The support network included tutors, each of whom worked with a group of approximately 20 students both at a distance, using snail mail, the telephone and fax, and face to face at tutorials. Other centrally provided support mechanisms included telephone help lines, residential schools, and regional centres that students could visit. The quality of the OU's educational provision depended upon the academic quality of its materials and the personal quality of the support provided to students.

Within this 'traditional' OU course model it was normal practice for a course to be prepared and course materials produced over a long time scale and at substantial expense prior to any students actually taking the course. Thus, for example, an undergraduate course might take three years and half a million pounds to develop before students started to be enrolled on it. Once the course had been produced it would be taken by thousands of students over its lifetime, a period of five or more years. The rationale for the long lead-time was that the course and its materials had to be perfect before it was used because it was not feasible to alter the course materials once students had started working on it. This was largely due to the practical and financial problems with sending out thousands of sets of revised materials.

Towards the end of the twentieth century the status quo within the OU started to change. This was due to developments in the wider education community, many of which related to developments in Information Communication Technology (ICT). New technologies were leading to increasing competition in the distance education market, and, perhaps more importantly, there was a strong belief in the wider educational community that Information and Communication Technology (ICT) had the potential to have a substantial impact on learning (e.g. Davis *et al.*, 1997; Schacter, 1999; Scrimshaw, 1997b; Trilling and Hood, 1999). This was reflected in the financial value of investments that were being made in ICT across all sectors of education in the industrialised world (e.g. Lemke and Coughlin, 1998; Twining and McCormick, 1999). This belief in the potential of ICT to enhance learning was underpinned by a growing body of research evidence (e.g. Schacter, 1999; Scrimshaw, 1997b). These pressures prompted the OU to start an ongoing process of exploring ways of using ICT in its courses for academic advantage.

Introducing the use of ICT to OU courses potentially has significant implications for the traditional OU course model, both in terms of course development processes and the pedagogy that underpin that model. Given the success of the traditional OU course model and the substantial sums of money involved in developing new courses any changes to that model require clear evidence that those changes will be an improvement. In order to explore these issues further we are going to focus on the development of one specific OU course – E211: *Learning Matters – challenges of the information age.*

Planning 'E211: *Learning Matters – Challenges of the Information Age*'

E211 is a second level undergraduate course that explores learning, and in particular the potential impact of new technologies on learning. The course team, whilst all holding different views on learning, could all be broadly described as constructivists. We all believe that learning involves the learner in constructing their understanding(s) of the world and developing their skills through their mental and physical actions within the social context in which they exist.

In the light of our views of learning and our knowledge of the literature on ICT in education, we were keen to make effective use of ICT as a vehicle for learning as part of E211. The focus of the course on the potential impact of new technology on learning meant that we felt it was important for students on the course to have personal experience of using new technologies in their own learning. This fits in with Scrimshaw's (1997a, p. 100) view that 'the computer is not simply another curriculum innovation;

it is also arguably the most important technical aid to teachers wishing to explore their own practice.'

Conole and Oliver (1998) describe a pedagogical framework for embedding ICT[1] in the curriculum. They identified the need to focus on courses at the level of educational activities, which they called 'learning scenarios'. They describe a learning scenario as being 'any educational interaction (e.g. a lecture, a discussion, a group project)' (p. 7). They go on to identify that every learning scenario is defined by a number of 'characteristics, including: media type; use of media; the preparatory work required; the educational interactions which are supported; the delivery constraints' (p. 7). They state that the interaction of the media type and the way in which it is used will determine the other three characteristics of a learning scenario.

The interaction of media type and the way in which they are used in education has been the focus of a good deal of research at The Open University (see for example: Burt, 1998; Goodfellow and Kukulska-Hulme, 1996; Laurillard, 1993; Taylor, 1991; Taylor and Salanki, 1994). One of the outcomes of this is a better understanding of the educational affordances of different media (Laurillard *et al.*, 1999). For example, print (on paper) lends itself better to long passages of text than does screen-based text due to 'readability' factors. Similarly, if you wish to convey enthusiasm or allow learners to 'experience' another culture video is likely to be more effective than print. This understanding of media affordances had already been used to inform the design of E211. The key to the E211 course team's deliberations was a concern to ensure that we made decisions about our use of media based on the learning outcomes for each learning activity and the affordances of each of the different media types. In addition, we were at pains to closely integrate different media so that they extended and enhanced each other. This is illustrated in the extract from the original course plan, which is outlined below.

Activity 7 The Trunk Flick Through **Multimedia**	This is an exploratory activity where the students are presented with a range of 'media artefacts' belonging to Bob McCormick (a member of the 'Learning Matters' course team). They are asked to explore the artefacts and select the five that they think tell them the most about Bob as a learner. They are expected to make notes about why they chose those five items.
Activity 8 Email re *Activity 7* **CMC**	The students share the items they selected in Activity 7 and their reasons for their selections in groups of 3, via email. At this early stage in the course they are not expected to enter into in-depth discussions electronically.
Activities 9 & 10 Reader Articles 1 & 2 **Paper**	The students read the Reader Articles, which address aspects of 'knowledge', 'learning' and 'achievement'. The students are asked to create a set of notes that relate their views of 'knowledge', 'learning' and 'achievement' from Activities 7 and 8 to the views expressed in the Reader Articles.

Activity 11
Tutorial
Face to face

This will be the first time the students and tutors will have met face to face (at least in relation to the course!). The aims of the tutorial are:

- to help students build relationships with each other and with their tutor in order to facilitate future computer conferencing (e.g. in Activity 13);
- to extend students' thinking about 'learning', 'knowledge' and 'achievement' and the concept of a 'setting' (i.e. to extend work done during Activities 7 to 10).

The activities in the tutorial will include: working in the same groups of three that shared emails in Activity 8 and discussing the similarities and differences between the choices they made in Activity 7 and their reasons for them.

Activity 12
The Trunk Sort
Multimedia

The students are presented with a subset of the items that they explored in Activity 7. The software takes them through a series of progressively more refined sorting activities: they are asked to focus on categories relating to 'learning', 'knowledge' and 'achievement'. As the students move further into the program more options are made available. Throughout the activity the students' ideas (as revealed by the ways in which they classify the objects) are used to further extend their thinking by reflecting it back to them in a variety of ways. The outcomes from The Trunk Sort are output in a format that the students can annotate (using the dedicated hypermedia software which they use throughout the course for taking notes, writing assignments, annotating media objects, etc.).

Activity 13
Conference re *Activity 12*
CMC

The students share the outcomes from Activity 12 via a computer conference. Using the 'Learning Matters' hypermedia software the students can look at:

- the categories other students used;
- how other students assigned items to each category;
- other students' annotations on the above.

The aim of this activity is to extend the feedback that the students receive and to help them further develop their ideas through discussion with other students (moderated by their tutor).

Activity 14
Tutor Marked
Assignment
CTools

The students create a hypermedia 'essay' using the 'Learning Matters' hypermedia software. This allows them to make links to the digital resources used in the Trunk as well as to sections of the Reader Articles that are supplied to them in electronic form on the course CD ROM and to the any notes they have made in digital format during previous activities.

One of the key concerns for the course team was to reduce the extent to which students were asked to 'absorb' content that was presented to them in the course materials. We were keen to reduce the emphasis on the transmission of 'knowledge' and increase the level of learning through activities. One way in which we planned to do this was to incorporate interactive multimedia within the course in order to develop what Sewell (1990) describes as 'empowering environments', which should act to engage intellectual activity, to encourage learners to take control of their own learning and to reflect on the consequences of their activities; to reflect on their own thinking' (Sewell, 1990, p. 19). Heppell's (1993) taxonomy of modes of interaction that integrated media should support is helpful here in distinguishing between different types of media use. The taxonomy consists of three levels of interaction:

- Narrative, where the learner is passive in the sense of only having the ability to attend to the media (or not);
- Interactive, where the learner has navigational control, as would be the case when browsing or searching the web for example.
- Participative, where the learner can contribute information and represent their ideas, as would be the case when authoring hypermedia.

Heppell (1993) highlights the need for greater emphasis on using ICT in this third, participative mode within education. This supports the claim by Jonassen, Myers and McKillop (1996, p. 94) that

> producing hypermedia and multimedia products is among the most complete and engaging of the constructivist/constructionist activities. Additionally . . . the process of researching, organizing, and constructing such knowledge . . . necessarily engages learners in high-order, critical thinking and literacy.

Whilst there is some research evidence that suggests that exploring hypermedia presentations that have been created by someone else does not enhance learning (e.g. Jonassen and Wang, 1993; Whalley, 1990), there is substantial research evidence that supports the view that the process of authoring hypermedia does enhance the author's learning (e.g. Turner and Handler, 1997; Jonassen and Wang, 1993). The course team therefore decided to include hypermedia authoring as one of the vehicles for student learning within E211.

One of the reasons why hypermedia authoring is educationally worthwhile is that creating effective hypermedia presentations involves making explicit the relationships between 'discrete chunks' of information. In order to do this one has to think clearly and deeply about one's understanding of those relationships. Thus hypermedia authoring involves metacognition. However, interactive multimedia can also support metacognition in other ways. Sewell (1990) claims that computers are powerful metacognitive tools because they can record and play back our actions thus allowing us to reflect upon them – 'the technology has the power to reify or to make concrete one's own thinking' (p. 21). Hazzan

(1999) stated this more forcefully when he wrote that 'thinking about complex issues can be enhanced if one has the means to externalize his or her mind-view and scrutinize it as an external and tangible entity' (p. 58). This is an implicit feature of hypermedia authoring.

The course team also wanted to utilise the power of interactive multimedia to overtly engage students in making explicit their understandings about learning (the subject matter of the course) and reflecting upon them. Thus we planned to use a metacognitive tool called the Elicitation Engine, one instantiation of which is included in the original course extract above under the name The Trunk (see Twining *et al.*, 1998, for further details). A prototype of the Elicitation Engine had already been developed and proven to be effective in the Institute for Educational Technology in the OU (Durbridge and Stratfold, 1996).

A second approach that the course team intended to take in order to increase the active participation of students in their own learning on E211 was to incorporate computer mediated communication, including text-based computer conferencing. This would provide a mechanism for students (and their tutors) to engage in two way communication, thus reducing the emphasis on one way transmission of information found within the traditional OU course model. Evidence from a variety of sources suggests that the use of computer mediated communication (CMC) can enhance learning (e.g. Parker, 1999) even in traditional face-to-face contexts such as schools (e.g. DTI, 1997). Clearly, in the context of distance education, CMC helps to reduce the isolation of the learners by providing them with an additional means of communicating with their peers and tutor. Asynchronous computer conferencing, which is what the E211 course team intended to use, does not require that the parties concerned are available at the same place or time. This enables students to work at convenient times and locations as well as allowing them to pace their interactions (and learning) (Parker, 1999). CMC also provides the opportunity for introducing collaborative activities (Scrimshaw, 1997a). Importantly, CMC potentially changes the students' and tutors' roles and relationships, for example by providing access to a wider range of sources of expertise (Scrimshaw, 1997a).

Inevitably, the incorporation of new technologies, as proposed by the E211 course team, introduces new skills for the students (and tutors). These obviously include the 'technical' skills associated with operating the software itself, but perhaps less obviously include new ways of working. For example, in authoring a hypermedia presentation the students not only have to learn how to operate the authoring software but they also have to grapple with new views of literacy associated with hypermedia (O'Neill, 1998). This has implications for the students not only in terms of the learning curve that they have to go through in order to engage with the course content, but also in terms of what represents appropriate assessment of their learning. This quote from Heppell (1994, p. 154) clearly illustrates the point:

Imagine a nation of horse riders with a clearly defined set of riding capabilities. In one short decade the motor car is invented and within that same decade many children become highly competent drivers extending the boundaries of their travel as well as developing entirely new leisure pursuits (like stock-car racing and hot rodding). At the end of the decade government ministers want to assess the true impact of automobiles on the nation's capability. They do it by putting everyone back on the horses and checking their dressage, jumping and trotting as before. Of course, we can all see that it is ridiculous.

Thus the course team also needed to ensure that the assessment of students on E211 was appropriate, including ensuring that it addressed the learning processes as well as content within the course.

All of the evidence from examination of the existing literature supported the course team's view that it was appropriate to use ICT in the way that we planned to do so. However, it was also clear from the research literature that ICT *per se* does not necessarily lead to educational enhancement (e.g. Maddux, 1993; Warschauer, 1998). The key determinant of the educational value of ICT is how it is used in specific contexts (Schacter, 1999; Squires, 1997) and the context within much of the literature is very different from the context of E211. Thus the course team needed to provide additional evidence, based on an analysis of our planned use of ICT, in order to justify the substantial costs and risks involved in such a radical departure from the traditional OU course model.

We looked to the literature on pedagogic re-engineering (Collis, 1996) to provide a framework that would enable us to analyse the impact of our proposed use of ICT on student learning within the course. Pedagogic re-engineering is based on the premise that courses are built up of instructional components combined together in particular sequences and that by changing these components you can change and enhance the course. These components are in many ways directly comparable with (Conole and Oliver, 1998) learning scenarios. Thus a key element in pedagogic re-engineering relates to the media types used in a course.

Laurillard (1996) combined the notions of media affordances and pedagogic re-engineering when she developed a framework for analysing the impact of changing the balance of media on OU courses. This framework, which I refer to as the Media Mix Model (Twining, 1999), is closely linked to Laurillard's conversational framework (Laurillard, 1993). It analyses the use of each media type within a course in terms of the modes of student interaction that they support. Laurillard identifies four modes of student interaction:

- attending
- practising
- discussing
- articulating.

Figure 8.1 illustrates how an analysis of 50 hours of student study time on a 'traditional' OU course looks within the Media Mix Model.

Key to abbreviations in Figures 8.1 and 8.2

Pr	Print
A/V	Audio vision: audiocassette plus artefacts to explore
TV+	Television programme plus notes
Video	Video programme plus activities
Tut'l	Face-to-face tutorial(s)
TMA	Tutor marked assignment
CMA	Computer marked assignment
Ctools	Computer tools (e.g. word processor)
Cres	Computer resources (e.g. digital versions of reader articles)
MM	Multimedia
CMC	Computer mediated communication (e.g. email, conferencing)

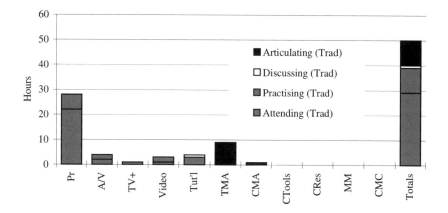

Figure 8.1   *Analysis of 50 hours' student study time on a 'traditional' OU course*

Laurillard's Media Mix Model seemed ideally suited to the needs of the E211 course team. It provided a framework that would allow analysis of our planned use of media on the course. In addition, as the framework had been developed within the OU itself, any analysis resulting from its use was more likely to be viewed as being valid, notwithstanding any limitations with the Media Mix Model (see Twining, 1999, for a discussion of some of these limitations). Thus the E211 course team applied the Media Mix Model to the first 50 hours of student study time that we had originally planned for E211. The results of this analysis are shown in Figure 8.2.

Comparing the amounts of time that the Media Mix Model predicted students would spend engaged in each of the four types of activity on a 'traditional' OU course and the first 50 hours as originally planned for E211 indicated that (see Figure 8.3) the amount of:

- attending would be reduced on E211
- practising would be increased on E211
- discussing would be increased on E211
- articulating would be increased on E211.

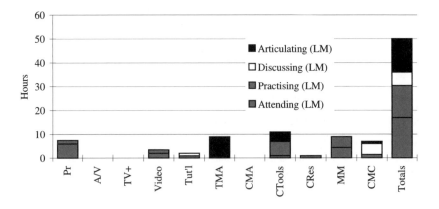

Figure 8.2   *Analysis of the first 50 hours' student study time originally planned for E211*

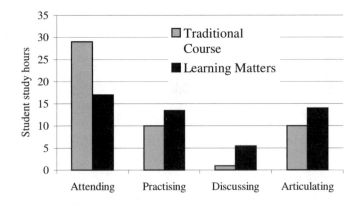

Figure 8.3   *Comparison of student activity on a 'traditional' OU course and E211*

From a constructivist view point, this analysis suggested that the plan to reduce the amount of print material on E211 and replace it with activities that made use of ICT would provide a better balance of student activity than a 'traditional' OU course.

Production and Developmental Testing of E211

Armed with this evidence the production of E211 went ahead as originally planned. However, all the evidence supporting the planned use of ICT on E211 was only theoretical. As Taylor and Laurillard, quoting Laurillard (1987), have pointed out 'the kinds of analysis which an instructional designer needs to go through to produce interactive events which result in meaningful learning for students . . . depends upon proper evaluation of the system in use with real learners' (Taylor and Laurillard, 1995, p. 243). Thus throughout the production of E211 the activities underwent developmental testing. This testing took two forms: first, individual testing of multimedia components; and secondly testing of sequences of activities by groups of students working through them as if they were actually taking the course.

The individual component testing was mainly focused on usability issues, though where possible evidence of the educational effectiveness of the components was also collected. The group testing, which took place on two separate occasions, on each occasion involved a group of 20+ students and a tutor working through 40+ hours of the course. This group testing aimed to collect additional evidence about the educational effectiveness of the course and the impact that the use of ICT was having.

Round 1 of Group Testing

The first round of group developmental testing focused on the use of ICT in the first two Blocks of E211, as it was originally planned.

There were serious technical problems with the main hypermedia-authoring tool (MetaNote) during this first round of group developmental testing. Given the central role of MetaNote in the original design of the course this resulted in the outcomes from this round of developmental testing being skewed. One of the students summed up the situation nicely when she wrote: 'I am finding dealing with the buggy software puts up barriers that make learning difficult – even learning how to use the software!' Nonetheless, the outcomes of this first round of group testing strongly supported the outcomes of the analysis in Laurillard's Media Mix Model, in terms of the shift in emphasis from content to process within the course.

It was clear from student feedback that some of the students on this first round of group testing did not like the change in emphasis from content to process. At times they were not sure that they had learnt anything, as summed up in these two comments: 'I did not know if I was doing it properly' and 'most of the time I felt I was not learning. I needed more reassurance that I was doing OK.' This was despite the fact that there was plenty of evidence that indicated that they had in fact learnt a great deal.

This developmental testing also drew attention to a number of other issues, which had not been addressed by the theoretical analysis of E211. Many of these related to the practicalities of studying a course that utilised ICT to the extent that was the case for this original version of E211, whilst others focused on the educational effectiveness of the software itself.

Educational Effectiveness Issues Emerging from Round 1 of Group Testing

Whilst the overall evidence from the developmental testing indicated a shift towards constructivist models of learning it was not always clear that the way in which the software was being used was appropriate. Thus, for example, some of the students perceived that the software sometimes distracted them from focusing on the main objectives of the activity whilst others felt the software enhanced those objectives. This is reflected in comments about FirstClass, the conferencing system that was used:

> Modern technology really is wonderful – I can see the useful possibilities of a set-up like FirstClass.

> I spent so much time on software and connection problems.

Similarly, there was a difference of opinion amongst the students about the appropriateness of using MetaNote, one of the hypermedia authoring tools, for some of the activities:

> I felt that the method of working of the software was excellent in developing conceptual thinking.

> I believe it is very important not to let the technology dominate – the writing and storing of notes can be achieved very easily with a pen and paper, and a file to keep them in remember!

The use of the Elicitation Engine (in the form of the Trunk Sort activity) was viewed predominantly as being educationally effective:

> The 'Sort' activity is interactive – good getting feedback and having challenge.

> Multimedia can stretch thinking (Sort).

> This (The Trunk Sort) is the first time for me that software has been really challenging since it reacts to my inputs.

> Bob's trunk was an example of learning via multimedia being interesting.

> The Trunk did make us think, but how useful are the categories devised?

However, this view was not universal. One student argued that 'you could have a page of pictures of items in the trunk – it is a bit of a gimmick'.

A number of factors seemed to come into play in determining the extent to which students perceived the use of ICT to be enhancing their learning. First, the level of technical difficulties they encountered when using the software, which was a significant problem in the case of MetaNote due in part to the number of bugs in the developmental testing version of the software. Secondly, owing to failings on the part of the course team, some students did not understand the role that the software played. As one student put it: 'you need to have a conceptual knowledge of how the technology works to get the most out of it'. The last comment about the Trunk in the previous paragraph may be a good example of this. The student appears to have overlooked the key role that the software plays in scaffolding the categorisation and reflection process in the way that it structures the students' activity, records their choices and provides them with feedback. Thirdly, the course team may indeed have overplayed the use of ICT in some instances.

Practical Issues Emerging from Round 1 of Group Testing

At the most basic level, it was clear that all of the students spent far longer working on the activities that involved software use than had been anticipated by the course team. Some of this can be accounted for by technical problems, but this was only part of the story. Even where students reported no problems using the software, as for instance with the Trunk, they still spent far longer working with it than expected.

Where time was an issue it was typically the case that the first thing the students omitted was the computer conferencing, even when they saw it as being valuable:

> The conferencing became a secondary and less important activity in my mind. I felt guilty about this which meant that I was even less able to partake – I lurked but I was not confident enough about my ideas to put them in the conference (I did make some contributions and got thought provoking answers. It was very worthwhile).

Not only was the amount of time required to do the activities in the first round of developmental testing problematic, but so too were the constraints that were imposed on when and where the students could study. Thus, the fact that most of the activities involved an ICT element meant that students needed to have access to a computer in order to do them. Their flexibility was further reduced by the way in which computer conferencing had been tightly integrated into the course. As one student remarked, '[Conferencing was] too demanding on time – very tiring trying to go on conference every night'. As this quote suggests, the students needed to log in frequently (though perhaps not every night) and this proved problematic. This was particularly noticeable where the conferencing was part of a collaborative activity in which students were dependent on each other's contributions. One student, for example, reported that she was not able to complete the next activity because the two students she was meant to be working with had not sent her the information she needed.

Revisions to E211 in the Light of the First Round of Group Testing

The first round of developmental testing did support the theoretical analysis, which suggested that the use of ICT as originally planned would result in a shift from a didactic to a constructivist model of learning. However, it also highlighted some significant issues which meant that this might not lead to an enhanced student experience. The consequences of the radical change from the traditional OU course model seemed to place too great a burden on the students, both in terms of practical constraints and in terms of their need to adjust their views of what studying on an OU course involves. As a result of this it was decided to:

- reduce the number of activities overall and increase the time allocated for those involving ICT
- significantly reduce the emphasis placed on MetaNote throughout the course, in favour of a longer paper-based study guide and more extensive use of another hypermedia authoring package called HyperNote;
- loosen the coupling between the computer conferencing and other course components, whilst still retaining it as a compulsory element that linked with and built upon other course components;
- generally scale down the compulsory ICT elements in favour of 'traditional' paper-based components, though still leaving over one-third of the study time on the course as a whole involving ICT as an essential ingredient.

These significant changes shifted the emphasis back toward 'attending' within the Media Mix Model, whilst still moving away from the didacticism of a traditional OU course model and towards a constructivist one (as illustrated in Figure 8.4).

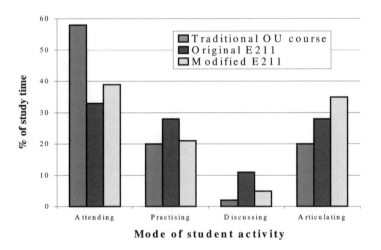

Figure 8.4   *Graph comparing modes of student activity*

Round 2 of Group Testing

The second round of group testing focused on the use of ICT in the latter parts of the revised course. The outcomes of this second round of group testing also supported the view that the use of ICT, even after the reduction in emphasis on ICT, did result in many of the changes initially anticipated for the original course plan. Thus there was a shift in emphasis from content to process, though this was less marked as a result of the changes made to the course. These quotes from three students sum the situation up nicely:

> I have found the last two weeks interesting, and can honestly say that I know more about learning situations now than I did last month! It is a very different sort of course to any I have taken before. I find it hard to express myself when analysing the different situations, but I think I am getting there, albeit slowly.

> I am much more used to reading-based courses and it was therefore unusual for me to be doing so much in activities but, as the software (HyperNote in particular) became more familiar, it was a rewarding exercise.

> Overall I like the activity based approach here but it does tend to depend on a high amount of keyboard time which might not suit everyone's situation. I think the activity base in the learning does bring it alive and gets it into the bloodstream a bit more than just reading and note-taking.

This last quote also highlights the issue of people's personal situations. As in the first round of group testing, this round emphasised the shortcomings of the original theoretical analyses, which did not deal explicitly with the practical implications of integrating ICT into the course. Thus, for example, the original analysis did not address issues relating to problems with students' hardware:

> Sorry, Joane,[2] for the delay in replying. My PC has been extremely poorly, and as a result I have only just got to the stage where I am ready to load the software again!

> My machine isn't that great either – hope it's not contagious – think we need a new power supply – Daniel has heaved himself off his sick bed to get a new box for the beast!! (Amazing how they recover when 'puters need fixing isn't it?)

> As I am behind because of technical difficulties i.e. no computer for several days, my TMA will be later than I had hoped.

An unexpected finding, given the emphasis placed on the essential nature of conferencing within the developmental testing, was that only around half of the students were active posters of messages. In addition, those students who were not active posters were also found not to be reading other people's messages. This suggests that vicarious learning by students 'lurking' in conferences is unlikely to be as widespread as one might have expected (Perkins and Newman, 1996).

As anticipated by the original literature review and despite the lack of full participation by all the students, the introduction of computer conferencing did lead to changes in roles for both the students and tutor. Joinson (2000), in his independent analysis of the conferencing during this round of developmental testing, found that the tutor played an active role in encouraging and directing student contributions to the conference. The tutor's role became more that of a 'facilitator of peer tutoring' rather than that of 'provider of answers'. Indeed, the students very often became the 'teachers' as well as being the 'learners'. Initially this tended to focus on technical problems, such as advising each other how to set up their computers most effectively, as illustrated by this short sequence of messages below:

22 October 1999 12:10:06
I Have just found an interesting problem. I have two CD Drives on my machine at work. The Hypernote programe seems to only want to access the resources disk on one of these. I don't know if it only looks on Drive D: which could be a problem if you have 2 hard drives. Or does it only look at the first CD Drive. I wanted to use my drive E: coz its faster.

Student 1
22 October 1999 12:38:48
Student 1 writes:
I Have just found an interesting problem. I have two CD Drives on my machine at work. The Hypernote programe seems to only want to access the resources disk on one of these. I don't know if it only looks on Drive D: which could be a problem if you have 2 hard drives. Or does it only look at the first CD Drive. I wanted to use my drive E: coz its faster.
It does not look only at drive D:, as my CDROM is set up to F: (so by process of elimination, it must look at the first CDROM drive)
Student 2

22 October 1999 20:19:28
Student 1 writes:
I Have just found an interesting problem. I have two CD Drives on my machine at work. The Hypernote programe seems to only want to access the resources disk on one of these. I don't know if it only looks on Drive D: which could be a problem if you have 2 hard drives. Or does it only look at the first CD Drive. I wanted to use my drive E: coz its faster.
My CD is drive F: too so it must look at the first CD, though I don't know, perhaps there is a way to point it elsewhere to a hard drive for instance if you want really fast access. If it is a real problem you could muck about in control panel or the BIOS of your machine and remap the CDs in software, or redo the cables if they are both IDE drives.
Student 3

As the developmental testing progressed the peer support gradually shifted to focus on the course content itself, as illustrated by this email message:

Student A writes:
Student C in her 'experience' commented on the fact that some of the material in the section on identity was difficult to grasp.
Could someone please explain to me the meaning of the first sentence in the paragraph commencing 'Certain anthropologists . . .' on page 17.
Sorry if mine is long on waffle, itsl ate and I'm tired – i want my bed!
Student A
Hi Student A
I'm in the mood to have a bash at answering your query <G>
I understand this paragraph as referring to the idea that within Western culture, the individual is important (as an example – our tendency to clothe ourselves in a variety of styles, fabrics and colours) where as in some cultures (for example Mao's China) the individual is not as important as 'the whole' – 'the whole' could mean country, city, town or village, or family.

In referring to the 'cult of youth' I imagine this is drawing attention to the attitude some youngsters these days have towards a total lack of consideration for other's needs outside of their own 'sect' or culture (Just think of those lads with their loudspeakers in their cars, with the bass turned way up LOUD!!! – I think you know what I mean :-)) Then you put a whole bunch of these 'oiks' together and see how much power the group has, and how much more fearful an ordinary Joe will be of asking them to turn the volume down . . . Would their reaction be any different if the request came from a person of near their own age compared with an Old Age Pensioner?
Does this help?
Student B
PS – as an ex riding instructor – i loved your personal experience – I hope i didn't yell at any of my kids like your instructor did though :-)

This change in roles encompasses changes in the recognised sources of expertise. For example, it is clear from the first set of emails about configuring CD drives that some of the students have a high level of technical expertise, perhaps more than members of the course team and the tutor.

The introduction of additional sources of expertise raises issues about the quality of the information that students have available to them. In the traditional OU model the course materials are the main source of information and the quality of that information is carefully controlled. The introduction of computer conferencing shifts some of the quality control responsibilities to the tutor and students. The students thus become not only consumers of information, which they need to evaluate the quality of, but also providers of information. This places additional responsibilities on them and may require that they refine their evaluation skills.

It was not just the computer conferencing that led to changes in roles and sources of expertise. Several students reported working with other adults on some of the multimedia activities, and some reported working with his children, as the quotes below illustrate:

> In my case it was also made more enjoyable as I used my children, aged 4, 6 and 9 as helpers. We spent two hours having good fun and we all contributed ideas. I then just had to spend half an hour 'tidying up' Modes of Learning,[3] mainly to make it more 'grown up' and reduce titles to one word. They were very reluctant to stop 'playing Modes'.

> After having done an awful lot of my thinking for me, my girls all want to know if my 'work' has got any more good games!

There were differences of opinion between the students about the different ICT components within the developmental testing, both in terms of its ease of use and its educational effectiveness, as illustrated by these contrasting messages:

Quotes re Modes of Learning:

> It was extremely straightforward and the software was easy to use and intuitive.

> Could not get it to work properly.

> The first few sorts were easy, but then as the software made me think harder, things became less easy.

It was difficult at first to try and categorise the different clips so that I could carry out a sort function.

Quotes re FirstClass:

The activity was not structured enough and there was no need to collaborate so the small groups in this instance failed to work.

I felt that the conference activities were a bit stilted – we were told what to talk about, and when to do so.

Inevitably, some changes needed to be made to the course as a result of this developmental testing. Overall, however, it did appear that the use of ICT in this revised version of the course did move the students towards a more active mode of learning whilst making the transition from the traditional OU course model manageable for students.

Conclusion

All of the evidence that the course team collected, whether it be from the initial theoretical analyses or the developmental testing, did indicate that incorporating ICT in the course would alter the nature of students' learning on the course. It would move away from a didactic 'deliver mode' to a more active and communicative one. This could be summarised in a shift from a 'presentation' mode of course deliver within the traditional OU model towards a 'transaction' mode in this new, ICT facilitated model.

The first round of group developmental testing demonstrated that the potential impact of this new ICT facilitated model, as implemented in the original version of E211, was even greater than anticipated. Indeed, it involved such huge changes to so many aspects of the students' learning that it was too much for a typical student to cope with. In the light of this the course was re-designed in order to reduce the overall impact of the integration of ICT, whilst still taking advantage of some of its potential to engage students in a more active mode of learning.

The second round of group testing suggested that the reduction and re-organisation of ICT use on E211 still built on the potential of ICT to change what and how the students learnt. However, it also kept the changes to manageable proportions for the majority of students and the tutor.

The key messages here seem to be that ICT does indeed have the potential to radically alter our learning, but as with any change we need to find ways to manage the transition from the old to the new.

Notes

1. Conole and Oliver (1998) refer to C&IT (Communication & Information Technology) as is the convention in OU higher education.

2. All names have been changed in order to protect the students' anonymity.
3. A multimedia application, similar to the Trunk, that is based on the Elicitation Engine.

References

Burt, G. (1998). *Do Media Matter in Distance Education?* Newport Pagnell: Open and Distance Education Statistics.

Collis, B. (1996). *Tele-learning in a Digital World: The future of distance learning* (1st edn). London: International Thomson Computer Press.

Conole, G. and Oliver, M. (1998). A pedagogical framework for embedding C&IT into the curriculum. *ALT-J*, 6(2), 4–16.

Daniel, J. (1997). VC's view. *Sesame*, Oct/Nov p. 9.

Davis, N., Desforges, C., Jessel, J., Somekh, B., Taylor, C. and Vaughan, G. (1997). Can quality in learning be enhanced through the use of IT? In B. Somekh and N. Davis (eds), *Using Information Technology Effectively in Teaching and Learning: Studies in Pre-Service and In-Service Teacher Education* (pp. 14–27). London: Routledge.

DTI (1997). *Schools Online Project: Summary of Report on Phase 1*. London: Department of Trade and Industry.

Durbridge, N. and Stratfold, M. (1996). Varying the texture: a study of art, learning and multimedia. *Journal of Interactive Media in Education*.

Goodfellow, R. and Kukulska-Hulme, A. (1996). *Evaluating New Technology in Learning and Teaching: A summary of recent research at IET* (IET Report – Tracking Technology for Academic Advantage): The Open University.

Hazzan, O. (1999). Information technologies and objects to learn with. *Educational Technology* (May-June 1999), pp. 55–59.

Heppell, S. (1993). Eyes on the horizon, feet on the ground? In C. Latchem, J. Williamson and L. Henderson-Lancett (eds), *Interactive Multimedia: Practice and promise* (pp. 97–114). London: Kogan Page.

Heppell, S. (1994). Multimedia and learning: Normal children, normal lives and real change. In J. Underwood (ed.), *Computer based learning: Potential into practice* (pp. 152–161). London: David Fulton Publishers.

Joinson, A. (2000). *Evaluation of 'E211: Learning Matters' pilot computer conferencing*. Milton Keynes: The Institute of Educational Technology, The Open University.

Jonassen, D. H. and Wang, S. (1993). Acquiring structural knowledge from semantically structured hypertext. *Journal of Computer-Based Instruction*, 20(1), 1–8.

Jonassen, D. H., Myers, J. M. and McKillop, A. M. (1996). From constructivism to constructionism: Learning with hypermedia/multimedia rather than from it. In B. Wilson (ed.), *Constructivist Learning Environments*. Englewood Cliffs: Educational Technology Publications.

Lane, M. (1999). OU's teaching of engineering rated the best. *Sesame*, April/May p. 1.

Laurillard, D. (1987). Pedagogical design for interactive video. In D. Laurillard (ed.), *Interactive Media: Working Methods and Practical Applications*. Chichester: Ellis Horwood Ltd.

Laurillard, D. (1993). *Rethinking University Teaching: A framework for the effective use of educational technology*. London: Routledge.

Laurillard, D. (1996). *How should UK Higher Education make best use of new technology?* Paper presented at the ALT-C 1996, Glasgow.

Laurillard, D., Stratfold, M., Luckin, R., Plowman, L. and Taylor, J. (1999). Affordances for learning in a non-linear narrative medium. *Journal of Interactive Media in Education*, http://www–jime.open.ac.uk/99/laurillard.index.html

Lemke, C., and Coughlin, E. C. (1998). *Technology in American Schools: Seven Dimensions for Gauging Progress – A Policymaker's Guide.* Santa Monica: Milken Exchange on Education Technology.

Maddux, C. D. (1993). Past and future stages in educational computing research. In H. C. Waxman and G. W. Bright (eds), *Approaches to Research on Teacher Education and Technology*, Vol. 1, pp. 11–22. Virginia: Association for the Advancement of Computing in Education.

O'Neill, B. (1998). New ways of telling: multimedia authoring in the classroom. In M. Monteith (ed.), *IT for Learning Enhancement* (pp. 141–152). Exeter: Intellect.

Parker, A. (1999). Interaction in distance education: the critical conversation. *Educational Technology Review* (12), pp. 13–17.

Perkins, J. and Newman, K. (1996) The archetypes in E-discourse: lurkers and virtuosos. *International Journal of Educational Telecommunications*, 2, 2/3, pp. 155–170.

Schacter, J. (1999). *The Impact of Education Technology on Student Achievement: What the most current research has to say.* Santa Monica: Milken Exchange on Education Technology.

Scrimshaw, P. (1997a). Computers and the teacher's role. In B. Somekh and N. Davis (eds), *Using Information Technology Effectively in Teaching and Learning: Studies in Pre-Service and In-Service Teacher Education* (pp. 100–113). London: Routledge.

Scrimshaw, P. (1997b). *Preparing for the Information Age: Synoptic Report of the Education Departments Superhighways Initiative.* Milton Keynes: The Open University.

Sewell, D. F. (1990). *New Tools for New Minds: A cognitive perspective on the use of computers with young children.* London: Harvester Wheatsheaf.

Squires, D. (March 1997). *An heuristic approach to the evaluation of educational multimedia software.* Paper presented at the CAL-97, Exeter.

Taylor, J. (1991). *Programme on Learner Use of Media: Annotated Bibliography* (PLUM Report 1a). Milton Keynes: The Institute of Educational Technology, The Open University.

Taylor, J. and Laurillard, D. (1995). Supporting resource based learning. In N. Heap, R. Thomas, G. Einon, R. Mason and H. Mackay (eds), *Information Technology and Society* (pp. 237–248). London: Sage Publications.

Taylor, J. and Salanki, H. (1994). *Programme on Learner Use of Media: Annotated Bibliography* (PLUM Report 1b). Milton Keynes: The Institute of Educational Technology, The Open University.

Trilling, B., and Hood, P. (1999). Learning, technology, and educational reform in the knowledge age or 'We're wired, webbed, and windowed, now what?'. *Educational Technology*, May-June, 1999, pp. 5–18.

Turner, S. V. and Handler, M. G. (1997). Hypermedia in education: children as audience or authors? *Journal of Information Technology for Teacher Education*, 6(1), 25 – 35.

Twining, P. (1999). 'Learning matters' – Adjusting the media mix for academic advantage. *ALT-J*, 7(1), 4–11.

Twining, P. and McCormick, R. (1999, March 1999). *Learning Schools Programme: Developing Teachers' Information Communication Technology Competence in the Support of Learning.* Paper presented at the 10th International Conference of The Society for Information Technology & Teacher Education, San Antonio, Texas.

Twining, P., Stratfold, M., Kukulska-Hulme, A. and Blake, C. T. (1998). SoURCE: Software Use, Re-use and Customisation in Education. *Active Learning*, 9 (November), pp. 54–56.

Warschauer, M. (1998). Online learning in sociocultural context. *Anthropology and Education Quarterly*, 29(1), pp. 68–88.

Whalley, P. (1990). *Models of Hypertext Structure and Learning* (PLUM Report 9): The Open University.

9

Online Learning in Sociocultural Context

Mark Warschauer

Proponents of online learning claim that it can transform education by promoting student-centred communication, collaboration, and inquiry. Yet these claims must be weighed against the actual implementation of online learning, which is influenced by a broad range of sociocultural factors. This study investigates sociocultural factors that helped shape a computer-based English as a Second Language (ESL) writing course in a conservative Christian college, factors that included a complex relationship between teacher, researcher, and students.

Since the late 1970s the educational literature has been replete with articles about the promising potential of new applications of microcomputers in the classroom, only to be followed a year or two later with disappointing reports of the actual implementation. As Cuban has ably documented (1986, 1993), the actual use of new technologies in the classroom is sharply constrained by broad sociocultural variables such as the role of school as an instrument of social control and sorting, the general culture of teaching, and the beliefs of classroom teachers. As a result, new media are usually introduced in a top-down fashion at odds with sound educational principles, and microcomputers are frequently used for drill-and-practice activities requiring low-level cognitive skills of rote memory and application (Cummins and Sayers, 1990).[1] And, as studies have shown (see, for example, Mehan et al., 1985; Roberts 1987), it is ethnic and language minority students who are least likely to have access to computers or to use them for challenging, problem-solving activities.

Now in the late 1990s, with the rapid growth of the Internet, one wonders if the cycle of praise and disappointment is beginning again. Online learning has quickly become the most-touted current application of computers in education (see, for example, Berge and Collins, 1995; Cummins and Sayers, 1995; Harasim, 1990b; Harasim et al., 1995). According to its supporters, online education 'introduces unprecedented options for teaching, learning and knowledge building' (Harasim, 1990a, p. xvii) and can help 'create communities of inquiry capable of stimulating intellectual, moral, and educational growth among rich and poor alike' (Cummins and Sayers, 1995, p. ix).

Yet these positive assessments of the potential of online education have not yet been sufficiently backed up by systematic studies of the actual uses of online learning in the schools. Within my own area, second-language learning, published studies of online education have mostly consisted of innovative teachers reporting anecdotally on their own successful practices (see, for example, Barson *et al.*, 1993; Kern, 1995b; Soh and Soon, 1991; Warschauer, 1995). More methodical research (see, for example, Chun, 1994; Kern, 1995a; Warschauer, 1996) has tended to examine one or two particular aspects (for example, the discourse in an online session) rather than provide a grounded, longitudinal, and contextualized account of the overall implementation of the online activities and of the students' experiences. And the very few contextualized ethnographic studies that have been published in this area (for an excellent study see Tella, 1991) have examined the experiences of 'mainstream' middle-class students rather than ethnic or language minorities.

To help fill this gap, I conducted a semester-long ethnographic study of an English as a Second Language (ESL) composition class at Miller College,[2] a medium-sized Christian institution of higher learning in Hawai'i. I chose this particular class for the study because (1) it was largely taught through online activities; (2) the students were a culturally diverse group from a broad range of Pacific, Asian, and South American countries; and (3) the teacher of the course, Ms. Sanderson, was enthusiastic about inviting me in as a researcher and collaborator. That Miller College was a conservative Christian institution was not a factor in my selection of the class, although I realized that that was part of the sociocultural context that could affect the way classroom instruction was carried out.

In conducting the study, I was not a neutral observer. First of all, I had my own well-developed beliefs about the potential of online learning, based on a sociocultural perspective that emphasizes the importance of creating communities of practice and semiotic apprenticeship in the classroom (Bayer, 1990; Wells and Chang-Wells, 1992). I felt that computer-mediated communication, by giving students opportunities for co-operative writing with each other and with distant partners, provided an excellent tool for promoting critical, collaborative learning. Beyond this belief, I was biased in an additional sense. The teacher of the course (Ms. Sanderson) and I agreed that I would actively work with her in sharing my thoughts and ideas about the learning objectives and activities throughout the planning and implementation of the course. Rather than being an outside researcher, I would thus be a partner in collaborative education and inquiry. Though in the end this process of collaboration did not develop in quite the ways we had imagined, it nevertheless proved to be an important factor that had some influence on the outcome of the course.

A Walk Through Miller College

A first-time visitor to Miller College – with its well-manicured lawns, quiet and clean grounds, and polite, conservatively dressed students – gets the sensation of entering a small town in the 1950s. A walk through the campus dispels any lingering doubts that this is a conservative institution. The college's dress code is posted prominently on all buildings. (For example, 'Sideburns should not be long or bushy, and should not extend below the bottom of the ear'.) Signs posted in the cafeteria urge students to 'Stop legalized abortion' and to say 'No to legalized gambling'. A front-page headline on the school newspaper asks, 'Judgment Day: Will you want justice or mercy?'

A visit to the campus bookstore confirms the conservative orientation of the campus. A recent book, prominently displayed near the entrance, contains chapters such as 'One True Church' and 'Teaching Pure Doctrine'.[3] The book explains that doctrine cannot be learned through experience or active interpretation, but must be taught from above. Another recent book (also on prominent display) emphasizes the importance of teaching the principles of the gospel rather than teaching ethics. Other books discuss the church's active role in working to bring this doctrine and its principles to the peoples of developing nations.

According to the college catalogue, the church's institutes of higher learning, including Miller College, were established for the purpose of assisting these goals, both by training students in church doctrine and preparing them to serve the church. The catalogue states that 'All students at Miller College should be taught the truths of the gospel of Jesus Christ'. The church president is quoted as saying that 'those who are blessed to attend [Miller College] have a great responsibility to make certain that the Church's investment in them provides dividends through service and dedication to others as they labor in the Church and in the world'.

Miller College thus plays a prominent role in the church's missionary work, especially in the Asia-Pacific region. American students who attend Miller are generally involved in missionary work in Asia and the Pacific. The majority of Miller's students, however, are not Americans, but are rather foreign students from the Pacific. Most have been involved in church activities in their countries and are learning the church's principles and developing leadership skills so that they will return to their countries as more capable church representatives.

Ms. Sanderson's Class

Ms. Sanderson's class is composed entirely of international students. Ten are Pacific Islanders from Tonga, Pohnpei, Palau, Samoa, Tahiti, and the Cook Islands, with the remaining six from Japan, Indonesia, Mongolia, Korea, and Brazil. The course is an advanced ESL composition class in the college's English Language Program. Students in this program have been admitted to the university, but due to low test scores are required to complete some special ESL classes. The purpose of this particular class is that students sufficiently master the genres of US academic writing so that they will be able to succeed in regular college classes.

Ms. Sanderson's class meets four times a week, twice in a computer lab and twice in a regular classroom. I visited the class once every one to two weeks throughout the semester, and between classes I stayed in touch with Ms. Sanderson and the students via e-mail. I received copies of nearly all the e-mail messages and texts the students wrote throughout the semester. I interviewed students in four rounds throughout the semester on a voluntary basis, with 12 out of the 16 students participating in one or more of the interviews. I also talked informally with students before or after class, in the computer lab, and in the cafeteria.

In the end, the course developed in ways that I had not expected, but the experience of discovering and working through this proved to be a valuable one for the teacher, students, and me. The process revealed a great deal about the sociocultural context of collaborative computing, as shaped by both institutional goals and values and also by ongoing negotiation between teacher and researcher. The following, then, describes my experience in Ms. Sanderson's class.

Discipline and Order in the Classroom

The atmosphere of discipline and obedience that pervades the college is apparent in Ms. Sanderson's class as well. The students work quietly and in an orderly fashion, without getting out of their seats to work with classmates at other computers. They raise their hands politely when they want to ask a question or need assistance. A wall display in the computer lab contains gold stars for students who have successfully completed their assignments.

Every class in the computer lab begins with a five-minute assignment or quiz, which is sent to the students over e-mail (for example, 'Correct the following sentence: It was not until the 1970s that the International Cultural Center become one of most popular visiting sites'). Students must complete the quiz and send it back within the allotted five minutes or they receive no credit. After the five minutes are up, Ms. Sanderson announces that no more credit will be given for the quiz. She explains that 'the class meets really early in the morning, and I'm worried about them coming late. This helps make sure they get here on time'.

These quizzes were of great frustration to many of the students, especially the ones who were new to computers and could not work very fast. Don, from Tonga, had never worked with computers before and was always a little bit behind in class. While other students were completing their quizzes, he was often still trying to figure out how to log in. Inevitably, when the five minutes were up, he still could not complete the assignment, no matter how hard he tried. I never saw Don smile in class.

The standards of discipline and hard work are applied to the quantity of assignments as well. A handout students receive the first day (which warns them twice to respect the dress code) explains in great detail an exhaustive list of assignments to be completed during the semester, including 60 grammatical exercises, five typing tests, 10 take-home essays, five in-class essays, two reading reports, 20 'key pal' (e-mail pen pal) letters, and a final research paper. Ms. Sanderson works extremely hard correcting all of these assignments, on occasion staying at her office all night in order to keep up with her work.

Ms. Sanderson's concern with rules and order also extends to her view of composition. She is not a proponent of freewriting or discovery writing. Rather, her verbal instructions and handouts explain to students exactly what is expected in a composition, as can be seen in this handout:

> Remember that in *comparison* writing, you are presenting similarities (not differences!).
>
> Your *organization* is important:
> * an *introduction of three sentences* with a *thesis statement at the end,*
> * *development* paragraphs (2–3) with
> * keyword and 'most important' transitions in each paragraph
> * *comparison transition* in the body of each paragraph
> * a *conclusion* of at least *three sentences.*
>
> Your ideas should be thoroughly developed (5+ *sentences per paragraph)* for high 'content'.

The focus on correct form and organization corresponds with what the students seem to expect of the class. When asked what good writing entails, or what they need to improve their writing, most students mentioned features related to organization or mechanics. One student, when asked what he liked most about the class, said, 'I like how she gives us the structures of essays. For example, putting a comma before the word *and* in a series. I was taught not to put the comma in my country'.

Peer editing is conducted, but without any opportunity to discuss the ideas in papers. Rather, students are given five minutes to both read a paper and assign it up to 20 points each in five categories (content, vocabulary, organization, language use, and mechanics). From observations and the students' comments, it is clear that these peer evaluations are conducted without much thought.

Uses of Technology

During the first week of class, a quiet Polynesian student made the exciting realization that she could use the computer system not only to write to her classmates but also to her faraway friends. She quickly jotted out a note to a friend at another university, using colloquial language, and asked how to fill in the e-mail address and send it. Ms. Sanderson glanced at her letter and sternly told her to check her grammar first. The class ended without the student learning how to address the message, and it went unsent.

A similar example occurred later on when the students first learned how to use the World Wide Web. Clearly, one of the most exciting features of the Internet is how the World Wide Web can be used to quickly gather information from a great variety of sources from all over the world. Ms. Sanderson's students did not discover this fact on that day, nor, to my knowledge, until the very end of the semester. Rather, they were instructed exactly how to navigate through the college's web pages to an online grammatical exercise that they then completed.

These two examples illustrate how electronic technology was used as a tool to implement and reinforce the rule-based functions of the class. Students spent about four hours a week completing computer-based grammar exercises. They also spent additional hours completing Typing Tutor exercises, which were mandatory even for those students who knew how to type. Most important, however, was the fact that almost all electronic communication, whether between the students and teacher, among the students in the class, or with long-distance pen pals was directed toward correct form rather than expressing meaning.

For example, the students worked in small electronic groups throughout the semester, e-mailing paragraphs back and forth which their classmates corrected for grammar and spelling and then e-mailed back. The students also decided in advance their topic sentences for each paragraph, and e-mailed these to their classmates for correction and feedback. The students wrote weekly essays that they e-mailed to the teacher for correction and comment. The students then sent the corrected essays, with a sentence or two of introduction, as letters (of a sort) to their long-distance key pals. Each letter was retyped (or, for the more computer-literate students, cut and pasted) in four different messages with a slightly different introduction to four different key pals, and then given a grade. A bold print warning on the first handout notified students that 'The instructor will *not* give credit for e-mailed key pal letters which have not been submitted in draft form for prior response on the due date', (emphasis in original).

Although students were generally interested in improving their grammar and form, they still chafed at the tremendous amount of time 'they spent at computer tasks they saw as weakly related to developing their writing skills. As Katina, a Samoan student, said,

> The whole thing is a big overload. There's a typing 101 class, so all this typing is a big overload. For some of us who know how to type, it's a big waste of time. But if it's helping us with our grade in the class, we do it. But why should we spend our time on this instead of on something useful?

Many students found the posting of essays to key pals particularly frustrating. As Minda, a Tongan student, commented, 'I'm just trying to write the same thing to eight people, to write the same thing in a little bit different ways. It's a waste of time.'

Topics and Content

Following a suggestion I had originally made, the writing assignments for the semester were all built around the theme of 'culture'. This did not lead, however, to the kind of critical sociocultural analysis I had intended. Rather, the view of culture that pervaded the class was in perfect accord with the state's International Culture Center, where tourists from around the world sampled foods, music, and dance in a variety of Pacific Island villages. As Ms. Sanderson wrote on the board one day, in her class culture consisted of

1. climate
2. food/clothing
3. music/dance/entertainment
4. school/education
5. family/values

Students' essays thus tended to focus on describing tourist sites in the United States and their country, comparing food, music, and entertainment, and describing why they chose to come to this college. The essays were inevitably in a standard five-paragraph form, with the first paragraph introducing the three points (i.e., three main reasons why I want to get an education are . . .), the next three paragraphs explaining each point, and the last paragraph repeating the points. The essays were often coherent and cohesive, but to an outsider's eye lacked creativity or originality.

Students' Impressions

At the beginning of the class, students were generally excited about the opportunity to work with computers, which they saw as important to their academic success and careers. As one student told me, 'Using computers, learning different things, e-mail, everything, I hated it before, but there's a saying, "Conquer or you'll be conquered". So I wanna conquer [rather] than be conquered, so I have to learn. I love it. I think it's so important for me'.

As the semester went on, though, nearly all the students became frustrated at the tremendous number of assignments, many of which seemed peripheral to learning how to write. As Katina told me,

> I think this class is called writing. Essay writing is what we should be doing, something that would help us learn how to write. Computer grammar exercises are a waste of time. The style of writing to key pals, just redoing the essays and sending them to the key pals, its a waste of time. She doesn't see what's going on. On my essay, I always get 19 out of 20. But I fell behind because I couldn't do all those other assignments.

It was at the time of my second round of interviews, right in the middle of the semester, that student dissatisfaction seemed to be strongest. Though the students were not accustomed to complaining to the teacher, nor the teacher accustomed to soliciting their views, the very fact of conducting the interviews seemed to prove a catalyst for change. On the one hand, the students, merely by having the opportunity to voice their opinions to a sympathetic outsider, seemed to gain confidence in their opinions. On the other hand, the teacher, consciously or unconsciously aware that the students were unhappy, now had to contend with the realization that their unhappiness was somehow coming out for inspection.

Thus, immediately after the second round of interviews (which were conducted privately between me and the students), Ms. Sanderson sent me an e-mail urging me to 'help us strengthen the positive and improve, as well as help me continue to build the class rapport I've been working at the last couple of weeks'. Two days later, following the next meeting of the class, she wrote to me that

> The class seemed a bit glum when we started and wouldn't look me in the eye this morning. . . . A couple of them admitted they were discouraged with the key pal bit, so I told them this week's key pal assignment is the last one with an assigned topic . . . after that it's free correspondence as long as they get the information they need for a good comparison-contrast research paper and have at least 20 exchanges total among the two to four key pals. They seemed satisfied with that.

The change, which meant that students could now write what they wished to key pals instead of submitting letters to her for grades, greatly satisfied the students. Other improvements were implemented in the following weeks, including allowing the students a good deal of autonomy in shooting and editing their own video to be sent to the partner class. (The topics of the video – climate, food, music, education, and family and values – were still determined by the teacher.) The teacher posted the students' essays on the World Wide Web, which brought them a lot of pride. And the students were finally taught how to navigate the web to find articles related to their own interest, which they also enjoyed very much.

By the end of the semester, a number of students expressed general satisfaction with the class. Others, though noting some improvement, still had strong criticisms. The variety of student experiences is captured by looking at two students, Jon and Paolo.

Jon

Jon, 21 years old, was born in a small village of the Cook Islands. He has been a member of the church all his life and saw coming to this college as a natural but wonderful opportunity. He worked in construction for three years after high school in order to save enough money for him and his wife to come study at Miller College.

Neither Jon nor his wife, Linda (who was also in the class), had any experience with computers, and both seemed disoriented the first weeks of class. Yet both worked extremely hard and received excellent marks. Jon beamed with pride as he talked of his accomplishments:

> We learned a lot of tricks on the computer with Ms. Sanderson, how to do e-mail and things. The other day, I was in the computer lab, and there was some guy who has been here a long time and he didn't know how to do it. And its my first year here and I was showing him how to do things!

Unlike some of the students, Jon did not find Ms. Sanderson overly strict. In fact, he found her to be lenient compared to his village teachers back home. In general, the limited opportunities that he had on his island made him highly motivated to succeed at Miller College and to appreciate what Ms. Sanderson had to offer. That he succeeded in learning how to write essays that were well organized and even had a certain flair is seen by the following excerpt of his writing:

> Each year, people from all over the world travel vast distances in search of a place that offers natural beauty, unique experiences, and an environment for relaxation. When thinking of such a place, the Cook Islands, which is a group of 15 tropical islands found in the South Pacific Ocean, comes to mind. The capital and largest of these islands is Rarotonga, the island of my birth. Rarotonga has an unblemished natural charm, pristine ocean, and unique culture, which offers welcome to people that arrive.
>
> Due to its unspoiled state, the island of Rarotonga offers a unique opportunity for people from the crowded cities of the world to experience a different type of attraction. The rugged green mountain terrains offer excellent mountain climbing and fabulous cross-island trekking. The aroma of the lush bushes and native plants gives us this sense of natural beauty. On hot summer days people can easily take a nice walk to a waterfall, where their bodies can melt into the cold fresh mountain waters. And if one was still not satisfied, he or she could head for the white balmy beaches of Muri.

The course helped Jon learn the culture of power that is often inaccessible to minority and immigrant students (Delpit, 1988). He mastered the genre of the five-paragraph essay and entered the discourse community of those who can produce an acceptable freshman essay. This is not a small accomplishment for many foreign students (though it should be noted that, in Jon's case, his previous education was also in English and, judging by his earlier essays, he came into the class with a fair amount of writing skill).

There is no indication, however, that in this course Jon was ever encouraged to tackle the larger problems of writing: for example, how to explain a difficult concept or argue a controversial point. He was not challenged to develop the skills of abstraction, system thinking, experimental inquiry, or collaboration that are crucial in today's economy (Reich, 1991). He was not challenged to 'talk and write about language as such, to explain and sequence implicit knowledge and rules of planning, and to speak and write for multiple functions in appropriate forms' (Heath, 1992). Nor was he encouraged to think about his homeland as anything but a tourist destination. Facing these challenges might have assisted Jon to master other genres and enter into a discourse community that values the content of writing and not just its form.

Paolo

A view opposite to that of Jon was expressed by Paolo, a 19-year-old student from Brazil. Unlike most of the students, Paolo had been in the church only a short time, joining a few months before he entered Miller College. Paolo had previous experience with computers, and, from the first week of class, he impressed me as a confident, quick-learning student who could practically finish an assignment before the other students had even figured out how to get online. His initial writings also seemed to be among the least stilted and most sophisticated in the class. But Paolo, who was extremely communicative and really enjoyed trying to express an idea, became frustrated with what he saw as the busy work of the class.

> We have so many little assignments. They're not important. But because you get graded on every little thing, I lose my focus, I can't concentrate on the big things. I like to do more essay writing, just give us a chance to write more. . . . In the beginning I was motivated. I'm motivated in all my other classes, I like them. It's only this class I don't like. Reading – that's the best class. We sit around and discuss. It's personal, no machine.

Paolo resented the strict organization Ms. Sanderson imposed on students' essays:

> She says, it's gotta be like this, especially like in the beginning of the paragraphs, when you have to write certain words, like linking words. The organization's gotta be like . . . that's hard for me, like you got the thesis statement, you gotta repeat, why do you have to repeat it in each one of the paragraphs? . . . It's boring. You start the essay writing on this, then you, by the middle of the essay, you just get bored, and you can't write any more.
>
> It's funny because when you read all the essays or whatever we read, it's not like that, so it's different. I'm writing something that I don't read, not very often. Even though it helps a lot, it should be helping a lot to understand organization, but there are some things I don't think are needed.

Paolo was the only student who attempted to deviate from the pre-selected topics on his essays, once choosing to write about the contradictions between rich and poor in Brazil rather than describing tourist sites there. As I read over the paper, he confessed to me that he was worried that Ms. Sanderson would not accept it because it was not on the main topic. Later, when I asked what happened to the paper, he said that it had apparently been misplaced because he never received it back from the teacher.

Paolo often told me that he did not like to write, but I suspect that it was Writing (the course), not writing (the activity) that he actually disliked. His early e-mail messages indicated that he enjoyed writing to communicate and was eager to express his views. His enthusiasm plummeted, however, during the first half of the semester, and was only slightly resuscitated when the teacher made some changes.

The Social Context of Learning

In trying to make sense of the teaching and learning practices I observed in Ms. Sanderson's class, I found it necessary to examine four overlaying contexts: (1) the church and college, (2) Ms. Sanderson's personal teaching philosophy, (3) the role of the English Language Program and (4) the triangular relationship that developed between teacher, researcher, and students.

The church and Miller College

The overall culture of the church and college, with an emphasis on funda-mentalist doctrine and missionary zeal, is clearly an important part of the context that influenced how Ms. Sanderson chose to develop online learn-ing projects. Students at Miller College lead a regimented life. In addition to the aforementioned dress code, they also make a commitment to abstain from physical familiarity outside the bonds of marriage; to eschew alcohol, drugs, and tobacco; and to regularly attend church meetings, support church leaders, and fulfil callings. Students are also required to complete a course on religious education every semester.

Concepts such as learner autonomy, creativity, and empowerment are at odds with Miller College's overall mission of developing obedient servants of the Lord and the church. In a sense, then, Ms. Sanderson's emphasis on discipline, order, and principles in classroom behaviour and in writing are a perfect reflection of the overriding goals of the college.

Yet I believe it would be a mistake to view Ms. Sanderson's behaviour as being strictly determined by the culture of the church. I met other teachers at the college who appeared to have a more open teaching approach. For example, I visited the course of a Spanish instructor who also teaches via computer-assisted activities, but in his case the online activities focus on student-student discussion rather than mastering of rules. To understand why such differences among teachers might occur, it is necessary to exam-ine both Ms. Sanderson's personal teaching philosophy as well as the more immediate context of the college's English Language Program.

Ms. Sanderson's teaching philosophy

Ms. Sanderson occasionally talked about her own teaching philosophy, which emphasized prescribing structure to students. This philosophy apparently stemmed from her own preferred learning style. As she once explained to me,

> When I was in college, I took a composition class. I didn't know what the teacher expected or required. I kept getting C's, then eventually I got an A. But I didn't know why. I was really bothered by the lack of structure. That's why I wanted this to be structured. Perhaps that's why I took German, because it was so structured.

The English Language Program

While Ms. Sanderson's teaching style is thus based in part on her own personal outlook, there is another factor that can account for differences in instruction between Spanish courses and ESL courses at Miller College. Unlike the American students in the Spanish program, the students in the English Language Program were newly arrived international students at Miller College. As Atkinson and Ramanthan (1995) have pointed out, ESL departments often emphasize a basic-skills approach to writing, rather than the more sophisticated approaches found in writing courses for native speakers. This seemed to be the case at Miller College. For example, Ms. Sanderson reported that a colleague in her department reacted very negatively to her idea to grade students on take-home essays, which students would have a chance to revise, since that would be grading them on 'effort' rather than product. Ms. Sanderson took this advice to heart and decided to base most of her grade on the more traditional in-class essays (and other assignments such as typing and grammar).

The department indicated its conservative nature not only in its writing courses but also in its reading courses; the department's language lab recently jettisoned a meaning-based approach for practising reading skills in favour of a computer-based activity involving memorization of isolated, decontextualized vocabulary words.

From a broader social view, however, it should be noted that the English Language Program within Miller College plays a particular socializing role beyond that played by ESL programs in secular colleges. The English Language Program is closely tied to the church's overseas role. Ms. Sanderson and other members of the department spend their vacations travelling to developing countries to teach at special church-sponsored institutes. Promising students from those institutes are then recruited to come to Miller College to study. They are required to abandon aspects of their native culture in order to conform to church policy. This entails learning appropriate rules of behaviour, both inside and outside of class.

It is thus not surprising that they are subjected to strict discipline and in fact are expected to conform to a pattern found to have existed throughout the twentieth century, where minority and immigrant children are forced to endure frequent tests and quizzes; teacher-directed procedures for seat work, recitation, and reports; and numerous other rules and regulations that 'enable schools to socialize and sort these students to meet the requirements' of society (Cuban, 1993, p. 250). In contrast, the students studying Spanish at Miller College are overwhelmingly white, American, and native-English-speaking, and thus are more likely to fit another pattern noted by Cuban whereby opportunities for 'individual choice, expressiveness, group learning skills, derivations of knowledge from many sources, joint student-teacher decision making, and student participation in both the verbal and physical life of the classroom' are generally reserved for American, upper-middle-class students since these 'classroom practices and student behaviors . . . are tailored for future professionals, managers, and executives' (1993, pp. 250–251).

Finally, it should also be mentioned that the historical relationship between the church affiliated with Miller College and the non-white minorities who are represented in the English Language Program has not always been based on equality and mutual respect. It could certainly be considered risky to the church's interests to foster a critical approach to education among groups of people whose focus of criticism could very well become the church itself.

The Relationship Between Teacher, Researcher, and Students

The last element of sociocultural context I want to examine is the relationship that Ms. Sanderson and I developed, and the possible influence this relationship had on the class. As indicated earlier, our initial conversations were quite fruitful, and we both agreed to view this as a collaborative experience. In those early discussions, however, I failed to recognize what differences there may be between us, both in outlook and in background. And as these differences became more evident in the first few weeks of the course, I continued to shy away from the difficult task of acknowledging and working through our different views.

As Briggs notes, 'Humanity is gained as the world, in the spaces between people, is acknowledged rather than denied or pushed away' (1996, p. 6). I pushed our differences away rather than confronting them, and Ms. Sanderson collaborated in this process of denial. My failure to help bring about an 'articulation of difference' made it difficult for us to heal the split between us (Minh-ha, 1994, cited in Briggs, 1996).

In a sense, it was the students themselves who rescued us from this situation when, in the interviews, they forthrightly shared their thoughts and opinions of the class. This created a context where Ms. Sanderson and I could no longer easily afford to ignore the difficulties, and Ms. Sanderson felt obliged to make some changes – even though the complaints had not been made to her directly. It seems that Ms. Sanderson's actions are explained in part by the metaphor of the *panopticon* (Foucault, 1979). Foucault selects Jeremy Bentham's circular prison, with the prisoners on the periphery under a potentially constant, but unverifiable, gaze from the guards in a central observation tower, as a metaphor for how power is wielded and knowledge shaped in the real world. According to Foucault, the guards too are always subject to an unverifiable gaze, not only from their supervisors but even from outside society, thus guaranteeing the control of the controllers.

Ms. Sanderson found herself caught up in the panoptic gaze of the outside research community. Simply knowing that I was interviewing the students, without being able to verify the content of the interviews, made her aware of the need to conform to outside standards. But while in Foucault's metaphor the outside and inside controllers are all part of one more-or-less homogeneous system, Ms. Sanderson was in a sense caught up in two competing panopticons – that of her college and church, with its own set of values, and that of the outside university research community, with a different set of values.

This does not suggest that the two sets of values are totally contradictory, and that only one set is accepted by Ms. Sanderson personally. Rather, it appears that Ms. Sanderson is trying to find her way through a number of different paths and thus eclectically applies a variety of approaches and perspectives. In this case, though, the triangular interaction of students, teacher, and researcher did seem to help introduce a critical perspective that resulted in Ms. Sanderson reassessing her teaching in midstream and making some necessary adjustments.

This minicrisis around the time of the second set of interviews, followed by changes in class procedure, helped bring about more openness between Ms. Sanderson and me, and we discussed more frankly our views about how the class should be taught. As the third round of interviews approached, Ms. Sanderson once again started to grow more distant, and she even sent me an e-mail message (that I did not receive until later) asking me not to come on the day of the interviews since the students were 'stressed'. After this third round was over, tensions receded and we spoke more freely again, and later began to engage in some interesting discussion about the class.

Thus over time, and with many pushes and pulls, we slowly achieved a degree of intersubjectivity, which, as Eugene Matusov points out, is 'a *process* of coordination of individual contributions to the joint activity rather than a *state* of agreement between the participants' (1996, p. 26, emphasis in original). The challenge for me, one I never fully met, was to maintain a critical perspective without attempting to impose it, to acknowledge the borders between us while still venturing into the borderlands (Rosaldo, 1989).

Socialization and Situationally Constrained Choice

Susan Jungck reminds us that 'computer literacy is theoretically an empowering concept; its development in practice can have contradictory effects' (1987, p. 492). For Ms. Sanderson's ESL composition students, the introduction of computers into the curriculum did indeed have contradictory effects. It brought them some knowledge of basic computer skills, but it did little to advance their abilities of systemic analysis, critical inquiry, or cross-cultural collaboration. Instead, they learned to come on time, follow rules of studying and rules of writing, talk and write about culture from a superficial standpoint, and use technology as a tool to accomplish busywork.

The students seemed aware that their success was due in large part to figuring out the rules of the game. As Jon told me, 'This semester we didn't know what to expect. We sort of have an idea [now] of how the system works, and the teachers'.

Students who did poorly in the class were not necessarily the worst writers but rather those who failed this socialization process. One example is Sun, a student from Korea, who told me early on that she really liked to discuss ideas and hoped that the class would include more discussion. Sun always tried to find ways to express her personal thoughts in her e-mail messages, even if that was counter to the particular assignment at hand. Sun either could not or chose not to keep pace with the frequent grammar exercises, typing assignments, and repetitive key pal mailings. She showed up to class less and less frequently as the semester continued. Another frequent no-show was Don, the Tongan student who could not complete the quizzes within the five minutes allotted. And then there is the case of Katina, who did well on the essays but complained about the large amount of busywork assignments; Katina received an F in the course despite writing an excellent final research paper that received a mark of 98 out of 100.

The failure of Katina, Don, and Sun should not be construed to mean that the course was not a success, at least from the point of view of Ms. Sanderson and the institution. The majority of students did make it through the initiation period and learned the appropriate behaviours and attitudes for Miller College. They also learned to write cohesive and coherent essays, with few controversial ideas but with correct transitional phrases. They are thus well prepared for their remaining courses at Miller College.

This result is explained well by Cuban's (1986, 1993) model of constancy and change in US schools, originally developed for K-12 schools though applicable to the highly structured environment of Miller College. Cuban studied previous educational innovations over 110 years, including the introduction of film, radio, and television, and found that none of these innovations qualitatively altered US education. Cuban suggests that deeply held cultural beliefs about the nature of knowledge, how teaching should occur, and how children should learn, steer policy-makers and teachers toward certain forms of instruction, and that these forms of instruction are guided by the broader role of the schools to 'inculcate into children the prevailing social norms, values, and behaviors that will prepare them for economic, social, and political participation in the larger culture' (1993, p.

249). Technologies are thus almost always implemented in a top-down fashion, which leaves in place traditional teacher-centred instruction, especially when the students are members of lower-socioecononic-status ethnic and language minority groups. Cuban's model does not suggest that all teacher behaviour is strictly determined from above, but rather that teachers have 'situationally constrained choice' (1993, p. 260), in other words, a degree of autonomy within the constraints of established school and classroom structures. This model accounts for variation among teachers (i.e., the fact that the Spanish teacher was able to choose a different approach than Ms. Sanderson) and also explains the type of changes that teachers are most likely to implement. According to Cuban, when changes are adapted they are most likely to affect issues of peripheral importance rather than decisions that 'touch the core of the teacher's authority' (1993, p. 270). Cuban points out that changes are also often made in the middle of the semester, once teachers feel they have already exerted a certain amount of control over the class.

In this example, we can see that Ms. Sanderson faced numerous sociocultural constraints, such as the strict disciplinary atmosphere of the church and college, the role of the college as a training school for missionaries, the relationship between the college and the international students, and the conservative expectations of colleagues in the English Language Program. Ms. Sanderson did indicate a willingness to make changes, but only in the middle of the semester and only on peripheral issues, such as how many papers students wrote, rather than on more central issues of control, such as who would determine the content of lessons. Adapting technology to her own sociocultural milieu and outlook, Ms. Sanderson continued teaching in a way that served to socialize international students into the roles established for them by the church and college.

In spite of the differences that we had, I certainly do not view negatively Ms. Sanderson's efforts to better her teaching. Rather, I endorse Cuban's view. 'That teachers even initiate incremental changes in the face of considerable constraints speaks of their strong impulses toward improvement' (1993, p. 287). Ms. Sanderson demonstrated her impulses toward improvement by devoting hundreds of extra hours to introduce new technologies to her students, by bravely inviting an outside researcher to observe her class the entire semester, and by admitting mistakes and changing some course policies that were upsetting to her students. Her courage to consider new ideas continued after the class. When I mailed her a report that included in summarized form many of the points from this article, she wrote me back saying that

> I like the report very much. . . . Your words helped me to understand ourselves a bit more as well! . . . I am going to keep your report in my professional development folder where I can refer to it frequently and think about my search for self-improvement in teaching. . . . The learning experience was good for the class I taught the following spring term, with more reason in balancing the students' homework load and in emphasizing the writing, with the computer used more in support of learning as students felt they wanted to use it.

Later, we even co-authored a short paper that summarized what we had learned from the experience, including the need to involve students in decision making when integrating Internet-based activities into the curriculum.

The Internet and Education

It is important to consider what may be unique about this situation, and what might shed light on other educational situations and contexts. As indicated earlier, few qualitative studies have been published of online learning, but I can draw on studies of two other classrooms I have recently conducted (Warschauer, 1997; Warschauer and Ortega, 1997). These two courses, also involving language and composition, were taught at a public university by two instructors who had very different teaching philosophies than Ms. Sanderson; both of them could be said to favour the development of collaborative, critical communities of inquiry and learning. And in both cases I found that the teachers were able to harness the power of the Internet to bring about important positive results, including increased apprenticeship learning (i.e., more opportunities for students to learn from interaction with peers and teachers), the development of important new literacy skills (e.g., learning the genre of academic e-mail communication, learning to read and write hypertexts), and increased student motivation.

The differences between these classes and Ms. Sanderson's class can be accounted for by a number of factors, including the institutional differences between Miller College and the public university, the varied approaches toward language and writing that were prevalent in the different departments, and the personal and educational backgrounds of the teachers involved. Clearly, though, one important factor is the teachers' beliefs about the nature of teaching and learning, a factor elsewhere demonstrated as critical to effective uses of technology in education (see the ten-year study by Sandholtz *et al.*, 1996). It appears that while societal and institutional expectations influence how technology is implemented, this takes place in large part through the shaping of teacher beliefs and attitudes. It can take a long time for teachers to change their beliefs, and their willingness to do so is greatly affected by attitudes within their department, institution, and school district. But when teachers are able to change their beliefs about the nature of education, new technologies can be implemented in ways that better tap their potential for aiding student-centred learning. In this light, it seems that Ms. Sanderson has begun a journey toward reconsidering some of her beliefs about teaching and learning, though whether in her environment she will continue to find the support for further change and development appears questionable.

Finally, I should point out that while no technology is all-powerful, bringing about changes independent of human agency, neither are technologies merely an add-on to human activity and relations. Rather, the tool we use to complete a task nevitably transforms the task itself (Bateson, 1972). For example, studies have shown that electronic discussion tends to feature more equal and balanced participation than does face-to-face discussion and can thus serve to democratize organizations (for a review, see Sproull and Kiesler, 1991). Thus, at Miller College one might wonder whether students' use of e-mail and the World Wide Web could in some small way eventually undermine teacher-centred approaches, even without the kind of pressures that were brought about by the nature of this research project (just as authorities in China and Singapore worry about how use of the Internet might threaten centralized state control). On the other hand, whether in countries or in classrooms, the powers that be can generally find a way to bend technology to their own interests, and the Internet can be harnessed for spying on citizens or students just as readily as for empowering them (Janangelo, 1991). I would conclude that the prevalence of interactive technologies such as the Internet can be one more element creating pressure for institutional change. But whether and how changes are implemented will depend on many other broader contextual factors.

Conclusion

As Cuban (1986, 1993) has documented, educational innovations, especially those involving new technologies, have been implemented in US education in a top-down, teacher-centred fashion for more than 100 years. First film, then radio, and then television were all purported to have the potential to radically transform education, but none ended up altering the fundamental way schooling is carried out in the United States.

Online learning similarly has been touted as the key to grand transformation of US education. And it may indeed be the case that online learning, when used by teachers committed to a critical perspective, has the potential to 'support and enhance a project of possibility that actively challenges the hegemony of the dominant group' (Cummins and Sayers, 1990, p. 26).

This study, however, suggests that such results are unlikely without the teacher and students having some degree of critical awareness of the sociocultural influences on the classroom. Rather, it seems probable that online technologies will frequently be implemented in a restrictive, teacher-centred fashion, and that ethnic and language minority students may be the least likely to use computer networking in ways that enhance critical thinking and collaborative problem solving.

But this study also suggests that educators who do have a critical awareness can actively intervene – not as outside experts but as collaborative trainers and researchers – to help introduce this awareness and thus provide some small counterbalance to the weight of conservative institutions. Indeed, students' own resistance is likely to call forth such intervention. Efforts to induce change may be more effective, and certainly humane, if we 'recognize and articulate contradictions, complexities, and differences' (Briggs, 1996, p. 17) between researcher and classroom teacher, thus practicing the same critical, collaborative communication that we hope to bring about through involving our students in online learning.

Notes

Acknowledgments. I am extremely grateful to Ms. Sanderson and her students for their openness in inviting me into their classroom. I am also grateful to Kathryn Davis of the University of Hawai'i, who provided valuable support, advice, and encouragement for this project.

1.   Top-down, as used by Cuban, means controlled from above. This is distinct from another use of *top-down* in education, which can mean looking at things from a holistic perspective.
2.   All names of individuals and institutions have been changed.
3.   Citations and references for church-related books are not included so as to protect the anonymity of the institution.

References

Atkinson, Dwight and Vai Ramanathan (1995) Cultures of Writing: An Ethnographic Comparison of L1 and L2 University Writing/Language Programs. *TESOL Quarterly* 29(3), 539–568.

Barson, John, Judith Frommer and Michael Schwartz (1993) Foreign Language Learning Using E-Mail in a Task-Oriented Perspective: Interuniversity Experiments in Communication and Collaboration. *Journal of Science Education and Technology* 4(2), 565–584.

Bateson, Gregory (1972) *Steps to an Ecology of Mind: A Revolutionary Approach to Man's Understanding of Himself*. New York: Ballantine.

Bayer, Ann (1990) *Collaborative-Apprenticeship Learning: Language and Thinking across the Curriculum, K-12*. Mountain View, CA: Mayfield.

Berge, Zane L. and Mauri P. Collins, (eds.) (1995) *Computer-Mediated Communication and the Online Classroom*. Volume 1: *Overview and Perspectives*. Cresskill, NJ: Hampton Press.

Briggs, Kaitlin (1996) Geography Lessons for Researchers: A Look into the Research Space for Humanity Lost or Gained. *Anthropology and Education Quarterly* 27, 5–19.

Chun, Dorothy (1994) Using Computer Networking to Facilitate the Acquisition of Interactive Competence. *System* 22(1), 17–31.

Cuban, Larry (1986) *Teachers and Machines: The Classroom Use of Technology since 1920*. New York: Teachers College Press.

Cuban, Larry (1993) *How Teachers Taught: Constancy and Change in American Classrooms 1890–1980*. New York: Longman.

Cummins, Jim and Dennis Sayers (1990) Education 2001: Learning Networks and Educational Reform. *Computers in the Schools* 7(1–2), 1–29.

Cummins, Jim and Dennis Sayers (1995) *Brave New Schools: Challenging Cultural Illiteracy through Global Learning Networks*. New York: St. Martin's Press.

Delpit, Lisa (1988) The Silenced Dialogue: Power and Pedagogy in Educating Other People's Children. *Harvard Educational Review* 58(3), 280–298.

Foucault, Michel (1979) *Discipline and Punish: The Birth of the Prison*. Alan Sheridan, trans. New York: Vintage Books.

Harasim, Linda (1990a) Introduction to Online Education. In *Online Education: Perspectives on a New Environment*. L. Harasim (ed.) pp. xxvii–xxiii. New York: Praeger.

Harasim, Linda (ed.) (1990b) *Online Education: Perspectives on a New Environment*. New York: Praeger.

Harasim, Linda, Starr Roxanne Hiltz, Lucio Teles, and Murray Turoff (1995) *Learning Networks: Field Guide to Teaching and Learning Online*. Cambridge: Massachusetts Institute of Technology Press.

Heath, Shirley Brice (1992) Literacy Skills or Literate Skills? Considerations for ESL/EFL Learners. In *Collaborative Language Learning and Teaching*. D. Nunan (ed.) pp. 40–55. Cambridge: Cambridge University Press.

Janangelo, Joseph (1991) Technopower and Technoppression: Some Abuses of Power and Control in Computer-Assisted Writing Environments. *Computers and Composition* 9(1), 47–63.

Jungck, Susan (1987) Computer Literacy in Practice: Curricula, Contradictions, and Context. In *Interpretive Ethnography of Education: At Home and Abroad*. G. Spindler and L. Spindler (eds.) pp. 475–493. Hillsdale, NJ: Lawrence Erlbaum Associates.

Kern, Richard (1995a) Découvrir Berkeley: Students' Representation of Their World on the World Wide Web. In *Virtual Connections: Activities and Projects for Networking Language Learners*. M. Warschauer (ed.) pp. 355–356. Honolulu: University of Hawai'i, Second Language Teaching and Curriculum Center.

Kern, Richard (1995b) Restructuring Classroom Interaction with Networked Computers: Effects on Quantity and Quality of Language Production. *Modern Language Journal* 79(4), 457–476.

Matusov, Eugene (1996) Intersubjectivity without Agreement. *Mind, Culture and Activity* 3, 25–45.

Mehan, Hugh, Louis Moll, and Margaret Riel (1985) Computers in Classrooms: A Quasi-Experiment in Guided Change. NIE Report 6–83-0027. La Jolla, CA: Interactive Technology Laboratory.

Minh-ha, Trinh T. (1994) Critical Rhythms of Borderlands and Permitted Boundaries. Paper presented at Smith College, Northampton, MA, November.

Reich, Robert (1991) *The Work of Nations: Preparing Ourselves for 21st Century Capitalism*. New York: Knopf.

Roberts, Linda (1987) *Trends and Status of Computers in Schools: Use in Chapter 1 Programs and Use with Limited English Proficiency Students*. Washington, DC: US Congress, Office of Technology Assessment.

Rosaldo, Renato (1989) *Culture and Truth: The Remaking of Social Analysis*. Boston: Beacon Press.

Sandholtz, Judith Haymore, Cathy Ringstaff and David C. Dwyer (1996) *Teaching with Technlogy: Creating Student-Centered Classrooms*. New York: Teachers College Press.

Soh, Bee-Lay, and Yee Ping Soon (1991) English by E-Mail: Creating a Global Classroom via the Medium of Computer Technology. *English Language Teaching Journal* 45(4), 287–292.

Sproull, Lee, and Sara Kiesler (1991) *Connections: New Ways of Working in the Networked Organization*. Cambridge, MA: Massachusetts Institute of Technology Press.

Tella, Seppo (1991) *Introducing International Communications Networks and Electronic Mail into Foreign Language Classrooms*. Research Report, No. 25, Department of Teacher Education. Helsinki: University of Helsinki.

Warschauer, Mark (1995) *Virtual Connections: Online Activities and Projects for Networking Language Learners*. Honolulu: University of Hawai'i, Second Language Teaching and Curriculum Center.

Warschauer, Mark (1996) Comparing Face-to-Face and Electronic Communication in the Second Language Classroom. *CALICO Journal* 13(2), 7–26.

Warschauer, Mark (1997) Computer-Mediated Communication and Language Minority Students: A Sociocultural Perspective. Paper presented at the Annual Conference of the American Association for Applied Linguistics, Orlando, FL, March.

Warschauer, Mark, and Lourdes Ortega (1997) Apprenticing into Academic Discourse: An Ethnographic Study. Paper presented at the Annual Convention of Teachers of English to Speakers of Other Languages, Orlando, FL, March.

Wells, Cordon and Gen Ling Chang-Wells (1992) *Constructing Knowledge Together*. Portsmouth, NH: Heinemann.

10

Kaleidoscope People: Locating the 'Subject' of Pedagogic Discourse

Soraya Shah

Knowing thyself as a product of the historical process to date which has deposited an infinity of traces, without leaving an inventory . . . Each individual is the synthesis not only of existing relations but of the history of these relations (Gramsci, 1988)

Introduction

This chapter is a tentative exploration of the politics of personal location, the concept of pedagogic space and changing identities. It focuses on one mature student's experience of returning to education and examines her perceptions of identity and self-development in relation to this process.

Questions around the nature of the complex subject position(s) we inhabit and their personal and political implications are not new. Gramsci in his exploration of how hegemonic power structures develop and function saw the starting point of a critical consciousness as acquiring an understanding of the ways in which we are produced or constructed. Gramsci's work, while neo-marxist, does not theorise hegemonic power structures in binary terms. Arguably, his recognition of the complex and contradictory positions we inhabit lends itself more to poststructuralism.

Using a poststructuralist, theoretical framework, with its conceptual critique of the 'centred' individual, I will explore the notion of fragmented or plural identities. We are implicated by, and constructed within, a multiplicity of complex and contradictory discourses or 'networks of power' (Foucault, 1979; Forgacs, 1988), each positioning us in different ways. I will be arguing that we are all what I term 'kaleidoscope people' and highlight some of the implications of this for access and Access provision for adult learners.

The intention here is to raise a number of polemical questions rather than to provide any definitive answers. The chapter will also look at some of the practical issues related to Access provision such as pre/post-Access information and guidance, course design and delivery, and the possible implications for change in these areas.

The (fragmented) structure of the chapter is intended as a formal complement to the shifting conceptual terrain of 'kaleidoscope people'. It is in part autobiographical; an account which in metaphorical term both places and displaces; speaking from the centre and from the margins (Sarup, 1988; Rutherford, 1990).

Autobiography: the Mature Student

Our identity (the way in which we conceptualise our subjective self, or are conceptualised by others), often understood as given or fixed, is always constituted within and across a range of narratives. By definition, in the UK adults over 21 years of age who enter the formal education system become 'mature students', but mature students, as we know, do not constitute an homogenous group, they inhabit enormously diverse histories and positions. Each has their own particular story.

Initially, when asked whether I would be interested in writing a chapter about my experience within education and how this subsequently changed my sense of self, my immediate reaction was . . . YES! Flattered at the idea of myself as a writer, the task itself seemed to pose no immediate problems. What could be more simple than writing a semi-autobiographical account of my personal journey through education?

Almost two months on, the chapter was nowhere near completion. In fact, it had hardly been started. By this time I was getting desperate, and the deadline was getting closer. I had to face the fact that maybe I was not destined to be a writer. How else could I explain my inability (not for lack of trying) to put together a simple sequence of events taken from memory and experience? Committed to the belief that society and the position(s) we inhabit within it shape us into the kind of individuals we are, I have on occasion argued quite passionately against the concept of natural or innate ability. How then could I explain this crisis of my intellect without resorting to the view, still held by some, that 'writers are born, not made'. The chapter eventually got written thanks to the perseverance of a close friend who in purely pragmatic terms stressed that I was almost duty bound to help dispel the mystique, and the fear, which surrounds writing. Writing, like any other trade, is about learning the necessary skills and having the confidence to apply these skills. Learning and confidence are the key words, both of these are acquired skills.

Many mature students feel inadequate in both of these areas when they return to education. As an Access tutor I should at this point in time have overcome such obstacles. After all part of my job is to teach students how to do this. However, writing this chapter confirmed to me that titles can be misleading and being a 'lecturer' doesn't necessarily mean that subjectively you feel the 'all knowing' one. Whilst writing this piece I felt more akin to a student, rather than the antithesis of one.

What is a 'mature student'?

Formal education constitutes only a part of the vast spectrum we call the learning process. Learning is not something specific to schools, colleges, or universities, outside of these institutions there is also learning, but of a very different kind. Within the formal education system, the value given to this other learning will depend on the perspective held, by practitioners, about what constitutes knowledge. Ryle and Stuart (1994) directly address the importance of not only recognising this as knowledge, but also *using* it as an integral and valuable resource upon which to build. The women's studies Access course at Sussex has incorporated this aspect of the mature student's prior learning and experience into the framework of their course, through the use of autobiography, and reflexive self-assessment.

All mature students going back into formal education take with them a vast, and valuable, pool of other learning experience through which their own sense of symbolic and subjective self has been constructed. Coming myself from a background which in terms of formal education was extremely limited, returning to education some 20 or more years later, and now working as a lecturer in further education and higher education, I have found myself constantly re-negotiating my sense of self-identity. The recurring contradictions that I have experienced through this have made me realise there is no singular or definitive 'real' me. Poststructuralist theory has given me a framework within which to articulate this process of ongoing change.

The 'subject'

Central to poststructuralist thinking is the concept of the 'subject', providing a critique of the humanist conception of the unified and autonomous individual, in possession of a human nature which transcends society. Poststructuralist theory disrupts this essentialist position, arguing that the 'subject' is constructed in and through language and discourse, is fragmented, rather than fixed, and is always in process (Sarup, 1988; Culler, 1983). The term 'subject' plays ambiguously between the subject/object dichotomy, subject of the state and subject to the law(s); it is both central and de-centred.

The formation of identity; a good girl

Gender, religion and ethnicity marked the parameters around what I did or did not learn during the formative years of my life. The informal education I received was that deemed appropriate for a respectable Muslim girl from a family which proudly claimed direct descent from the prophet. I read the Qu'rān, was taught daily prayers, how to cook and clean competently, and spare time was spent embroidering pillow cases, tablecloths and bed sheets, under the sharp experienced eye of my grandmother. Formal education was not a necessary requirement; in fact, within that context it was seen as socially and morally unacceptable for girls from my family to go 'out' to school. I was instilled with a particular set of values and beliefs, which entailed caring for younger members of the family, respecting elders without question, being modest and obedient; a 'good girl'. The values I learned were gendered; my twin brother seemed to inhabit another world than mine. For him, action rather than submission was encouraged, thinking rather than accepting, and access to wider forms of knowledge through school was thought imperative for his future career prospects. These differences were made to seem natural and fixed; the 'norm'. At times both my brother and myself fitted uneasily into our expected roles. He hated aggression, I hated embroidery. A combination of patriarchal power and religious discourse were central to the formative construction of my sense of self; it was not until years later that I began to conceptualise and deconstruct certain parts of this formation.

The ultimate vocation

For all of the girls from my background, marriage was unquestionably our future destiny, and motherhood the primary role through which our status as respected women would be fully recognised. Marriage was sacrosanct. The question of it 'breaking up' or not working was unthinkable. Marital problems were resolved by the intervention of the immediate family, in-laws would reinforce the sanctity of marriage and stress the moral duty of both husband and wife to preserve this. In the eyes of the extended community divorce brought shame on the girl's family. The moral status of some women was actually enhanced by their dutiful suffering and fatalistic acceptance of an unhappy marriage. Some years after my marriage I left Pakistan, the geographical space of my early formation, and came back to Britain to join my husband.

The unthinkable happens

The narratives which contribute to the formation of identity are also paradoxically those which can result in its eventual fragmentation. The unthinkable happened. The break up of my marriage signalled a rejection of the fatalism with which I had entered into marriage, and constituted a complete re-negotiation of my sense of self and the values I held. Overnight I became different things to different people, a 'fallen woman', an 'independent woman', a member of the 'underclass', a 'victim', a 'single parent'. However contradictory these identities may seem, they are all partially true.

The break up of my marriage radically changed the everyday dynamics of my life. My role as a single parent demanded new practical skills, as well as new communicative skills which required a degree of self-confidence and assertiveness on my part. I had to confront the public world of men, social security offices, school open evenings, council housing officials and solicitors. It was frightening, but at the same time it gradually influenced my decision to enter the formal education system. When the youngest of my children started nursery I enrolled on a course at the local adult education centre. That moment was the beginning of my journey as a 'mature student' *en route* through education.

A fresh start; back to basics

Initially, my decision to return to education was made for practical reasons. Official forms brought me out in a cold sweat and the inability to complete them without help was a particularly belittling experience. Being unable to help my children with their homework was another motivating factor. Some women friends I knew told me that they had been learning English one morning a week at a local adult education centre, that anyone could join the class, and it was inexpensive. I had no idea what to expect but I rang up and made an appointment.

From personal experience, and in the light of friends' experiences, the initial steps taken to return to education are the most difficult with commonly held perceptions creating barriers. For many, like myself, the concept of adult education seemed quite alien. Returning to adult education in this sense is a public exposure of one's ignorance, believing as I did then, and many others still do, that the formal skills of reading, writing, maths and so on should have been acquired in school during childhood, and on leaving school education inevitably comes to an end. The other major obstacle to those who feel they do not possess adequate literary skills is another widely held view, that adult education, or basic education, is about teaching the basics to people who are 'thick' and many find crossing this humiliating barrier impossible.

I enrolled in a basic English class but decided to leave after only a few sessions. Although in practical terms it was exactly what was needed, I found the lessons on sentence construction, apostrophes, prefixes and suffixes, extremely boring; they didn't engage me. My tutor persuaded me to stay in adult education but referred me to another course called 'Fresh Start For Women'. This group was small, it did not feel intimidating, and it was all women. Along with some basic literacy skills, we had stimulating group discussions on a variety of topics ranging from 'snuff' movies to romantic poetry. Most important, the tutor who ran the group created an informal learning environment, particularly suited to the needs of women like myself who were returning to education after 20 or more years and lacking in self-confidence. There was a general consensus amongst the group that being women only made it easier for some of us to speak openly about certain issues. This aspect of women only courses must be addressed, but in a way that does not homogenise 'women' and takes into consideration and recognises the vast differences that exist between them. By the end of the year my literacy skills had improved, I had gained in confidence, and was motivated to carry on.

A visit to the local further education college which entailed an informal group meeting with an Access co-ordinator proved invaluable for the Fresh Start group. Unfortunately, many mature students today are still unaware of the existence of Access courses. It is important that all adult education centres make sure this information along with advice and support is made more widely available to their students in order to more effectively bridge the vast gap that exists between adult education and further education, and assist in facilitating the crossover. Without having had an insight into Access, and the constant support of the Fresh Start tutor, the move out of adult education into further education might never have happened for me.

Access to Cultural Studies

For adults returning to education a combination of both personal and practical reasons will bear upon the particular course they choose. I chose the Access to Cultural Studies course. It was a part-time course which ran only two days a week and as a single parent I felt it would fit in with the practicalities of bringing up a young family. A full-time course would have been impossible to combine with child-care, particularly in the absence of a local tea-time club where the children could be supervised until I got home. Financial circumstances ruled out the possibility of a child-minder. On a personal level, the thought of plunging into full-time study was too daunting to comprehend. I had gained a certain amount of confidence through the Fresh Start course, but certainly didn't feel anywhere near ready to commit myself so drastically. I had no idea what I intended to do after Access, I had not thought that far ahead, or in terms of future job prospects. I simply wanted to learn as much as possible about as many different things. On an immediate day-to-day level, Cultural Studies seemed ideal.

Many adults return to education for the learning experience itself, and at that point many do not possess enough of an understanding of higher education to be clear about the direction they intend to take after Access. The fact that Cultural Studies was not an Access course geared towards a specific vocation such as teaching or social work, but was more open-ended, appealed to me. What also appealed was the fact that the course explored a wide range of different themes: industrialisation, democracy, imperialism, class, race, gender and education, rather than concentrating on one subject area alone.

En route: *the real thing?*

My identity as a student was ambiguous; I felt I wasn't a *real* student but an imitation. The image I held of real students – calm, collected, and completely submerged in study – did not fit my own experience. A closer approximation of this reality might have been 'manic mother in transit'.

This scenario involved getting five young children up, fed, clothed and ready for school on time. Travelling to college via public transport to realise five minutes after the lesson had commenced that I had forgotten to give the youngest her packed lunch and the text I was supposed to have interrogated was still on the radiator drying.

The learning process in formal education was undoubtedly changing me, but at this point I never thought of myself as a 'mature student'. Gradually this changed, but not until I was well into the first year of my degree. I began more to conceptualise myself as a student during the time spent on site in lectures and seminars, or in the library; however, once out of the building this changed, particularly when amongst certain friends and family members who could not comprehend the dialectical juxtaposition of motherhood and studenthood – you were either one or the other, you couldn't be both. This uncertainty about whether or not one is a 'real' student is one experienced by many mature students. External views and attitudes serve to reinforce and perpetuate existing uncertainties about ability and identity; a friend and graduate who now holds a teaching position expressed this by saying, 'I think that one day someone will tap me on the shoulder and tell me I'm a fraud'.

Really useful knowledge

Access courses are specifically designed to facilitate the progression of mature students without traditional qualifications. Fundamental to the learning experience and progress of Access students are both the content of Access courses and the methods of teaching employed. Adults returning to formal education to improve their quality of life must feel able to interact with the course content on a personal as well as an intellectual level (Ryle and Stuart, 1994). The themes around which a course is structured, and the methods of teaching used to cover these, will inevitably influence students' progress. Return to study courses need to place equal emphasis on developing both the conceptual powers of critical analysis and the study skills necessary to express these competently in writing. From my own experience I know how easily the lack of basic study skills can lead to an undermining of one's ability, and despair. Anyone who has been on an Access course will identify with the dreaded 'first essay' syndrome, when it seems impossible to transfer onto paper what is in one's head. Reading skills are also a crucial part of formal education. Performing what may seem a simple task, such as reading a handout and detecting the important points, can result in pages of highlighted dayglow pink and yellow text, with a few solitary white lines remaining untouched. A lack of these basic study skills can be the most daunting part of a mature student's initial experience within formal education.

Early on in the Access course, after being given our first essay title, I realised I could not write essays. I did not know where to start. The same thing happened some weeks into the course with the first timed stimulus that had to be completed in class. My final contribution was one A4 page of half-finished beginnings of answers to the first question . . . there were five questions in all! I understood the subject and knew what I wanted to write, the problem was I did not know *how*. Throughout the year equal time was given to study skills, taught through the course content, as was given to exploring the historical issues and concepts. Without this grounding I certainly would not have been able to progress into higher education, or produce the standard of work required at that level, where it is assumed that one is already well equipped with these skills.

Access to Cultural Studies provided a broad historical and conceptual base from which students could approach different subject areas. By the end of the course most students were making the wider connections between the social, the economic, the political, and relating these to underpinning ideological factors. Through interaction with a body of texts, the process of critical analysis was generated by a combination of both past and present experiences.

Entering the text

On commencing the Access course I was introduced to a number of texts. I describe the way in which I experienced this reading process as *lived* 'intertextuality'; I entered these texts. Whilst reading Dickens' *Hard Times*, I felt Sissy Jupe's shame when her apparent ignorance stemming from her lack of formal education was publicly exposed in the classroom. I empathised with Louisa Gradgrind, bound up in the middle-class social conventions of the time which educated her to fulfil a role very different to that expected of her brother Thomas. This text was being read primarily in the context of industrialisation, the factory system and nineteenth-century British Utilitarianism. These were areas I then knew little or nothing about, but which were made relevant to me in other ways. The utilitarian philosophy of education encapsulated by Gradgrind's words 'Teach these boys and girls nothing but Facts. Facts alone are wanted in life' (Dickens, 1987) raised questions around knowledge and power, which I related back to personal experiences – who made the rules by which I grew up who defined what became constituted as fact, or 'common sense'?

From the late 1940s substantial numbers of people from all over the Commonwealth, the previous colonies, came to Britain either to study or in search of work. The break up of the British Empire signalled a new historical era. My father came to Britain three years after the nation state of Pakistan was created and Britain had simultaneously lost India, its imperial 'jewel in the crown'. He met and married my British mother soon after. I was very young when my father decided to take the family back home to Pakistan. Growing up, my historical knowledge of British imperialism was limited; it was never discussed by either of my parents. I never really understood my father's intense dislike of British attitudes, nor the early racism experienced as a mixed race, yet very 'Asian' child in Britain. I knew, through a combination of stories told by my grandmother and old family photographs, that all of the male members of my father's family had been in the Indian army and fought for the British. My grandfather had been killed in Hong Kong whilst serving under the Raj. Part of the Cultural Studies course content was an exploration of empire and included looking at the ways in which nineteenth-century visual and literary representations signified 'otherness' in relation to national identity and race. Rozina Visram's (1986) *Ayahs, Lascars and Princes* traces historically the interrelated history of India and Britain and her chapter on 'Soldiers of the Empire' examines how Britain established its hegemony through the establishment of a formal education system and an army organised along lines of caste and ethnicity. In Visram's soldiers I saw my uncles and my grandfather. The faded brown photographs my grandmother had often pointed out to me as a child took on new dimensions.

The historical context in which the formulation of my racial, national and ethnic identity had been constructed was given another perspective through texts such as Kipling's poem 'The white man's burden', and Hughes' *Tom Brown's School Days* with their implicit and explicit racial superiority based on an ethnocentric 'common sense' dichotomy of 'civilised' and 'uncivilised'. Through these I understand more clearly the historical basis of the different forms of racism, and racist views, I had personally encountered within the British and Asian community.

Undoubtedly, my own past and present experiences shaped the meanings I took from these texts, yet at the same time the texts themselves gave historical and conceptual shape to aspects of my racial, ethnic, class, and gender identity. The pedagogic process of deconstructing the text (Sarup, 1988; Culler, 1983), constituted simultaneously both a de- and re-construction of my self. The positions I occupied remained the same, but I re-located myself as a 'subject' and aspects of my self identity *qualitatively* changed. This interactive role of literature within adult learning, and the function it provides particularly on Access courses, has been explored by Bailey (1992).

This de/re-construction of identity is also partly an interactive group process. Other students' responses to the Cultural Studies course content and the meanings they constructed through the texts were crucial and provided a focal point for informal discussions. Critical analysis was often at its best at social gatherings outside of class time, over the phone, or on the journey home. The group also functioned as an important support mechanism, we openly discussed many of our problems, mutually counselling and coercing each other through them.

Kaleidoscope people

In our everyday lived experience we inhabit a number of positions, or 'mini-narratives'. These positions are often contradictory and do not necessarily fit neatly into the broader categorical 'grand-narratives' of class, race, and gender. For example, class and racial alliance can be disrupted by the narrative of sexuality. An example is a heated debate I witnessed between two 'mature students', both middle class by their own definition, and both white/British, over the implications of Clause 28; one was a gay male, the other a heterosexual mother, neither of them could find any common ground on which to agree. Both felt the subject affected them in highly personal terms on a day-to-day level. After that instance they could never really communicate with each other. Ultimately it was the issue at hand which determined which part of their identity was foregrounded above others. The response of the rest of the group was varied and did not by any means proceed smoothly along class, gender, or racial lines. To this extent we are all 'kaleidoscope' people, our shape constantly changing in accordance with how we are positioned, and position ourselves.

Moving on

After successfully completing the Access course I felt adequately prepared to move on into higher education in terms of self-confidence, study skills, and ability. During the first year at university, some of the mature students I met were finding it extremely difficult to overcome problems related to their lack of study skills, made particularly evident by younger students coming in straight after completing A levels who could turn out essays in a matter of hours, if necessary. Recently, I carried out a number of interviews with students who had entered higher education by 'alternative' or 'non-standard' routes (Webb *et al.*, 1993), some of whom had returned to education after a very long period. Many expressed their anxiety at 'keeping up' with others. A number of these students had not known, or been informed about, the existence of Access courses until they had already started their degree, at which point it was too late. Most of these students felt they would have gone in via Access had they known about it.

Theorising the Subject

Our identity(ies) are formed in relation to a number of both material and symbolic factors, and as such are complex and contradictory. Through them we inhabit a number of psychic and subject positions. Any politics of articulation must recognise the diversity that exists *within* these positions, and attempt to avoid essentialising them in simple binary terms.

On completing my degree the term 'mature student' no longer applied, I became a 'graduate'. Subsequently, this changed, and now I am referred to as a 'lecturer'. What I find interesting is the *deceptive* nature of these different frames of reference, and their incongruousness when translated into the realm of subjectivity. In terms of racial, ethnic and class location my identity is fragmented and ambiguous. I am of 'mixed race'. At times I am categorised as 'black' (meaning all non-whites), or referred to more specifically as 'Asian'. I am also described as 'white' due to my skin colour, the way I dress, and aspects of my present way of life. The same applies with regard to class. As as part-time lecturer I am still reliant on certain state benefits, and so still constitute part of the so called 'underclass'. I live in the inner city, on a large council estate where most, if not all, of the residents would define themselves as working class, either unemployed or working in the non-'professional' sector. However, even though my financial position has not changed, I have been told by some that I am no longer working class, but have become middle class, due to the fact that I am now a lecturer.

By placing myself outside any singular, dominant, metanarrative, am I guilty of retreating into a quasi-liberal position? Does attempting to engage in localised struggles mean I have been ideologically seduced away from the main battlefield? Is embracing Foucault and Lyotard merely 'tripping the light fantastic and entering into the haze of post-structuralist, post-fordist and post-modernist fog'? These are some of the questions raised by Clarke's 'Putting class back on the agenda', which concludes by provocatively posing the question 'are you a revolutionary or a reactionary'? Admittedly, some poststructuralist thinking has become so obscure that it is difficult to decipher the complex terminology used, let alone make it relevant to lived experience. But, on the other hand, to dismiss it all as 'folly' (Clarke, 1993) is to deny the conceptual insights it offers to counter certain dogmatic forms of empiricist thinking.

I am arguing here that as 'subjects' we are constructed kaleidoscopically within 'networks of power' and that the complexities and ambiguities of this construction must be recognised within the provision of education for mature students. Prioritising one particular discourse over another can be problematic, and lead to overly broad generalisations. The juxtaposing of two articles from one issue of the *Journal of Access Studies* illustrates this. Both articles (Clarke, 1993; Leicester, 1993) are set within clearly defined narratives, and both assert very similar arguments in their analysis of discriminatory practices within the education system. The difference between them is that Clarke poses a grand-narrative premised on class, and Leicester prioritises race. Both tend to set up a binary relation, between an 'us' and 'them', black or white, working class or middle class.

I agree completely with the view that full-time Access courses provide huge barriers to students with young children, or those on low incomes who need to work part-time (Clarke, 1993); but to assert that Access has been used successfully by middle-class women and has almost 'ignored the needs' of working-class women, is misleading. I am certainly not arguing that class is a 'non issue, out of fashion and politically incorrect' (Clarke, 1993). However, I am saying that care should be taken not to throw the baby out with the bathwater, by setting up a framework for action which excludes on the basis of non-'authentic' class location, which implies lack of 'real credibility'. To bring about change, the profession does need more working-class students entering it, but it must also construct more productive forms of alliances that will function across existing class barriers, rather than serve to close these into separate camps. Clarke argues that the 1980s 'equal ops' policies on race, gender, sexuality, class, disability and age were all achieved, with the exception of class equality (Clarke, 1993).

Leicester's argument runs counter to this assertion (Leicester, 1993). Using statistical evidence, she looks at how black students from ethnic minorities, relative to the population as a whole, are being underrepresented in higher education. In her view, commitment to access for black people is 'rhetorical, past the point of entry'. This is put down to what she calls the PLU (people like us) factor which operates discriminately through the procedure of discretionary interviewing of mature students; 'discretionary interviews of mature students, a supposedly facilitating device, which may work for white middle class women, could work against black adults' (Leicester, 1993). One way of redressing this racial imbalance, she argues, is to have more 'black' gate-keepers, on the assumption that 'white' gate-keepers may make biased judgments about people from different backgrounds. Institutional racism, as most of us know, exists, and must be addressed at every level. Racism is no more an illusion, or a nonissue, than class(ism) is. However, to assert that the majority of 'white' admissions tutors are 'unware' and 'potentially racist', is very sweeping. The concept of race itself, and the subject positions we take in relation to it, are so complex and contradictory, they can't possibly be explained simply by the PLU factor, which assumes we know who the 'us' is. 'Black' is a floating signifier, which operates in conjunction with other aspects of our material and symbolic being, or sense of collective consciousness. It can mean different things, in different contexts, to different people. Racism takes many forms, not just black against white.

The PLU factor is far too ambiguous, too broad and, paradoxically, far too narrow a yard-stick, by which to measure racial, or class, identity. Caste, ethnicity, nationality, gender, religion, and sexuality, are other important coexisting elements which constitute the 'people like us' factor. As 'subjects' we negotiate different personal spaces. Our subjective identities are constantly reproduced, through transformation and difference. I acknowledge that 'frames of reference' are necessary when engaging in any social or political struggle for change, but the positions we inhabit are multiple and fragmented, and the positions we foreground in localised struggles should equally be conceptualised as 'strategic' positions (Gramsci, 1932), rather than 'fixed' essentialised ones. In taking up fixed positions there is the very real danger of homogenising them and putting each into its own neatly labelled box. This, in my view, is reactionary. Working within and across the politics of difference means a revolutionary renegotiation of singular referential axes, or dominant metanarratives. Locating the 'subject' of pedagogic discourse will entail the opening of many boxes.

Conclusion

The intention in this chapter was to raise a number of complex polemical issues rather than provide any definitive answers. The theoretical basis from which I argue for the concept of 'kaleidoscope people' is one which is undoubtedly unsettling for those of us who appear secure in our sense of self or, on the other hand, who attempt to locate others in categorical terms. Given the importance of student/tutor dynamics in facilitating the process of learning and the further progression of mature students, it is necessary from time to time for us, as practitioners, to stand back and take a critical look at ourselves and to evaluate how, or to what extent, this sense of self location influences our perception and construction of others.

By drawing on some of my own experiences I have attempted to highlight some of the practical implications that might be taken up further, and in far more depth, by others. In particular, the question of more adequate provision of information and guidance, which would serve to link the progression from adult education/further education to higher education level more effectively, needs addressing.

References

Bailey, J. (1992) Literature: text and context in Access, *Journal of Access Studies,* 7(2), 193–203.

Clarke, P. (1993) Putting class back on the agenda, *Journal of Access Studies,* 8(2), 225–230.

Culler, J. (1983) *On Deconstruction: Theory and Criticism after Structuralism.* London: Routledge and Kegan Paul.

Dickens, C. (1987) *Hard Times.* London: Penguin Press.

Foucault, M. (1979) *The History of Sexuality,* Vol. 1. London: Penguin Press.

Forgacs, D. (1988) *A Gramsci Reader.* London: Lawrence and Wishart.

Gramsci, A. (1988) Notes for an introduction and approach to the study of philosophy and the history of attune. In D. Forgacs (ed.) (1988) *A Gramsci Reader.* London: Lawrence and Wishart.

Leicester, M. (1993) Anti-racist Access? *Journal of Access Studies,* 8(2), 220–224.

Ryle, M. and Stuart, M. (1994) An Access curriculum for women, *Journal of Access Studies,* 9(1), 79–90.

Rutherford, J. (1990) *Identity, Community, Culture, Difference.* London: Lawrence and Wishart.

Sarup, M. (1988) *Poststructuralism and Postmodernism.* London: Harvester Wheatsheaf Press.

Visram, R. (1986) *Ayahs, Lascars and Princes.* Australia: Pluto Press.

Webb, S., Davies, P., Green, P., Thompson, A. and Williams, J. (1993) *Alternative Entry to Higher Education.* University of Warwick.

11

Records of Achievement: Tracing the Contours of Learner Identity

Roger Harrison

Introduction

In recent years processes of profiling, action planning and recording achievement have touched almost all aspects of education and training, playing a part in strategies for teaching and learning in schools, further and higher education, informal adult education, careers and educational guidance. Their claim to authority is grounded in the assertion that it is through processes of self-assessment, forward planning, recording and reviewing progress, that individuals acquire personal autonomy in their roles as learners, workers and citizens. This is represented not only as personally liberating, in that learners are now 'empowered' to plan and evaluate their own learning and development, but also as essential preparation for the demands of the modern work environment, where economic survival will depend on individual 'self-reliance' (AGR, 1995). In this chapter I want to examine more closely not only the claims being made for these developments, but also the beliefs, values and assumptions about learning which underpin them, and their implications for the identity of learners.

Policy Concerns

Government policy statements have consistently supported the idea that individuals need to develop skills of self-reliance and self-regulation. For example, the Dearing Review of 16–19 qualifications specifically identified the National Record of Achievement (NRA) as 'an important instrument through which young people develop the practice of managing and taking responsibility for their learning' (SCAA, 1996, p. 15). The contemporary discourse of 'lifelong learning' positions the individual learner as actively planning and choosing learning opportunities and career changes. For example, the recent Green Paper 'The Learning Age' promotes the idea of a 'learning culture' in which 'individuals and enterprises increasingly take charge of their own learning' (DfEE, 1998a, p. 17). Central government funding has been instrumental in developing and integrating the processes

155

of action planning and recording achievement throughout the compulsory and post-compulsory curriculum. For example, in Higher Education the Employment Department's 'Enterprise' programme of the 1980s was followed up by the 'Guidance and Learner Autonomy' and 'Learner Managed Learning' programmes of the 1990s. The titles of these programmes are themselves illuminating, indicating a particular notion of the learning process and the type of learner who might be engaged with it. Introducing a recent round of funding aimed specifically at promoting records of achievement the DfEE makes it clear that despite changes in its political complexion, government aspirations remain the same:

> The emphasis will be on the need for students to develop reflective and learning skills which will assist them in future employment.
>
> (DfEE, 1998b)

These aims have been actively supported by a range of stakeholders, from the Confederation of British Industry which has proposed that 'individuals have to make it by themselves, taking ownership of their own futures' (CBI, 1995) to the Association of Graduate Recruiters which identified 'Self-reliance' and 'Career Management' skills as the key requirement for effective performance in the twenty-first century (AGR, 1995).

Rationalities

Acceptance of the validity of these policy aims is secured through an appeal to rationalities of efficiency and effectiveness. Efficiency in responding to the need of the economy for skilled and flexible workers. The emergence of a 'global economy', where competitive advantage is claimed to reside in the ability of organisations to respond to rapid and frequent changes in the market, has been used to support a demand for ever more flexible working practices and ever increased levels of flexibility by workers. The most efficient form of 'human resource' in this context is the self-steering individual, capable of learning and changing in order to maintain competitive advantage.

> Individuals are the key to the UK's competitiveness. Efforts must be focused on empowering them, and on encouraging self-development and lifetime learning.
>
> (CBI, 1993, p. 7)

A second aspect of 'efficiency' is the demand on public sector education to do 'more for less'. In further and higher education the dramatic rise in student numbers has been accompanied by a reduction in per capita resources. At the same time the growing diversity and complexity of lifelong learning, including flexibilities in curricula, institutional frameworks and forms of assessment, have created a growing number of choices in terms of when, where, what and how to study. Shifting some of the responsibility for these decisions to learners, often through the use of open learning packages in recording achievement and action planning, represents a re-source efficient means of reaching a wider audience (Ball and Jordan, 1997). It is also a convenient way of shifting the responsibility for career management and guidance away from the organisation and towards the individual, taking some of the load from teachers. For the Association of Graduate Recruiters, a direct effect of increasing learner autonomy 'will be to relieve the demands on teaching staff because students will have the skills to be self-reliant learners, (AGR, 1995).

Increased 'effectiveness' is seen as occurring through the beneficial effects on student learning of adopting a learner-centred pedagogy which foregrounds autonomy, choice, and the development of generic skills asso-ciated with self-directed learning. Hargreaves has summed up the hopes of educational 'optimists' for the effects of introducing records of achieve-ment into a school context:

> They offer . . . the hope, the possibility of placing young people at the centre of their own learning, giving them increased responsibility for their own develop-ment and assessment, empowering them with the capacity for self-determination.
> (Hargreaves, 1989, p. 131)

The idea of learners having power and a sense of ownership over their own learning is also evident in the conclusions of the 'Higher Education for Capability' expert seminar:

> Records of achievement should be created by the learner, owned by the learner and managed by the learner for the development of the learner.
> (Bull and Otter, 1994, p. 2)

It is a pedagogic approach which seeks to encourage an intrinsic orienta-tion towards learning, allowing learners to set their own goals and choose their own learning pathways. The educational rationale for embedding processes of reflection, forward planning and review into the curriculum draws on the humanistic appeal to the ideal of the autonomous learner; the rational, self-aware and informed decision-maker, freely choosing between learning opportunities and career destinations. In adult learners this has been represented in terms of a strong 'sense of self, intrinsic motivation, personal control and responsibility, high self perceptions of competence and self-esteem' (Fazey, 1996, p. 26). It is a vision of learning and the learner which appeals to those practitioners in education who have sought to value the experience and situation of the learner as a counter to more traditional, discipline-based pedagogical practices (Knowles, 1984). This ideological commitment helps to explain the almost religious fervour which has accompanied many initiatives in profiling and recording achievement.

By aligning economic necessity with liberal humanism a powerful dis-course is constructed which now occupies a central position within a 'pro-gressive' agenda for curriculum reform. It is a discourse which suggests learning as an individual rather than a social activity, and learners as en-terprising, flexible and adaptable individuals, capable of taking respon-sibility for managing the frequent transitions required by contemporary life and work. In critiquing this discourse I want to look first at the practical viability of some of these claims before going on to examine in more detail the work that they do in normalising a particular social and cultural understanding of what it is to be a learner and a person.

Managing Change

Processes of reflection and action planning ostensibly provide learners with tools for rational decision making which can be applied in the arenas of education and work, personal and social life. Individuals are presented with a set of techniques which offer the promise of 'empowerment' through choice; of taking the role of manager in the conduct of their own career as a learner, a worker, a person. The difficulty here is that a rational decision-making model is most effective when the information available is complete, and future trends are predictable. Analyses of contemporary social and economic conditions suggest that neither of these assumptions can be taken for granted. We have already touched on some of the reported effects of globalisation on economic conditions, which suggest instability and change as defining characteristics, and adaptation and flexibility as key strategies for individual and corporate survival. Contemporary social conditions have been characterised by the term 'detraditionalisation' (Beck, Giddens and Lash, 1994, p. vi); the expectation that nothing can be taken for granted, that traditions are 'routinely subjected to interrogation'. Whereas in traditional society occupation, social class and gender-based family roles provided the foundations of personal identity and economic and social relations, in the 'post-traditional order' (Giddens, 1991, p. 31) people's lives and the conditions in which they live become more varied and dynamic. For instance, people are no longer encouraged to aspire towards a career of steady progression in one field or with a single employer. Frequent job change and the development of 'multi-option flexilives' (Handy, 1984) are now presented as both normal and desirable. An understanding of people as 'human capital' encourages a view of individuals, not as rooted by ties of family and community to a single locality, work role or social position, but as a mobile and flexible resource, capable of deploying themselves where most appropriate in the cause of economic efficiency. Individuals are able, and expected, to manipulate their own images, using consumer choices to signal changing identities and lifestyles. An emphasis on the role of the individual in adapting to social and economic change has been contrasted with the way transitions are managed in traditional societies, where social norms are collectively established and maintained. In modern society 'the altered self has to be explored and constructed as part of a reflexive process of connecting personal and social change' (Giddens, 1991, p. 33).

This in itself would be unsettling, but it occurs alongside a crisis of confidence in the rational and scientific basis of industrial development.

Belief in progress through the application of science and reason is undermined by today's 'ecological crisis', raising questions about the nature of progress itself, as well as the ability of industrialised nations to control the trajectory of development they have set in train. In the 'risk society' described by Ulrick Beck,

> recognition of the unpredictability of the threats provoked by techno-industrial development necessitates self-reflection on the foundations of social cohesion and the examination of prevailing conventions and foundations of 'rationality'.
> (Beck, Giddens and Lash, 1994, p. 8)

As faith in the narrative of progress and the authority of traditional institutions has come into question, and as the security conferred by an established social and economic order has been eroded, the responsibility for shaping the self is located increasingly with individuals. It is precisely in these circumstances that forms of practice (profiling and recording achievement) and types of identity (the self-reliant learner) become both attractive and necessary. It is significant that their emergence as part of a powerful discourse of learning and learner identity has coincided with a set of social and economic conditions in which the possibility of their realisation appears to be uniquely problematic.

> Individuals are now held responsible for decisions with regard to their life course that are largely beyond their influence.
> (Jansen and van der Veen, 1997, pp. 265–266)

In this context individual choice around learning and career becomes a risky rather than a rational business, a process of *ad hoc* adaptation rather than rational planning. It is in this spirit of scepticism towards the mainstream discourse which accompanies processes of profiling and recording achievement that I now want to look at other interpretations of the work they do in shaping our understandings of learning and learners.

Recording Achievement and Surveillance

As a counter to the 'optimistic' view of some educational practitioners, Hargreaves (1989) has identified the potential role of records of achievement as a form of surveillance in which the actions, feelings and thoughts of students are available for scrutiny and comment by those in a position of authority. Referring to work within compulsory education he states:

> The personal record component of records of achievement also has an extraordinary capacity to restrict young people's individuality, to discipline and control them through the power of a pervasive and intrusive pattern of personal assessment.
> (Hargreaves, 1989, p. 133)

Hargreaves points to the ways in which records of achievement monitor affect as well as achievement, personality as well as performance, suggesting that they are 'bound up with a more generalised trend towards the development and implementation of increasingly sophisticated techniques of social surveillance within society at large' (1989, p. 133). He invokes the French philosopher and historian Michel Foucault, drawing on his notion of 'discipline' as a means by which social control is exercised in modern society. Whereas in earlier times direct coercion and violent punishment were the means of maintaining authority, contemporary forms of discipline are more subtle and pervasive. Discipline in this sense is a carefully regulated administrative system whose concern is with measuring, assessing and recording the conduct of individuals. Authority does not have to assert itself through grand gestures designed to intimidate its subjects. It operates through the power of the unseen observer who sees everything but remains invisible.

> In discipline it is the subjects who have to be seen. Their visibility assures the hold of the power that is exercised over them. It is the fact of being constantly seen, of being always open to be seen, that maintains the disciplined individual in his subjection.
>
> (Foucault, 1977, p. 187)

Foucault (1977) uses the architectural image of the panopticon, a nineteenth-century observation tower used in penal institutions and factories, to illustrate the principle of a form of observation in which the observer remains invisible to the observed, and where the observed never know when they are being watched.

In Foucault's terms, the observed becomes 'the object of information, never a subject in communication' (p. 200), and the effect is 'to induce in the inmate a state of conscious and permanent visibility that assures the automatic functioning of power' (p. 201). In the quest for more holistic and humane forms of assessment, profiles and records of achievement encourage students to record not only their performance in class, but also their emotions, personal relationships and work outside the educational institution. These details of the student are open to evaluation, monitoring and possibly intervention by the institution. Areas of students' lives that were once regarded as private are now subject to processes which are intrusive and judgemental, even where they might be represented as liberal and humane.

Foucault suggests that through the regular and detailed observation and examination of subjects they become objectified. Drawing on his studies of prisons and psychiatric hospitals, he notes how the construction of individuals as 'cases', the subjects of examination, classification and judgement, plays a key role in modern forms of power. It is through the 'normalising gaze' (p. 184) of the examination, and the creation of the written record, that the lives of individuals are opened up to closer scrutiny and control by those who have authority over them. This description comes uncomfortably close to the ways in which formative recording of achievement is currently being used in schools, involving the building of a written dossier which can be retrieved and referred to at any point in the future when guidance interviews are held, career choices are discussed, or disciplinary action is being taken. The application of computer technology to these mechanisms has the potential to further extend their reach, 'enabling schools to keep hi-tech tabs on their pupils emotional and behavioural whereabouts' (Hargreaves, 1989, p. 135). This is the nightmarish Orwellian vision of records of achievement, a mechanism which contributes towards a form of surveillance which is endless and from which there is no hiding place.

Recording Achievement and Self-Discipline

Hargeaves's analysis is focused on schools, where the contents of records of achievement are relatively public documents, often available to teachers, parents, careers guidance advisers and those with responsibility for disciplinary interventions. In post-compulsory education the surveillance aspects become less obvious. Here profiles, portfolios, action plans and records of achievement are linked with self-assessment, allowing students to disclose as much or as little as they wish to their tutors, advisers and assessors. Here, surely, is the context in which the self-reliant, autonomous learner can become a reality, and the personal record of achievement realise its emancipatory goal. Yet even as power appears to be devolving to learners and as they are invited to assume greater control over their learning and working careers, they are simultaneously enveloped in a discursive form of power, one which shapes the very ways in which they are able to think about themselves as learners, workers and citizens. It is precisely this form of power, 'the way a human being turns him or herself into a subject' (Foucault, 1983, p. 208) that came to occupy the attention of Michel Foucault in his later work. Foucault uses the notion of 'confession' to encapsulate 'all those procedures by which the subject is incited to produce a discourse of truth . . . which is capable of having an effect on the subject himself' (1980, p. 215–16). Discourses are understood here as the ways in which knowledge is organised to legitimate certain forms of truth; to establish what can and cannot be said or thought. Their power depends on how far they are able to confer 'common sense' or 'taken for granted' status on understandings which have specific historical and cultural origins. Language plays a central role in this process, since as Fairclough observes 'as one changes the wording one changes the meaning' (1992, p. 191). As learners start to incorporate the language, and work within the categories for self-description provided by profiles and records of achievement, they are internalising the 'normalising gaze'; coming to understand themselves in these terms.

The processes for recording and analysing achievement have become fairly standardised in terms of:

- recording of previous educational experience and educational decisions
- explicit self assessment using rating scales or questionnaires

- describing personal interests
- reviewing achievement and progress in the current course of study
- action planning for academic, personal or career development.

(Ball and Butcher, 1994, p. 25)

The aim of developing students' ability to 'take greater control of their learning and working careers' (Employment Department, 1994, p. 9) is to be achieved through strategies which are presented as objective and technically neutral. Contained in the record of achievement are mechanisms and templates through which personal experience can be processed, interpreted and coded, and which are presented as purely technical processes controlled by the individual learner. Yet to superimpose one's own experience onto these templates already constitutes it in quite specific ways, and to evaluate one's own progress according to these models is to confirm norms which are historically contingent rather than universally acknowledged. What is being put forward here is a powerful and far from neutral technology which is engaged in producing a certain sense of selfhood or subjectivity, whilst at the same time disguising its historical and cultural origins behind the humanistic discourse of empowerment and economic well-being. Here power is working 'from below' as individuals take on the role of self-surveillance; constantly scanning and adjusting their own thoughts, feelings and behaviour according to what they take to be normal and acceptable.

It is in this sense that techniques of self-assessment and reflection are most powerful as mechanisms for governing individual conduct; as 'techniques for assuring the ordering of human multiplicities' (Foucault, 1977, p. 218). They are effective in shaping the capacities and inclinations of individuals, not through coercion, but by engaging individuals in their own self-formation. In their analysis of the closely related practices of guidance and counselling Usher and Edwards note that

> the most effective forms of power are those which are not recognised as powerful because they are cloaked in the esoteric 'objective' knowledge of expertise and the humanistic discourse of helping and empowerment.
>
> (Usher and Edwards, 1998, p. 215)

It is a form of power which displaces the need for active containment or overt oppression, bringing not only the behaviour and external appearance of individuals, but also their inner lives, within the gaze of self-surveillance. Processes of profiling and recording achievement can be read as techniques for shaping particular 'dispositions and habits' (Ransom, 1997, p. 156) by bringing learners under their own critical, self regulating gaze, whilst that gaze is informed by a powerful discourse of individualism, self-reliance and autonomy. They provide a structure and a vocabulary which values and recognises certain kinds of subjectivity, bringing into view particular forms of experience and aspiration and suggesting certain kinds of outcomes. The spaces in which learners are invited to insert their own experiences and preferences are not, in this analysis, as innocent as they might appear, but already inscribed with certain expectations and understandings. The self-knowledge which is being elicited and validated here is only one among many possible accounts of the identity of the learner. Whilst recording achievement has the explicit purpose of opening up choice and opportunity, in so doing it also brings closure, both to understandings of what it means to be a person in the world, and also of what is 'realistic' for a person to expect from the world. Moreover, the closures and the categorisations which are imposed are not accidental, but reflect the priorities and goals of those who design and assess the process and its outcomes. Whether the intention is to produce emancipation or social control is less relevant here than that learner identity is already enclosed within discourses which are always on the move, and that these shifts are not under the control of the individual learner. Reviewing the history of such mechanisms in the context of vocational preparation for work, Stronach concludes:

> Thus, the indistinct figure that stands behind the profile and the vocational discourse is not the perfect worker, or even the ideal citizen. It is the outline of the tractable client . . . well motivated, adaptable, indefinitely prepared for an uncertain future.
>
> (Stronach, 1989, p. 172)

Ownership and Resistance

To achieve power discourses need to be 'owned' by those operating within them. Much of the literature on records of achievement therefore places an emphasis on the freedom which learners can exercise in using the process to reach their own decisions. The expertise of the professional helper – teacher, careers adviser, learning mentor – is invested in designing the templates into which learner experience is inserted and the algorithmic stages through which it is processed. Learners might be supported as they work through the process, but responsibility for the outcome rests with them. As Metcalfe (1992, p. 627) has commented in relation to career guidance,

> This double action, of demanding confession and then falling silent, is central to the confessional technology of the self. It tries to ensure that students take personal responsibility for the way they are, 'responsibility' being a key word in the careers guidance literature.

Perhaps unsurprisingly, evaluative studies on records of achievement frequently report that students themselves are sceptical of the discourse of empowerment through self-reliance. Research on first year undergraduate students reported by Rouncefield and Ward (1998) concluded that 'the majority of students do not link recording achievement to the learning process or see it as a mechanism for planning and managing learning' (p. 70). These students understood the process of recording achievement as less concerned with their own development and more with the bureaucratic and instrumental value of the record 'as a transition document' (p. 71). Other evaluations of projects designed to promote autonomy and self-reliance have similarly identified the insertion of institutional priorities and goals into the purportedly learner-centred processes of action planning and recording achievement (Garrigan, 1997; Carter and McNeill, 1998). No wonder Bullock and Jamieson (1998) identify 'ownership' of the personal development planning process as crucial to its success, but note that 'tutors may need to be continuously proactive in transfering this to the students' (p. 73). It would appear that assertions such as that of the Association of Graduate Recruiters that 'The process of recording achievement is designed primarily for the benefit of the individual'(AGR, 1994, p. 1) is not taken at face value by all learners.

It is perhaps in these small signs of resistance to the surveillance and self-disciplining power of records of achievement that opportunities for different kinds of learning, and forms of learner identity, are to be found. Foucault's analysis of the operation of modern power suggests that the techniques associated with self-formation are not simply designed to repress and manipulate, but also to create and develop capacities and dispositions which increase the power and productivity of individuals. The practices associated with governmentality not only constrain and categorise, they also produce possibilities for resistance and difference. Power may be omnipresent, but is not necessarily omnipotent. In positioning knowledge at the heart of power Foucault leaves open the possibility for disturbing power through challenging and reconceptualising knowledge. As Ransom has argued,

> the 'power-knowledge' sign marks a kind of weakness in the construction of modern power . . . If power and knowledge are intertwined, it follows that one way to understand power – potentially to destabilise it or change its focus – is to take a firm hold on the knowledge that is right there at the centre of its operations.
>
> (Ransom 1997, p. 23)

Through identifying and naming the assumptions and understandings which underpin individualised processes of self-assessment and forward planning their 'taken for granted' status as benign and helpful strategies is undermined. Foucault's analysis of the workings of power through surveillance and self-regulation produces a different form of 'knowledge'; one which calls into question the apparent neutrality and rationality of these pedagogic strategies, and which implicates them in the discursive construction of a particular kind of learner identity. Dominant ways of presenting the self are revealed as not simply descriptive, but also active in shaping people's self awareness and individuality, of constituting their subjectivities. For both teachers and learners Foucault's analysis suggests the need for a more reflexive engagement; one which is able to move beyond the narrow categories and options for being and doing offered by current forms of recording achievement, which refuses to take for granted dominant discourses of autonomy and self-regulation, and which is prepared to explore different sorts of spaces and discourses within which learner identities can be located.

References

Association of Graduate Recruiters (1994) *AGR Briefing: Records of Achievement and the Future of the Classified Degree.* Cambridge: AGR.

Association of Graduate Recruiters (1995) *Skills for Graduates in the 21st Century.* Cambridge: AGR.

Ball, B. and Butcher, V. (1994) *Developing Students' Career Planning Skills: The Impact of the Enterprise in Higher Education Initiative.* London: EHEI.

Ball, B. and Jordan, M.(1997) An open-learning approach to career management and guidance, *British Journal of Guidance and Counselling*, 25, 4, 507–516.

Beck, U. Giddens, A. and Lash, S. (1994) *Reflexive Modernisation: Politics, Tradition and Aesthetics in Modern Social Order.* Cambridge: Polity Press.

Bull, J. and Otter, S. (1994) *The Recording Achievement and Higher Education Project.* Cheltenham: UCAS.

Bullock, K. and Jamieson, I (1998) The effectiveness of personal development planning, *The Curriculum Journal* 9, 1.

Carter, K. and McNeill, J. (1998) Coping with the darkness of transition: students as the leading lights of guidance at induction to higher education, *British Journal of Guidance and Counselling* 26, 3, 399–415.

Confederation of British Industry (1993). *Routes for success; Careership – A Strategy for 16–19 Year Old Learning.* London: CBI.

Confederation of British Industry (1995) *Realising the Vision: A Skills Passport.* London: CBI.

Department for Education and Employment (1998a) *The Learning Age: A Renaissance for a New Britain*, DfEE: Sheffield.

DfEE (1998b) *Higher Education Development Projects.* Sheffield: DFEE.

Employment Department (1994) *Higher Education Developments: The Skills Link 2.* Sheffield: Employment Department.

Fairclough, N. (1992) *Discourse and Social Change.* Cambridge: Polity Press.

Fazey, D. (1996) Guidance for Learner Autonomy, in McNair, S. *Putting Learners at the Centre: Reflections from the Guidance and Learner Autonomy in Higher Education Programme.* Sheffield: DfEE.

Foucault, M.(1977) *Discipline and Punish: The Birth of the Prison.* London: Penguin.

Foucault, M. (1980) *Power/Knowledge.* New York: Pantheon.

Foucault, M. (1983) The subject and power, in Dreyfus, H. and Rabinow, P. *Michel Foucault.* Chicago: University of Chicago Press.

Garrigan, P. (1997) Some key factors in the promotion of learner autonomy in higher education, *Journal of Further and Higher Education*, 21, 2, 169–182.

Giddens, A. (1991) *Modernity and Self Identity: Self and Society in the Late Modern Age.* Cambridge: Polity Press.

Handy, C. (1984) *The Future of Work: A Guide to a Changing Society.* London: Blackwell.

Hargreaves, A.(1989) *Curriculum and Assessment Reform.* Milton Keynes: Open University Press

Jansen, T. and van der Veen, R. (1997) Individualisation, the new political spectrum and the functions of adult education. *International Journal of Lifelong Education*, 16, 4, 264–276.

Knowles, M. (1984) *The Adult Learner: A Neglected Species.* Houston: Gulf Publishing.

Metcalfe, A. (1992) The curriculum vitae: confessions of a wage labourer, *Work, Employment and Society* 6, 619–641.

Ransom, J. (1997) *Foucault's Discipline: The Politics of Subjectivity.* Duke University Press.

Rouncefield, M. and Ward, R. (1998) Recording achievement and action planning: a basis for progression to higher education? *British Journal of Guidance and Counselling*, 26, 1, 61–73.

School Curriculum and Assessment Authority (1996) *Review of Qualifications for 16–19 Year Olds* (the Dearing Review). London: SCAA.

Stronach, I. (1989) A critique of the 'new assessment': from currency to carnival? in Simons, H. and Elliott, J. (eds) *Rethinking Appraisal and Assessment.* Milton Keynes: Open University Press.

Usher, R. and Edwards, R. (1998) Confessing all? A 'postmodern' guide to the guidance and counselling of adult learners, in Edwards, R., Harrison, R. and Tait, A. (eds) *Telling Tales: Perspectives on Guidance and Counselling in Learning.* London: Routledge.

12

Disciplining Bodies: On the Continuity of Power Relations in Pedagogy

Jennifer M. Gore

Introduction

The history of educational reform is littered with discarded ideas and practices, with policies that were never enacted – at least not as they were intended – and with libraries of academic theories well past their shelf life.

Despite the diversity of educational ideas and enormous intellectual labor invested in educational change, the experience of schooling bears some remarkable similarities. For instance, what Philip Corrigan (1991) refers to as the 'tightening of bodies' that accompanies schooling is manifest in generations of former and current students who raise their hands to speak, who ask permission to leave rooms, who tense up in examination situations, who beam with the tiniest expression of approval. Our similar experiences of schooling are also evident in the quick recognition of teachers and students in a range of social situations, and our assumption of (or resistance to) those positions in adult pedagogical situations as diverse as teaching an adolescent to drive a car, sharing a recipe, or learning about parenting. One need only watch young children 'play school' to observe the longevity of certain schooling practices.

It is my contention that the apparent continuity in pedagogical practice, across sites and over time, has to do with power relations, in educational institutions and processes, that remain untouched by the majority of curriculum and other reforms. With the exception of Bernstein (1975, 1990), Bourdieu and Passeron (1977), and a handful of others who have drawn on their work, educational researchers have paid little attention to the microlevel functioning of power in pedagogy.

In this chapter, I address two specific questions that contribute to the investigation of power relations in schooling: How do power relations function at the microlevel of pedagogical practices? To what extent is the functioning of power relations continuous across different pedagogical sites? The arguments I construct in response to these questions will be informed by Michel Foucault's analytics of power and my own empirical study of four distinct pedagogical sites.

Foucault on Power Relations

Foucault's analytics of power was helpful in conceptualizing this study, for its focus on the micro-functioning of power relations. Once declaring himself a 'happy positivist', Foucault (1981) sought to ground his idea in empirical events. Methodologically and theoretically, then, I chose to explore pedagogical practices from a Foucaultian perspective on power.

Foucault (1977) argues that 'disciplinary power' emerged with the advent of modern institutions and extended throughout society, so that continuities in power relations are evident not only in schools, hospitals, prisons, factories, and other institutions, but also outside of these institutions.

Foucault's concept of disciplinary power explicitly shifts analyses of power from the 'macro' realm of structures and ideologies to the 'micro' level of bodies. Foucault (1980, p. 39) argues that unlike the sovereign power of earlier periods, disciplinary power functions at the level of the body:

> In thinking of the mechanisms of power, I am thinking rather of its capillary form of existence, the point where power reaches into the very grain of individuals, touches their bodies and inserts itself into their action and attitudes, their discourses, learning processes and everyday lives.

Using the exemplar of the panopticon, with its normalizing surveillance. Foucault describes disciplinary power as circulating rather than being possessed, productive and not necessarily repressive, existing in action, functioning at the level of the body, often operating through 'technologies of self'.

There is a scholarly debate over whether Foucault's analysis of power was particular to penal institutions or intended to characterize all of modern society. There is general agreement that Foucault provided a careful elaboration of specific techniques of power in penal institutions – techniques of surveillance, normalization, individualization, and so on. What seems to be in question is the extent to which his analysis of penal institutions was intended to apply to other institutions – the extent to which he was illustrating a general theory of society with the penal example, or tentatively proffering a general theory that emerged as a result of his investigation of prisons. Certainly, without doing the same kind of sustained analysis, Foucault (1983) made observations about the functioning of power in educational institutions:

> Take, for example, an educational institution: the disposal of its space, the meticulous regulations which govern its internal life, the different activities which are organized there, the diverse persons who live there or meet one another there, each with his own function, his well-defined character – all these things constitute a block of capacity-communication-power. The activity which ensures apprenticeship and the acquisition of aptitudes or types of behavior is developed there by means of a whole ensemble of regulated communications (lessons, questions and answers, orders, exhortations, coded signs of obedience, differentiation marks of the 'value' of each person and of the levels of knowledge) and by means

of a whole series of power processes (enclosure, surveillance, reward and punishment, the pyramidal hierarchy).

(pp. 218–219)

I interpret this passage as evidence that while Foucault illustrated his analysis of disciplinary power with reference to other institutions, he left the detailed analytic work to those 'specific' intellectuals with a closer attachment to education. The analysis of select passages from Foucault's vast (and sometimes contradictory) work is a common form of scholarly engagement with his ideas. Rather than contribute further to these debates on the basis of claims to have read Foucault better than others, I have taken up the question of power relations in pedagogy on the basis of an empirical study of contemporary pedagogical sites.

Power Relations in Pedagogy

Four diverse sites were selected in the hope of being able to construct some broad statements about power relations in pedagogy. The sites were high school physical education classes with an explicit focus on bodies; a first-year teacher education cohort, working with three lecturers; a feminist reading group; and a women's discussion group that met for the purpose of intellectual stimulation, usually via reading courses provided by community education organizations.

One part of the study[1] involved putting Foucault's techniques of power in penal institutions to the test of relevance for contemporary pedagogical functioning. Put simply, I was asking the question, 'Are the mechanisms of schooling like the mechanisms of prisons, in terms of the micro-practices of power Foucault identified?' It probably will not be surprising that my research yielded a 'positive' result – that I found the techniques of power that Foucault elaborated in prisons applicable to contemporary pedagogical practice. Finding what one looks for in research has been both a perennial problem and a source of comfort for many researchers. I would emphasize, however, that it would have been possible to not find these techniques of power, especially not in each of the sites, diverse as they were.

Techniques of power

In the remainder of this chapter, I briefly elaborate each of the eight major techniques of power that I investigated in order to demonstrate, first, that they are readily recognizable – that they exist in pedagogical interaction – and, second, that they were found in all of the sites studied. Next, I present some cross-context comparisons based on quasi-quantitative analysis. Finally, I make some statements about the usefulness and dangers of the approach I have taken.

As Foucault (1983) says, analysing what happens in the exercise of power relations is 'flat and empirical' (p. 217). The following segments of data, taken from field notes or transcripts,[2] are certainly that. While contextualizing and categorizing are joint components needed in qualitative research (Maxwell and Miller, 1993), demonstrating techniques of power in order to show that they exist in pedagogy requires only the systematic process of categorization. Furthermore, especially without the specific context of each session in which these data were collected, each event or episode is open to multiple interpretations and many episodes could appear equally legitimately in more than one category. Indeed, the majority of episodes were coded for multiple practices of power, indicating the co-incidence and rapidity with which power is enacted.

Surveillance

Without turning, the teacher says 'Zac, you know I can always tell your voice' (PE).[3] Surveillance was found frequently during our[4] observations – where surveillance was defined as 'supervizing, closely observing, watching, threatening to watch, or expecting to be watched'. Consider the following additional examples:

> The teacher goes to the board where she draws a smallish rectangle in the bottom right corner and writes inside it 'B1' to indicate that Bill has one demerit point. (PE)

> Elisabeth conducts a roll call. . . . She then conducts an exercise aimed at putting names to faces: each student, starting from the back row, must give his or her name and tell of one school experience. (TE)

> Because Judith is the only one who seems to be making any defense of the book, Carol continually looks at Judith when she critiques as if it is a personal debate. This goes on for some time until Judith says in protest, 'Don't look at me'. (FEM)

> 'Well, since then I've read about 10 other books. I just pushed the other one to the back.'
> 'It's not memorable, is what you're saying there, hey?'
> 'Well, it was for a time.'
> 'What page did you get up to, Elaine?'
> 'Did you get that far, Judith?'
> '127. I got to'. (noises of surprise)
> 'Oh, I only got to 75.'
> 'This is one-upwomanship!' (laughter)
> 'You only did half of what she did!' (in a self-mocking tone)
> 'I know.'
> 'Well, I didn't read it. That gives me the other end of the continuum.' (FEM)

In these examples, teachers monitor students, and students monitor each other. Surveillance singles out individuals, regulates behavior, and enables comparisons to be made.

It is important to remember the productiveness of power. Foucault (1977) declared: 'A relation of surveillance, defined and regulated, is inscribed at the heart of the practice of teaching, not as an additional or adjacent part, but as a mechanism that is inherent to it and which increases its efficiency' (p. 176). More generally, Foucault (1988a) said:

Power is not an evil. . . . Let us . . . take something that has been the object of criticism, often justified: the pedagogical institution. I don't see where evil is in the practice of someone who, in a given game of truth, knowing more than another, tells him what he must do, teaches him, transmits knowledge to him, communicates skills to him. The problem is rather to know how you are to avoid in these practices – where power cannot not play and where it is not an evil in itself – the effects of domination which will make a child subject to the arbitrary and useless authority of a teacher, or put a student under the power of an abusively authoritarian professor, and so forth. (p. 18)

At least some of the surveillance practices outlined above, such as getting to know the names of one's students and keeping students 'on task', can be seen as serving purposes productive for pedagogy.

Normalization

'Okay, so what we want and hope that you will have competence in by the end of your teacher education program, is that you'll be able to articulate and defend a personal theory of education, which is moral and socially just, because you are involved in a moral enterprise. You're making judgments all the time about goodness and worth, judgments about whether this particular learning activity is a worthwhile learning activity, whether a decision that you've made in managing . . . a learning difficulty in the classroom is a fair and just decision. So the whole notion of teaching as social practice is that it's an ethical practice. You'll be able to communicate effectively to your pupils, your peers, the people with whom you work, and the community at large. It's very important that teachers can justify what they do and that they can learn from each other' (TE). Foucault (1977) highlighted the importance of 'normalizing judgment', or normalization, in the functioning of modern disciplinary power. He explained that such normalization judgement often occurs through comparison, so that individual actions are referred 'to a whole that is at once a field of comparison, a space of differentiation and the principle of a rule to be followed' (p. 182). For the purposes of my research, normalization was defined as 'invoking, requiring, setting, or conforming to a standard – defining the normal'. The following examples, like the one above, should be readily recognizable:

> Ingrid also dislikes Eisenstein. She thinks a better feminist representative could have been chosen. She feels that Eisenstein is 'too giggly', not serious enough about the issues. (FEM)

> Kate gives an example of a student at the institution who, because of his religion and upbringing, believed that corporal punishment had a place in schools. Kate finds this 'hard to come to grips with'. She unpacks the assumptions behind this student's belief. Then she asks if his belief was justifiable: Educationally – No. Corporal punishment does not promote learning. Morally – No. He has no right to do this to another person. Socially – No. This behaviour does nothing to promote harmonious relationships in the world. Politically – No. It is against the law. She says, 'End of argument'. (TE)

Whether in relation to participants in these pedagogical settings, or in relation to other people or views, reference to standards appears to be a common feature of pedagogy. Educating is about the teaching of norms – norms of behaviour, of attitudes, of knowledge. Here, the productiveness of power would seem to be a fundamental precept of pedagogical endeavour.

Foucault's view of power relations as enacted at the site of the body also is readily demonstrated in the following examples of normalization:

> I hear the class teacher telling her, 'Success breeds success'. Clearly both teachers are urging her to try to improve her marks. Amy, her back to the class as she is 'encouraged' by the two teachers, pulls her windcheater hood over her head (as if to retreat into the security of it). (PE)

> A girl climbs on the stage behind the teacher and looks over his shoulder: 'Oh, you're writing reports'. He glances at her with an annoyed expression: 'Shh. If I blow this, it has to go right round to everyone again', he tells her (i.e., one mistake will require all those staff responsible for this student's report to rewrite it. No errors or crossing out is permitted on this 'official' document). (PE)

> A young girl is seen standing looking in from the door. The teacher's back is towards her, but the girls in the class see her and one calls out, 'Yes, can I help you?' (taking on the teacher's role). (PE)

The girl who pulled the hood of her jacket over her head while being singled out and challenged by teachers probably was doing so not because she was cold, but in response to an exercise of power. Similarly, it was a student's movement onto the stage and another's standing at the doorway that prompted reactions – or, in Foucault's terms, prompted 'actions upon actions' – and so set up relations of power.

Exclusion

There is a great amount of discussion as students fire questions or make observations about body building. One of the girls makes a statement about how 'disgusting' female body builders look and that it is 'not natural' (PE). The category of exclusion was used in my research to mark the negative side of normalization – the defining of the pathological. Foucault refers to exclusion as a technique for tracing the limits that will define difference, defining boundaries, setting zones. Exclusionary techniques are pervasive in pedagogy, as demonstrated in Tyler's (1993) research that found that, even in kindergarten, some children, some dispositions and behaviours, are constructed as 'better', while others quickly are excluded. One long-term aim of my research is to identify techniques of power that need not be as they are in pedagogy – to identify what Foucault (1988c) called 'spaces of freedom'. Examples of exclusion from my study follow:

> The women criticize the tutor, saying, 'There's no comment on our work' and 'he even has poor grammar'. Julie says, 'He just doesn't answer our questions; he's not extending us'. (WG)

> A boy was sent to sit on the side of the court. He seemed to go without much reticence, and also without the kind of spectacle some students create in these situations. (PE)

She said something I disliked and she's not a feminist, so I wrote rather a longish letter, pointing out that I wanted them to take it into account and also pass it on to her. (FEM)

Mrs. Fernley says, 'Come on. You cannot be chatting merrily and writing at the same time'. A girl says, 'Wanna bet?' Mrs. Fernley: 'You can't write and read'. A student says, 'We never do, we just write'. (PE)

Now when you look at some of the literature on viewing teaching as problematic, some people say that teachers operate at different levels. I do have some problems where people talk about levels because it implies a hierarchy and I think it's very difficult to rank teachers into some kind of hierarchy. . . . [I prefer] more of a continuum, that as teachers we can view our practice as ranging from this end of the continuum as quite unproblematic right through to this end of the continuum, extremely problematic. (TE)

In these examples, there is the exclusion of individuals – in one case the bodily removal of a student from the activity. Particular identities and practices also are excluded, as are ways of constructing knowledge.

Very often exclusion and normalization occurred together, where the pathological was named in the process of establishing the norm. A pedagogy that does not set boundaries, that does not normalize and pathologize, is almost inconceivable.

Classification

Ingrid offers the view, taken from a book she has read, that men are warlike and conquering by nature, while women are peaceful and sedentary. Therefore, women are much more likely to be forcibly oppressed (FEM). Differentiating groups or individuals from one another, classifying them, classifying oneself, is another common technique within Foucault's elaboration of disciplinary power and was found within the pedagogical sites investigated. Some additional examples are provided:

Kate states that the teacher who operates as a critical analyst will take on different roles: coach, mentor, facilitator, listener, questioner, comforter, model, etc. Some of these roles will be active, she said, others will be passive – depending on the situation. Kate continues by discussing the operation of teaching as totally unproblematic or taking a more critical approach. Those who operate under the latter will see teaching as far more complex. (TE)

But once again Ingrid disagrees, saying that the 'libertarians' promoted it. 'Libertarians' is said in a derogatory tone. . . . Maxine suggests that the author indulged in this sort of relationship because she was a 'creative type' and wanted to experience everything in life. (FEM)

Zac returns to his seat as a conversation develops about the awarding of some Australian beauty crown to a male. The teacher remarks that she sees it as a 'step ahead', but Zac is baffled about how a 'guy' could win the competition. The teacher explains that he had raised a lot of money for charity and that the competition 'has to be non-sexist'. Madeleine remarks that the winner 'is a Nancy'. (PE)

Helen asks if the others have seen a photo of the author – she describes her as a 'large, masculine, person'. One of the women jumps in with the comment: 'Well, someone married her!' (WG)

Mrs. Fernley arrives and says, 'Right-o. Your tests. Some of you did very well. Some of you didn't do very well'. (PE)

As these examples illustrate, pedagogy proceeds via classificatory mechanisms – the classification of knowledge, the ranking and classification of individuals and groups. A whole tradition of educational research has addressed problems associated with the reproductive sorting functions of schools. Examining specific micro-practices of classification may be one way of intervening in these problems.

Distribution

'What we've organized for the tutorials is . . . some second- and third-year students [who] would like to have a chance to share with you some of their experiences of the practicum. . . . We'll break into smaller groups and we'll actually withdraw, so you'll be able to say those things that you really do want to discuss that you might be feeling a bit tentative about' (TE). Foucault also argues that the distribution of bodies in space – arranging, isolating, separating, ranking – contributes to the functioning of disciplinary power. The exercise of power via techniques of distribution is evident in the following examples:

'The people who are going to be working with you are Kate, Elisabeth, and myself, and our room numbers and our phone numbers are there. And it might be now an opportune time to just mention who will be your tutor for the groups that meet at 12.30. . . . Um, Group 1, . . . you know which groups you're in don't you? You know which groups you've been placed in? (long pause) So Group 1, which has Katie Adams, and Sue Allan, and Michelle Alexander, and a whole lot of other people, you'll be with me and you'll be in room 32. So those I'm with are in 32. Those of you who are in Group 2 will be with Elisabeth in 50, and those of you who are in Group 3 will be with Kate in room 45A. Do you want me to repeat those? Has everybody got it?' (TE)

The teacher moves Robert's desk, apparently in an attempt to prevent him from talking to his mates, and to avoid his distraction from the questionnaire. (PE)

While the teacher is handing out sheets at the back of the room, one of the boys near the front gets up from his seat and hits another boy in the front row. The 'victim' calls out, 'Miss', but the teacher is busy, her back turned toward them as she distributes the sheets. The 'attacker' glances at her briefly to see if his actions have been detected, but seeing the coast is clear, he returns to his seat. (PE)

Another boy runs back from jumping and ever so subtly wheedles his way in, way ahead of the end of the line. (PE)

Madeleine asks other girls if they want to skip with her. A few decline. She then asks me and I decline too. Madeleine turns with some exasperation, it seems. Bill finally accepts her invitation. When Bill is done, Zac is called upon by Madeleine. He says, 'Do I have to?' and acts very reluctant, but skips anyway. Madeleine then asks Shaq to skip, saying, 'Shaq, come over here'. He comes over but says he wants to skip by himself first. He says he wants to get warmed up. Madeleine does not accept this. She skips double time and tells another boy to run in and join her. Several of the students laugh at this. Madeleine says to one boy, 'Go play with yourself. I'm skipping'. She is encouraged by Annalise to try 'double dutch' (I think that's with two ropes turning in opposite directions). Madeleine goes off to the storeroom and emerges with a huge, heavy tug-of-war rope. Both of the teachers seem to have left the hall at this point. . . . The students laugh raucously at Madeleine's new rope. Several others join in, swinging the huge rope, which makes a solid thump each time it hits the floor. (PE)

These examples illustrate a wide range of distributive techniques, from teachers assigning rooms, physically moving bodies, requiring students to form groups, to students moving themselves or imploring others to do so.

Individualization
'But when I was reading, I kept thinking, would I have the moral courage, or the emotional courage, to do what she has just done?' (WG). Giving individual character to oneself or another is a common technique of power in pedagogy, as illustrated below:

'I grew up in the ____ suburbs. I went to a country Teacher's College. I was sent to ____ area for my first school. I then went to the inner city. I'm now teaching on the ____. So, I've really come quite full circle around NSW, I think. And what it's done in the time that I've been teaching primary school is that I've had to change myself. I've had to rethink what I was doing as a teacher.' (TE)

She encourages a student to run and practice the jump, saying, 'Patrick'. As he unenthusiastically approaches the mat, walking rather than doing a proper run-up, the teacher calls out, 'Go Patrick!' He complies, but without putting any effort into the action. (PE)

Meanwhile a discussion has begun about Monica Seles suing German tennis for the injury that was inflicted upon her and the financial losses involved. Annalise says, 'She's pretty young', I think implying that she has time to recover and become Number 1 again. Curt says, 'I think she's pretty', an unusual admission from an adolescent male, I thought, until he continued with, 'I like the way she grunts, Miss!' (PE)

At this point another of the girls enters the class, saying, 'Sorry I'm late, Miss'. She explains that she has been to see one of the other teachers to see whether she could 'drop PD'. Madeleine interrupts, claiming, 'No she wasn't, Miss. She's been in the toilets.' (PE)

The group is unanimous in its dislike for the text. Somebody asks whose idea it was to read it. I think Carol points the finger at Ingrid, who says that she hasn't read it for a long time but doesn't remember it being that bad. (FEM)

Totalization
'Teaching as a profession requires us to go on engaging in professional development throughout our careers. . . . So I hope we can model for you what we're asking you to do in your own professional lives' (TE). At the same time as individualization as a common technique, totalization, the specification of collectivities, giving collective character, forms a readily recognizable element of pedagogical activity. Sometimes totalization is achieved through simple linguistic structures, such as using the word 'we', as in the following examples:

Elaine states that 'we think of dilemmas as a choice between two evils, but that it is now more appropriate to think of them as two alternatives'. (TE)

'But she's really the same as all of us. I mean, if we traveled in an area like that (Afghanistan), we would form our own opinion . . . and we'd then come home and tell it all, writing letters about what we thought.' (WG)

At other times, totalization involves addressing whole groups of particip-ants in the pedagogical site or elsewhere:

We enter the small video viewing room at the far end of the library with the students. I comment that the back row is already taken. One girl says, 'We are Year 11 students, after all!' (PE)

A boy remarks in relation to Mrs. Fernley's forthcoming long service leave, 'Teachers are always going away. It's a great life.' (PE)

'One of the main effects of alcohol is that it gives you a high. That's why people drink it. It's not because they love the taste, although some people do, but I would suggest that most people drinking beer for the first time, for example, probably wouldn't like its taste.' (PE)

'I think the Australian male has changed. . . . Lots of women didn't question things much then, because they weren't economically capable.' (WG)

As these examples show, while totalizing is clearly a technique used in pedagogy for governing or regulating groups, students and teachers also 'totalize' themselves by naming themselves as part of various collectives.

Regulation
'The subject, as you can see, is assessed on a pass/fail basis. And we're intending that to be the case because we hope that the course will be intrinsically inter-esting' (TE).

Regulation was defined in my research as 'controlling by rule, subject to restrictions, invoking a rule, including sanction, reward, punishment'. While all of the previous techniques of power could be seen to have regu-lating effects, this category was used specifically to code incidents in which regulation was explicit, as in the following examples:

'Madeleine, that's your fourth infringement'. Madeleine makes some excuse, asking the teacher, 'Did you see that?' Nevertheless, and without much further persuasion from the teacher, Madeleine collects her things and leaves the room, saying, 'And I'm not coming back!' (I don't get the impression that she feels too much animosity over the incident, as she was quick to comply with the teacher's decision. I was aware that one of the class rules involved allowing four infringe-ments in any week, and any further violations required students spending two lessons in the library and the expectation that they would catch up on the work that they had missed. Madeleine's exit precipitated a discussion among the boys about how many 'demerits' each of them had.) (PE)

'You've probably been told in all your other classes about the idea of plagiarism and cheating and things and it's very important that you start right from the first day, that you do get a copy of the referencing procedures and that you use them and you do reference your material correctly. And if you have problems with understanding the reference system, then you come to see me and I'll show you how to do it. But it is vital that you do reference your material, that you don't just use great big chunks of other people's work without acknowledging it. It's not appropriate and it won't be accepted.' (TE)

'That did change, but it wasn't until 1942 in fact, the early 1940s, that aboriginal people could actually legally, they were legally able to go to Western schools.' (TE)

When the discussion turns to the 'caring' argument relating to quarantining HIV positive people, Ingrid says that this is done in Sweden under a humanitarian guise. Most of the group seems incredulous over this policy. The group discusses the effect of such a policy. Carol says that people who thought they might be HIV positive would not submit for tests because of a fear that they would be interned in one of the separate HIV communities. Therefore, these people 'go underground'. Somebody points out that this is the converse of the Australian policy. (FEM)

'But it was because we decided to answer every question, he says here, "the topics for discussion at the end of each lecture are suggestions only, to be used as much as you require, to stimulate and guide discussion"'. (WG)

As with other categories, regulation sometimes involved reference to knowledge, not only reference to group rules or restrictions.

To the extent that this whole set of examples resonates with readers, conjuring up memories of similar incidents as teachers, students, or members of other groups, I trust I have demonstrated that these categories have been useful and relevant for the analysis of classroom power relations. In what follows, I outline some broader insights that have emerged from the analysis of data thus far conducted.

Continuities across pedagogical sites

Many educational theorists would expect quite different practices of power in the four disparate sites in which my study took place. For instance, some feminist, critical, and other radical pedagogues have argued that their classrooms should or can do away with power. From this perspective, where power is often an evil to be done away with, less power might have been expected in the feminist and teacher education[5] sites than in the others. From the perspective on power informing this study, however, no site was free of power relations and no site 'escaped' the use of techniques of power. Rather, as the examples demonstrate, the broad techniques used in the exercise of power relations were found in the radical and mainstream, and the institutionalized and non-institutionalized sites.[6] Hence, my speculative view that the institutionalization of pedagogy within schools and universities constrains radical agendas might not be supported by the study, as a generalized claim. Instead, it seems that pedagogy has some continuous features across quite different locations. This continuity might be accounted for, in part, by the fact that participants in the non-institutionalized sites were adults – people who had already been subjected to and had learned the governmental processes of pedagogy.

Finding these techniques in contemporary pedagogical practice is not surprising, given Foucault's view of the disciplinary techniques of prisons as having their beginnings in pedagogy:

> Foucault emphasizes in *Discipline and Punish* that the disciplines linked to the panopticon were first used in secondary education, then primary schools, then the hospital, then the military barracks, and only later the prisons. So the panopticon was not dispersed into society from the prison; on the contrary.
>
> (Kelly, 1994, p. 370)

While a continuity in pedagogical practices across time is suggested by this passage, and while there is certainly considerable evidence in popular literature on schooling, and in the memories of generations of students and teachers, of minimal change over time, my own study was not designed to 'test' continuities over time, but continuities across sites.

As the above examples illustrate, I am able to claim continuity in the broad 'techniques of power' for each of the four sites investigated. While the specific effects of those practices of power may have varied across sites, I can say with some confidence that power relations in pedagogy were enacted via techniques of surveillance, normalization, exclusion, distribution, and so on. These techniques were often productive for pedagogical (or other) purposes. Perhaps Foucault's (1977) statement about surveillance as inherent to pedagogy and as increasing its efficiency, holds also for the other techniques. Part of my ongoing analysis is oriented toward identifying specific forms of surveillance, normalization, and so on, that were necessary for teaching, and those that may have been peripheral, such as regulating students' dress and eating habits in classrooms, for instance.

The examples also demonstrate that each of the techniques of power, as I defined them, was employed in a number of ways: sometimes, they functioned in the construction of knowledge; at other times, they functioned in the construction of relations among participants in the various sites; at yet other times, they functioned in the construction and maintenance of particular subjectivities (often defining oneself). Moreover, as already indicated, these techniques of power also occurred frequently in combination, illustrating the rapidly circulating functioning of power relations, and highlighting Foucault's view that power relations are simultaneously local, unstable, and diffuse, not emanating from a central point but at each moment moving from one point to another in a field of forces (Deleuze, 1988). The complexity that this analysis embraces is, in my view, illustrative of the ways in which a Foucaultian analysis of power in schooling can complement and extend past analysis, and aid the empirical study of power.

In order to draw comparisons between and within sites, and between and among the techniques of power, the relative frequency of each technique of power was calculated, where each segment of data had been coded with the multiple techniques of power that could be discerned. When examining these frequencies across all sites, I found that individualization and totalization were the most common techniques. Foucault (1988b) writes of the kind of rationality in which institutions are grounded, a rationality characterized by the integration of individuals in a community or totality that results from a constant correlation between increasing individualization and the reinforcement of the totality. This 'rationality' was most obvious in the teacher education site, not surprisingly, given that we observed a first-year cohort of students in their introductory subject, where a certain kind of teacher was being produced.

Across all sites, there was also substantially less use of regulation (explicit reference to or enactment of rules, sanctions, etc.) and surveillance (observational techniques) than of the other techniques. This 'finding' is consistent with Foucault's elaboration of the increasing invisibility of governmentality in modern society. The 'Panoptic' operation of surveillance (which is invisible but constantly possible) may well have had an impact on specific practices enacted by participants, but was not visibly exercised as frequently as were normalizing and other practices. Observing that which is 'invisible' is, of course, a problem. Nevertheless, the subtle techniques that I have called, after Foucault, normalization, classification, exclusion, and so on, were much more frequently observable than direct surveillance and regulation.[7]

As already stated, I am not attempting to argue that the techniques of power were configured identically regardless of pedagogical site. Differences were evident between sites, even in the few decontextualized passages I have presented above. Foucault's view of power as operating in capillary style, from the infinitesimal, does not imply that there are no patterns in the circulation or functioning of power. For instance, the examples provided, however open to multiple readings, suggest that teachers and students exercised power differently. That is, in many cases, students' power was 'reactive' rather than 'active' (Deleuze, 1988). Power circulated in these sites, but the exercise of power certainly was not equal for all participants.

Conclusion

Documenting the techniques of power outlined in this chapter, identifying which seem essential to pedagogical enterprise and which might be altered, is my own contribution to thinking about how educators might exercise power differently. In bringing about educational reform, I argue that we must know what we are and what we are doing (in education), in order to begin to address adequately how we might do things differently. I recognize the potential enactment of the very governmental processes of modern society that Foucault studied, and in part criticized, with this attempt to document techniques of power in pedagogy. But pedagogy's governmental influence, both within and beyond schooling institutions, is enormously powerful in the control of populations. Attempting to understand those processes and remove those that are harmful cannot, in my view, be any more dangerous than maintaining what already exists.

The microlevel focus of Foucault's analytics of power, therefore, not only is useful for understanding power's operation in specific sites, as demonstrated here, but also has clear potential in addressing change possibilities. That is, the Foucaultian approach enables us to document what causes us to be what we are in schools, and hence, potentially, to change what we are. Given the continuing widely documented negative effects of schooling for many students and teachers, such change seems a worthy pursuit.

Notes

I am grateful to the Australian Research Council for the funding that has supported this study, to all who participated in the research, and to James Ladwig, Gavin Hazel and Marie Brennan for their comments on earlier drafts of this chapter.

1. I want to emphasize that the scope of the overall project is clearly much larger than can be conveyed within this chapter. There are many other theoretical and methodological concerns that I am addressing elsewhere.
2. These episodes have been selected randomly by simply opening, for each category, the file of data segments that were coded with that technique of power. The number of coded segments per category per site ranged from four episodes of regulation in the feminist site to 746 episodes of distribution in the physical education site.
3. Pseudonyms are used throughout and other identifiers have been removed or changed. The data source is coded PE for the physical education site, TE for the teacher education site, WG for the women's discussion group, and FEM for the feminist reading group. Transcripts are distinguished from field notes via quotation marks. The transcripts have been edited slightly, in order to facilitate reading. Given the multiplicity and complexity of pedagogical events, no truth claims are made for these data. As Bourdieu, Chamboredon, and Passeron (1991) say, we need to 'renounce the impossible ambition of saying everything about everything, in the right order' (p. 10).
4. My research assistants, Erica Southgate and Rosalie Bunn, and I spent approximately six months in each of the sites, during 1993, making detailed observational notes and audio tapes of all group meetings during that period.
5. The teacher education programme was driven by strong critical and feminist educational perspectives.
6. For further examples that substantiate this point, see Gore (1994).
7. Average proportions for each category indicate the following as the most to least common practices across all sites: individualization, 24.7; totalization, 17.8; exclusion, 16.5; classification, 15.8; normalization, 15.7; distribution, 14.0; surveillance, 5.4; regulation, 4.8.

References

Bernstein, B. (1975). *Class, codes and control: Towards a theory of educational transmissions*. London: Routledge & Kegan Paul.
Bernstein, B. (1990). *The structuring of pedagogic discourse*. London: Routledge.
Bourdieu, P., Chamboredon, J.-C. and Passeron, J.-C. (1991). *The craft of sociology: Epistemological preliminaries*. Berlin: De Gruyter.

Bourdieu, P. and Passeron, J.-C. (1977). *Reproduction in education, society and culture*. London: Sage.

Corrigan, P. R. (1991). The making of the boy: Meditations on what grammar school did with, to, and for my body. In H. A. Giroux (ed.), *Postmodernism, feminism, and cultural politics* (pp. 196–216). Albany: State University of New York Press.

Deleuze, G. (1988). *Foucault*. Minneapolis: University of Minnesota Press.

Foucault, M. (1977). *Discipline and punish: The birth of the prison*. New York: Pantheon.

Foucault, M. (1980). Prison talk. In C. Gordon (ed. and trans.), *Power/knowledge: Selected interviews and other writings by Michel Foucault, 1972–1977* (pp. 109–133). New York: Pantheon.

Foucault, M. (1981). The order of discourse. In R. Young (ed.), *Untying the text: A post-structuralist reader* (pp. 48–78). Boston: Routledge & Kegan Paul.

Foucault, M. (1983). The subject and power. In H. L. Dreyfus and P. Rabinow (eds), *Michel Foucault: Beyond structuralism and hermeneutics* (2nd edn, pp. 208–226). Chicago: University of Chicago Press.

Foucault, M. (1988a). The ethic of care for the self as a practice of freedom. [Interview]. In J. Bernauer and D. Rasmussen (eds), *The final Foucault* (pp. 1–20). Cambridge, MA: MIT Press.

Foucault, M. (1988b). The political technology of individuals. In L. H. Martin, H. Gutman and P. H. Hutton (eds), *Technologies of the self: A seminar with Michel Foucault* (pp. 145–162). Amherst: University of Massachusetts Press.

Foucault, M. (1988c). Truth, power, self: An interview with Michel Foucault. In L. H. Martin, H. Gutman and P. H. Hutton (eds), *Technologies of the self: A seminar with Michel Foucault* (pp. 9–15). Amherst: University of Massachusetts Press.

Gore, J. M. (1993). *The struggle for pedagogies: Critical and feminist discourses as regimes of truth*. New York: Routledge.

Gore, J. M. (1994, November). *Power and pedagogy: Within and beyond the schooling institution*. Paper presented at the annual conference of the Australian Association for Research in Education, Newcastle.

Kelly, M. (1994). Foucault, Habermas and the self-referentiality of critique. In M. Kelly (ed.), *Critique and power. Recasting the Foucault/Habermas debate* (pp. 365–400). Cambridge, MA: MIT Press.

Maxwell, J. A. and Miller, B. A. (1993). *Categorization and contextualization as components of qualitative data analysis*. Unpublished manuscript.

Morey, M. (1992). On Michel Foucault's philosophical style: Towards a critique of the normal. In T. J. Armstrong (ed. and trans.), *Michel Foucault philosopher* (pp. 117–128). New York: Harvester Wheatsheaf.

Tyler, D. (1993). Making better children. In D. Meredyth and D. Tyler (eds), *Child and citizen: Genealogies of schooling and subjectivity* (pp. 35–60). Griffith University, Brisbane: Institute of Cultural and Policy Studies.

Index